100 VOICES

100 women share their stories of achievement

Edited by Miranda Roszkowski

unbound

First published in 2022

Unbound
Level 1, Devonshire House,
One Mayfair Place, London W1J 8AJ

www.unbound.com

Text design by Ellipsis, Glasgow

A CIP record for this book is available from the British Library

ISBN 978-1-80018-102-1 (trade pbk)
ISBN 978-1-80018-104-5 (ebook)
ISBN 978-1-80018-103-8 (limited edition)

Printed and bound in Great Britain by Clays Ltd, Elcograf S.p.A.

To anyone who has found it hard to be heard,
we lend you our voices

With special thanks to Paula Hawkins

CONTENTS

VOICES THAT TAUGHT

VOICES THAT WENT THE DISTANCE

FOREWORD

Deborah Frances-White

In a world that's on socially distanced fire, it's easy to feel like your voice is a drop in the ocean. But a hundred drops can make a wave. All the ocean can ever be is a collection of drops that finds a depth, a calm, a power, an energy – a tidal wave even. This anthology of voices is just that. Women singing solo and finding harmony in the strength of a choir.

Women have always had to band together to find the alchemy that would turn their voices into influence. We are just over one hundred years on from some women getting the vote in Britain and still seven years away from all women over twenty-one reaching the same milestone of being given that tantalising power. The vote has brought us so many rights, as politicians don't tend to legislate for those who can't help them at the ballot box. Before suffrage a man could declare us insane, lock us up and throw away the key if he were done with us, and not before taking our children away. Our employer could do with us what he wanted and often what he wanted was a horrendous, wilful abuse of power. But the vote hasn't brought us all the representation we'd rightfully expect. Not by a long way.

Virginia Woolf said that in a hundred years' time no one would notice if a novel were written by a man or a woman – it'd just be a novel. Just shows how wrong an icon can be. I can't help wondering (like Carrie Bradshaw – another icon with a typewriter) what the suffragettes would think of us. In some ways we've surpassed their most implausible dreams. In others we're working at a glacial pace that in some lights looks a lot like the status quo has pitched a tent. The stories in this book reflect the struggles, shackling and frustrations of contemporary women but also our ambition, rebellion and decadence. They include reflections on family, creation, sex and friendship. They speak to art, sport, heritage and the human condition. Because sometimes, as women, we are so focused on our identities, it's easy to forget to nourish our humanity. We can either conform to gender stereotypes or live our life rejecting them – both paths are exhausting, and I can't think of a third. Inside every woman is a hungry, libidinous, angry, mischievous human spirit. There's a primal scream in all of us that's shrieking, 'I'm human too – not just female!!!'

This book adds to the canon of female voices through the ages with our own unique twenty-first-century fears, feasts and follies. Spend time with a sister who craves being heard and find a flash of understanding, as you devour her story. Learn from those who live further in the margins than you and then reach out to lift up voices who echo these sentiments in your community.

Now for the instructions. Pick up this book. Turn off your phone. No, not just on silent. All the way off. Actually off. Now put it in another room and sit by a window with a cup of tea or – better still – walk to your nearest park and lie on the grass under your favourite tree. In fact, if you can, take more time for yourself – go to your closest ocean and hear the water lap on the sand as you read A Hundred Drops Making a Wave in these rustling pages. Here you will find a depth, a calm, a power, an energy – a tidal wave even. Let it lift you up and fill your rage for resistance, your joy for resilience and your peace for empathy. Then open your mouth and see what comes out. Put pen to paper, fingers to keyboard and surprise yourself. Liberate your female spirit and roar.

INTRODUCTION

WHAT ARE YOU PROUD OF?

Miranda Roszkowski

Well, this is awkward. We're not really meant to be proud, or brag about things. Especially as Brits. Especially as women.

In February 2018, to mark 100 years since the first women were allowed to vote in the UK, I launched a podcast. It ran for 100 days, from the ice-cold of February into a heatwave of May. Every day, for over three months, I broadcast an audio clip of a different female-identifying writer sharing a story of achievement, to an audience which grew into the thousands and internationally. Running a podcast was something completely new; it terrified me and delighted me in equal parts. But I did it. This is the book of those stories, and a few others. It is 400 pages of inspiration. And I'm quite proud of that, though I know it's a bit crass to say.

So I prefer to talk of achievement; it sounds more serious for a start. It's a hard thing to define. Until I started this project, the only achievements I thought about were on job applications, or remembered by dusty swimming badges that appeared at the bottom of old boxes when I moved house. Though I was proud of some of those things (it took an embarrassingly long time to get those swimming badges) I didn't feel like these achievements defined me as a person. When I launched *100 Voices for 100 Years*, I had to be a bit clearer. I had to consider if an achievement is something that needs to be realised in the face of difficulty, or is it just the act of having done something – of having a plan and executing it correctly? Sometimes the smallest things can feel hugely significant, in the same way that the tiniest slight can knock you off track for days.

What I learned, putting the podcast and subsequent book together, was that achievement is all about the context. Because for us as women, there are invisible trip wires everywhere as we go about our lives attempting to achieve things – are we too loud, too messy, too quiet, not good enough? Strangers literally stop us in the street to explain what's wrong about us (I don't think I'm alone in that?). We are so often defined by things we *should* be and don't quite make the grade. I speak from personal experience, as a non-Disabled, white woman who has many privileges. It is far harder for others, including people of colour, those who are Disabled or have queer identities. I wanted to do something to tip the balance a bit, to show the remarkable resilience, the creativity and above all the ambition of women.

Courage calls to courage everywhere, and its voice cannot be denied.

These are the words of Millicent Fawcett, given in a speech following the death of the suffragette Emily Wilding Davison who died while protesting for women's right to vote. I only discovered the quote as I was setting up the *100 Voices for 100 Years* podcast. The words perfectly summed up the idea of the project, which was all about voices coming together to inspire each other to be brave. I put the quote on the website, surprised that I hadn't come across it before, as it is so inspiring, not just for women but for everyone whatever their gender or goal. It was probably big at the time Mrs Fawcett was kicking about, I thought, but do people really preserve the legacy of women's words? Which made me a bit angry, and made me even more driven to go ahead with the project. Here was an opportunity to preserve for the future a large number of inspiring words written by women, about their real lives. I wanted to look at women now, and not just those we would deem 'exceptional' because society already knew about them, they'd beaten the system. I felt that there were more unheard stories about real women than we were allowed to see. There had to be, given the monocultural representations we got in film, fiction, art, business and politics.

This book is about personal stories because the stories we tell define the society we get. When I started my career, first as an actor, then as a writer, I had few role models to inspire me to pursue the work I wanted. Of course there were brilliant female actors, especially in Britain, but what roles were there to demonstrate their skills? And when I got into writing fiction, there were plenty of women I could track down to inspire me, but in the high street bookshops, the 'good books', the ones that were popular *and* respected (and importantly, sold) were by men. Now that's not necessarily the case – there's been a sea change in the industry, helped by changing attitudes following

Covid-19. In 2020 the bestseller lists were dominated by women, and significantly, women of colour were right at the centre of that. Institutions are adapting – over the last decade women have won the Booker Prize on four occasions (with Bernardine Evaristo and Margaret Atwood having to share the award in 2019), but if you look at the statistics since 1969, a woman is about half as likely to win as a man. Women's voices are still under-represented in so many areas. In the UK, only 14 per cent of films have a female director. Looking further afield, in the US, which dominates the global film industry, the percentage of films with a female protagonist was only 29 per cent. Films with female characters in speaking roles in 2020 was a depressing 36 per cent. That's how many women were allowed to speak on screen. This isn't a phenomenon that is limited to art – by coincidence, a similar percentage of people allowed to speak in our Parliament were women. In the UK, just 34 per cent of elected Members are female. Out of twenty-three Cabinet Ministers, six are women. I don't want to depress you, but I do want to stress that women's voices are still, literally and metaphorically, unheard in many situations, 100 years after getting the right to vote. It is not just that low numbers of women get to tell their story, but that only certain types of women make the cut and because of that we get little diversity in those stories.

We need to read about the achievements of women, not least because we are constantly reminded of the achievements of men, who are more confident in asserting their views, their voices and their bodies into our cultural space. Moreover, we need role models of all female identities, ethnicities, class and personality types to remind our younger generations that they are not starting from scratch, that women have gone before them, and that where they are ambitious, someone might have already blazed a trail, even if it is overgrown.

I was lucky to have grown up with a strong female role model in my mother, who took a lot of chances, and on the occasions where things didn't work out, she got back up and had another go. I'm even luckier that she's agreed to share a small section of her story in this book. Yet one role model is not enough to appreciate the range and depth of strength, ingenuity and bloody-mindedness that women have shown, and continue to show every day. And what if you don't have that role model in your life? Research shows that seeing positive role models has an amplified benefit for women, perhaps due to the negative stereotypes we have lived with for generations. Seeing a woman doing something that inspires them is likely to empower other women to go for it. This book aims to show the many different ways women experience achievement, what makes them proud and how they have built on these experiences in order to take their next steps, whatever they may be.

Achievement is sometimes accidental, or inspired by external forces. By giving myself the external challenge to publish 100 stories over 100 days, I gave myself permission to be bold. When I started the podcast I didn't know 100 writers. I brazenly introduced myself to people I would never have dared to talk to. I even approached someone in the changing rooms of a swimming pool when I over-heard her mention being a writer on the phone. I was naked. Luckily she's very open-minded. And above all, she's a first-class writer.

I approached writers and people who used storytelling in their day-to-day lives, be it bloggers, theatre professionals or those working with words professionally. The writers shared the call-out with their own networks. That means that some of the writers share identities with me, being from Wales, having worked in theatre or lived in London. Overall I tried hard to ensure a good geographical spread of writers, from all over the UK. I approached additional writers to increase representation of people of colour and different gender identities in the book. I refer to this collective as women, as that is how we want to present ourselves here, but there are many identities within this. Of course others will define themselves in their own words.

The book is not a perfect representation of what it is like to be a woman today, because it never could be. There is not one single female story and this is the point – we are being treated to a snapshot of these individuals and their lives. I hope, though, that in showcasing such a wide range of writers, it will go some way to expanding the reader's perceptions of women's experiences, and perceptions of what achievement is as a whole. The pieces are about personal triumph, from learning how to make lemon curd, use a 'fork and knife' or speak Bengali, to steeling yourself to take the mic at a poetry gig. They are reflective, considering how the authors have learned to 'speak me'. But they are also difficult, dealing with trauma and recovery. They are hilarious, from breastfeeding competing twins, to the fallout from a childhood of winning dance competitions. Like women, these stories are many things, often at once.

Achievement doesn't mean winning and neither is it about constant positivity. The writers in this collection didn't always feel they had 'found their voice' and in the editing process often questioned the confidence with which they had written their original piece.

Achievement is slippery, the feeling of having 'conquered' something comes and goes. Achievement often feels best appraised at a distance. Sometimes we need someone else to tell us how impressive our achievement really is. Other times we might need the distance of time to see it ourselves. And yet, once we have achieved something, that success can never be taken away.

That is why it was so important to create this book, which has been edited and curated to stand as a testimony, a solid, undeniable artefact of these stories. I hope it will inspire others to create their own and shout their own stories of achievement with loud voices.

ENDNOTES

1   The Women's Victory – and After: Personal Reminiscences, 1911–1918 by Millicent Garrett Fawcett, Chapter 5: The Pilgrimage and the Derby Day, p. 66. https://archive.org/details/womensvictoryaftoofawcuoft/page/66/mode/2up

2   I was wrong. Part of the quote has been immortalised by Gillian Wearing's statue of Fawcett, which stands in Parliament Square, London. https://plinth.uk.com/blogs/in-the-studio-with/courage-calls-to-courage-everywhere

3   'Since 1969, 32 men and 18 women have won the prize.' https://thebookerprizes.com/facts-figures

4   Across 3,452 films in production in the UK between 2003 and 2015, only 14 per cent of all directors were women. Furthermore, just 1 per cent of all directors were women of colour. Findings from *Calling the Shots: Women and Contemporary Film Culture in the UK*. https://womencallingtheshots.com/

5   It's a Man's (Celluloid) World: Portrayals of Female Characters in the Top Grossing U.S. Films of 2020, Center for the Study of Women in Television & Film, San Diego State University. https://womenintvfilm.sdsu.edu/wp-content/uploads/2021/04/2020_Its_a_Mans_World_Report_v2.pdf

6   Ibid.

7   'There are 220 women MPs in the House of Commons. At 34 per cent, this is an all-time high.' https://commonslibrary.parliament.uk/research-briefings/sn01250/

8   Six ministers in the current Cabinet (26 per cent) are women. The highest proportion of women in Cabinet was 36 per cent between 2006 and 2007.

9   'To Do or Not to Do: Using Positive and Negative Role Models to Harness Motivation' by Penelope Lockwood (University of Toronto), Pamela Sadler (Wilfred Laurier University), Keren Fyman and Sarah Tuck (University of Toronto), Social Cognition, Vol. 22, No. 4, 2004, pp. 422–50.

VOICES
THAT STARTED IT ALL

The following story was the first I received (on my birthday!) and was broadcast on 6 February 2018 via the 100 *Voices for* 100 *Years podcast, marking* 100 *years since the first women could vote in the UK.*

LEMON CURD

Rachel Barnett-Jones

Kettle's on – what'll it be?

Coffee, tea, chamomile, peppermint, lemon and ginger,
    something to help with digestion, something else to help
    with digestion. Hot water with a slice of lemon?

Oh. No. Actually. I'm out of lemons.

I made lemon curd.

Yes. I did.

Had loads of lemons.

Thought I'd make lemon curd.

Bit stressful.

Juiced the lemons.

And a couple of ancient limes for good luck.

Texted Mum, 'do you like lemon curd?'

She doesn't.

Thought she did. Must have been being polite that time a
    friend gave her a jar.

3

Impressed I was making it.

BBC Good Food says it's easy though.

So.

Text best friend, 'I'm making lemon curd.'

She's equally impressed.

It's really not that hard.

So far.

I start to worry.

Text friend who's good at baking.

'Is lemon curd difficult?'

She doesn't reply.

Then she does.

'No. It's really easy, here's my recipe.'

Her recipe looks REALLY complicated.

I decide to press on with the three-step recipe I've found.

Cross-referencing it with Delia Online which is entirely

different and highly contradictory.

Anyway.

By now I'm flying blind so I decide to press on.

And I've already gone 'off recipe' because I've gone for a tiny

bit of maple syrup rather than a cupful of sugar – because

sugar is EVIL and maple syrup is less evil apparently.

So the butter is melting into the lemon juice.

I wonder about adding another flavour.

Decide not to.

Then I add the eggs.

Text best friend,

'my eggs are scrambling in the lemons.'

She sends a laughing yellow face with tears of mirth.

Text friend good at baking,

'what should I do if the eggs start scrambling?'

She doesn't reply.

Google it.

Should have tempered the eggs apparently.

Bloody BBC Good Food recipe three simple steps.

Whisk like my arm is powered by Duracell.

Eggs still scrambling.

Find the sieve.

Mum texts

'How's it going?'

I text back

'Brilliant. Looking glossy. Kitchen smells of lemons.'

Let the mixture cool down.

Sieve it.

Sieve it some more.

It looks like I've saved the curd.

Try a bit.

Bitter lemon pulls my lips back from my gums.

Tastes of lemons.

Smells of lemons.

Text friend

'Curd saved.'

She texts back

'Well done.'

Pour it

Carefully –

Big pot for us

Little pot for elderly next-door neighbour, I'll take it round
     tomorrow and get back the container for the chopped
     liver I gave him a couple of weeks back.

In the morning

I peek into the pot.

It's set, smooth and clear.

Triumphant.

My kitchen smells of lemons.

Kettle's boiled – what'll it be?

Rachel Barnett-Jones's work has been performed at theatres in
the UK and abroad, including the Royal Court, Arcola Theatre,
Manhattan Theatre Source in New York, Live Girls in Seattle,
Key City Public Theatre in Washington and Auroville in India.

Following a BA in English Literature from Cardiff University
and an MA in Writing for Performance from Central School of
Speech and Drama, she has specialised in working with young
people, people with disabilities and community groups. She shares
her time between playwriting, producing, workshop leading, lectu-
ring, copywriting, company management, consultancy and looking
after her little boy.

She co-founded and runs www.flyhighstories.co.uk.

CROSSING THE LINE

Sophie Haydock

Perhaps you've dreamed of running a marathon? It's possible that some of you, like me, have crossed that particular finish line. If not, maybe running 26.2 miles is on your bucket list? Whether you're a runner or not, it might surprise you to know that, for a very, very long time, women were banned from taking part in long-distance running. Experts deemed the activity 'damaging to health and femininity'. Some seriously thought the repetitive motion of running so far would make a woman's uterus fall out.

Let's take a moment to let that sink in.

(Just as an aside, I once interviewed an incredible American woman, Amber Miller, for the *Guardian*. She ran the Chicago Marathon in 2011 when she was nine months pregnant – and gave birth to a healthy baby girl later the very same day.)

In 1967 Kathrine Switzer became one of the first women ever to run an official marathon. The then-twenty-year-old had registered for the race using her initials, K.V. Switzer. Two miles in, Boston officials noticed, and she was physically pulled from the course. It didn't stop her, and she battled her way to the finish line that day, making history in the process. Later, she was disqualified from the

7

race and received hate mail. What did she do? She kept on running, won a marathon, set up her own club – and inspired millions of women worldwide to follow in her footsteps.

Forty-nine years later, I sweated for five hours in order to make it across the finish line of my first major running event – the New York City Marathon, in November 2016. It took place days before Donald Trump was elected President. Two million people lined the streets to cheer the race, which started on Staten Island and stretched through the city's five boroughs. Those crowds cheered me and more than 50,000 other runners on as we stomped through Brooklyn, Manhattan, the Bronx and up First Avenue. It's a testament to the rulebreakers of the past that 41.77 per cent (or 21,465) of those who finished that day were women.

The final stretch of that 26.2-mile course, through Central Park, with the autumn leaves glowing a special kind of gold in the dying light of that Sunday afternoon, with people cheering my name like my life depended on it – I'd carefully painted 'Sophie from the UK' on the back of my running top – is a moment I'll never forget.

As I burned into the last of my energy and gave it everything I had, the last 0.2 miles deliriously, agonisingly, tormentingly long, I thought about the women who never made it across that line, the ones who were denied their part in the race or told they weren't up to it, and the ones who broke the rules and didn't take no for an answer, who made it possible for me to run my heart out, cross the line, and accept a heavy medal for my efforts.

I still have the medal hanging in pride of place in my home. I look at it to remind myself that small steps can add up to something incredible. Since that day, I've added two new ones: I completed the Berlin Marathon in 2017, and set a personal best at the London Marathon, of 04:11:48.

I'm grateful to all those who made it possible. With every step, pounding the streets of Hackney, or wherever I find myself – it could be a snowy trail in Scotland or barefoot on a beach in Mexico – Switzer's words have always rung in my ears: 'Take the first step. And if you take the first step, you can then take three steps. And then you can take ten. And someday maybe you can run a marathon. And if you can run a marathon, you can do anything.'

Sophie Haydock is a journalist, author and marathon runner. She is passionate about short stories, and works as a digital editor for the *Sunday Times* Short Story Award and is associate director of the Word Factory short story organisation. Her debut novel *The Flames*, about the women who modelled for the Austrian artist Egon Schiele, won the 2018 Impress Prize for New Writers and will be published by Doubleday in February 2022 (follow @egonschieleswomen on Instagram for more). She has run marathons in New York City, Berlin and London, and intends to complete all six marathons in the World Marathon Majors series.

SUNDAY BEST

Emma Halliday

My voice quivered as the words started to jump around on the page. I couldn't keep the paper still. As the sun beamed into the classroom and the sweat rolled down my cheeks, I let out a wheeze mid-sentence and started to fall.

It was my first proper public speaking outing. I was reading a book report that I had spent countless hours writing and editing. That was some time commitment for a teenager with an 'active' social life. Well, we hung out at parks and shops around Leeds whatever the weather.

English was my favourite subject and I knew my report, a review of a young adult adventure book, was worthy of top marks if only I could get through sharing it with a class of teenagers. They were uniformed in navy and grey, everyone trying to find some way to show their individuality with badges and hairbands and sweaters draped on shoulders, bodies slouching or upright. I stood there, legs shaking, palms itching as beads of sweat started to gather at my temples. All eyes – some vacant, others interested or simply relieved it wasn't their turn – stared up at me. They resembled a pack of hyenas waiting for their next prey to fall. Well, in my case, faint.

That fainting episode clung to me for more than half my life. It stopped me going to university and I said no to interviews if I had to do a presentation. It started to seep into my mindset. Getting me down. I was scared to even say my own name in meetings. My own name! I would sit there listening intently as each person introduced themselves, while frantically repeating my name in my head. What if I opened my mouth and no words came out, or if I stuttered? My stomach would dance and lurch as my body heated up, leaving me dehydrated in the process. I was back in that classroom again.

A chance encounter with an old friend inspired me to take stock of my life. There was a moment while talking with her that it became evident that I wasn't living the life I wanted, including being in a job that didn't challenge me. Knowing that I was the obstacle holding me back in so many situations, I took the first step and found a 'fear of public speaking' class in Sheffield.

Little by little, with practice, persistence and a lot of perspiration, I did find my voice and with that many doors opened and my confidence soared. Which is why I wanted to stand up in front of a crowd and speak from my heart about hope and heartache.

So, in July 2015 I set up an event called Sunday Best. The slogan was 'Be your best – on your own terms'. I found the venue, a short drive from the city centre. It was a perfect size, with a car park and kitchen, and at a reasonable price. I managed to find an additional four speakers to join me and got people to buy tickets.

My nerves tried to take over as I stood up and addressed the room. I'd like to say it was a sea of people but there were about twenty of us including the speakers. So maybe a puddle of people but people nonetheless. I cleared my throat and then I said, 'Who has an item that you absolutely love, but save for special occasions – that rarely come?'

I could feel my voice fluctuating and my head starting to slowly spin but I continued. It was important that they got the message that sometimes we have to go out and create those special moments as they do not always come to us, and the more that you keep them hidden away the harder it is to bring them out again, a lot like vulnerability. I then invited them to listen as I shared a piece of me that had been locked away in the pages of a diary that I owned from the ages of eleven to fifteen years old. This particular piece was written by a fifteen-year-old me, not long after I had written the book report. It said:

My mother died in February – it was so sudden – not a lot of people know about it – I can't bring myself round to tell them. All the family are coping as best they can. My whole life was turned upside down. She was so healthy one day, the next she had died. We have to look to the future now, and my mother's death has made me realise that I should have fun now – as I'm only young once. I don't care what people think about me no more – it's my life and I will live it the way I want to live.

I read that piece to remind people that we don't know what is around the corner, so now is the time to wear those fancy clothes, eat from the best china, go out and dazzle as ourselves, because we are living on borrowed time. I stood there in awe of myself as the realisation washed over me that I had gone head to head with my fear and I'd won. Speaking on such a sensitive topic was a truly powerful moment and one of the proudest of my life. After so many years of playing small and keeping quiet, I faced a fear and, with that, I found my voice, which had been lost since I was a teenager.

Allow me to introduce myself. My name is Emma Halliday and I'm still really scared of public speaking.

Emma Halliday is a writer from Leeds, West Yorkshire. She shares her personal stories and journey to live authentically on her blog: www.thisvulnerablelife.com. She juggles her full-time job at the NHS working in Diversity, Inclusion and Health Inequalities with a part-time politics, philosophy and economics Open University degree. Emma is as obsessed with books as she is with memes, and is passionate about personal development, travelling and spending quality time with her friends and family.

SPEAKING ME

Yvonne Battle-Felton

I'm a bit of a me-connoisseur. I know what I mean when I say certain things. I know when I say coffee makes me a kinder person, that while I love the thought of creamy coffee goodness and sweet vanilla or hazelnut cream, the truth *may* be that I don't like drinking coffee as much as I like acquiring coffee.

I'm fluent in me.

I think that's why I didn't quite 'get' mindfulness. It felt like I was doing it: living in the moment, or at least worrying about what the moment was, where it was, and how I would make it last longer, all the time. As for appreciating moments while living them, well, I multi-task as much as the next person so I thought I was experiencing, appreciating, living all at the same time. Much like I cook, write, update statuses and text all at once. Or walk, talk, breathe.

I'm sitting here, relaxing, foot tapping, shifting, clearing my mind, eyes closed, being in the moment. Each time I find myself thinking about emails and applications, deadlines and projects, I mentally pull myself back. I'm focusing on my breathing. Reminding myself not of things to do but the cycle of my breath and concentrating on a word to describe how I want my research life to look. I'm in a plastic chair. I feel myself wondering how much more it costs to rent a cluster of leather chairs, comfortable ones with plush seats, maybe thick arms to squeeze and backs sturdy enough to hold— but no, I remind myself. It's a plastic chair. The temperature is cool, there are about twelve people around me, are their eyes also closed as the facilitator has suggested, or did he recommend keeping them open and closing them only if you had to? I could peek but wouldn't that prove I'm not relaxing? That I don't know how to? That I need a facilitator to facilitate relaxation?

I'm on a course designed to help me achieve my research life and to help recognise what that might look like. Today is session two. Both this week and in session one, two weeks or so ago, we were asked to sum up our thoughts into one word that might explain our present, past or future. Most of mine have been pretty painless. The past: fragmented or mosaic, depending on my mood. The present: hopeful, promising. The future: funded.

The facilitator asks why.

I'm a mom, I say. To me that sums up most discussions, really. It means people rely on me. It means I am responsible. Because I have multiplied it means I must at times add, subtract, divide myself, my goals. It means everything. Much of what I do stems from my idea of what being a mother means to me. At times, it completes me. At others, it consumes me.

There are times I can't remember who I am. Not Dr Yvonne

Battle-Felton, but who. What things I like to do in, what everyone else claims to have, my free time.

I'm present, actively engaging, listening, pondering that one word when I hear it. I heard it then too, on the bridge in Kendal with my children. *I like it better than I like Lancaster*, one of my children had said. The other one wasn't so sure it was better than or similar to Lancaster. A place, it turns out, my children like to visit but don't want to live in.

In Kendal, there was water that I didn't hear flowing, there were birds I didn't really hear singing, and the words of my children, that I heard but maybe didn't *hear* them. The way I would if I were, well, in a room, somewhere else, not rushing for the train but relaxing and searching for a word to describe that what I want most for my children is a place to call home: a place that doesn't rely on year-to-year visas, or letting contracts. A place less transient. A place to go back to.

For me, it's a structure. For them, it's me. My children will return to me like boomerangs and postcards no matter how they feel about where home is.

That day, while I am present, I realise what I *want* for them, I *need* for me.

I am the sort of person who plots major decisions the way others plot stories. I outline characters, with myself as the protagonist, strengths, obstacles and goals, because sometimes I forget that other people have motivations that differ from my own, and sometimes I forget that there are things outside of the many roles I take on at once: things that I want that are purely, unashamedly, undeniably for me.

And sometimes I forget that that's OK.

Yvonne Battle-Felton was born in Pennsylvania, USA, and is currently living in Sheffield, South Yorkshire, with her family. Yvonne holds an MA in Writing from Johns Hopkins University and a PhD in Creative Writing from Lancaster University. She is principal lecturer, Business and Enterprise lead in Humanities at Sheffield Hallam University where she teaches Creative Writing. Yvonne is founder of Book-able Space Middle-Grade Book Club and Bookable-Space African-American Lit-Literary Salon. Her debut novel *Remembered* won a Northern Writers' Award in 2017 and was longlisted for the Women's Prize for Fiction 2019 and shortlisted for the Jhalak Prize 2020. Yvonne writes fiction for children as well and her short story *So Your Mom Is a Superhero* was commended for the Faber Andlyn BAME (FAB) Prize in 2017. Find her on www.yvonnebattlefelton.com.

L'APPEL DU VIDE

Victoria Richards

When I became a mother I lost myself (*active*), I got lost (*passive*)
my mind broke and I went mad, I was mental, you know?
    I couldn't cope with the horror of loving this tiny thing so
    completely
it was like being INSIDE the news – like a hostage situation, where
    I'm the gunman and the bullet at the same time, where my life
    is narrated by David Attenborough, talking talking talking
as I am swallowed whole like a snake swallows a deer – inch by
    inch – until the deer is no longer a deer, but a giant bulge in
    the snake's stomach, and *Jesus Christ*, is it alive in there?
    Could it still be alive in there?
And on becoming a mother, after seven series of *Gilmore Girls*
    while *baby* slept twenty-three hours of every day,
while *daughter* went to school and came home crying
because she had to make all new friends and couldn't hug me
    because my hands were full of baby, my breasts so full of milk,
and it hurt for her to grip me tight with her pink-and-green
    bracelet arms.
After, they both got sick, heartbeats angry white-on-black:

170 — *no, you can't go home* —

200 — *we need to move you into resus* —

after that, a long time after that, while walking in the forest I

    realised I hadn't thought about the autumn leaves. Hadn't

    noticed the gold and red and soft brown crunch, or the swans

or that heron sitting on the post in his grey overcoat

    or the dogs running sideways with the wind in their ears

    or the bluebells in the woods that people travel for miles to see.

I hadn't spoken for days and I'd hardly eaten

and my mouth was a stone

and I lost myself somewhere between the bus stop and the A406

on that motorway bridge where traffic zooms by so fast it blurs —

and what's the word for the feeling when you stand too close to

    the edge and get the uncontrollable urge to throw yourself

    off?

Victoria Richards is a journalist and writer. In 2017–18 she was shortlisted for the Bath Novel Award and the Lucy Cavendish College Fiction Prize, was highly commended for poetry in the Bridport Prize and came third in the *London Magazine* Short Story Competition. A collection of her poetry was published in May 2019 alongside two other poets in *Primers: Volume Four*, with Nine Arches Press, and in 2020 she came first in the Nature in the Air poetry competition, first in the Retreat West Best Opening Page competition and second in the Magma Poetry Competition. Find her on Twitter @nakedvix and at www.independent.co.uk/author/victoria-richards.

1995

Katherine Vik

4 July 1995 and what better way to spend a balmy summer's evening than trekking up to north London to check out a Japanese noise band? I'd been living in London for less than a year and was going to as many gigs as my pitiful budget would allow, mainly in the back rooms of tiny pubs which no longer exist, named after manly men and their manly things. The George IV and Canterbury Arms in Brixton, the Goldsmiths Tavern and the George Robey were favourites, as was the glorious Prince Albert.

Occasionally I'd splash out on a gig in a bigger venue, queuing at the venue's ticket office (usually a hole in a wall, cut off by glass) to buy a real paper ticket ripped from a specially printed stub. I'd heard that the best gig in town that night was the Boredoms at the Garage in Highbury and knew that with their two drummers and a frantic shrieking singer thrashing about the stage I was sure to be impressed.

In my dingy beige Brixton room I dressed for the gig in ripped-up tights, a men's long black singlet top, sewn up at the sides to make a sort of sheath shape, with a brown crocheted see-through dress over the top. I completed this with the brown suede jacket that I'd picked up at Barnardo's for a fiver and my trusty Blundstone boots, the cheaper Aussie alternative to Docs. Tying my orange hair up in pigtails I applied layers of regulation black eyeliner and offset this with red lipstick, then hit the road.

Getting to the Garage was quick. It was a Tuesday and I got a few odd looks from the commuter crowd, but then it was across the road, ticket torn, and straight to the bar. The support band was on and I got chatting with some friends, watching the stage from the corner of my eye and sipping cider. The room was dark, hazy with smoke, the floor sticky, and the toilets lacking doors. A ceiling fan above the crowd swirled smoke around in mini hurricanes and threatened to decapitate crowdsurfers. That's when we got introduced. Alex said, 'Hey, meet Lil, he's the guy I put on gigs with,' and as we both put on gigs at the opposite ends of town, I was curious to see what this 'Lil' guy was like. So I turned my back to the band, said hello, and asked if he wanted a pint.

In those days my feminism manifested itself by offering to carry heavy amps, learning how to pee standing up, and always getting the first round in. I went to the bar and bought him that pint of Guinness, and though I remember watching the infamous Boredoms and jumping around down the front like a tightly wound spring, the thing I remember most about that night is meeting Lil. The mental snapshot remains of him standing there with that Guinness, a glint in his eye, a cheeky grin and the feeling that we were primed to take over the world.

As the cliché goes, good things don't come easy and relationships are all about compromise, which I've never been good at. Most of the time I'm stubborn and don't like to see things from the other side. At times it's been a struggle, and I still have days when I hate him as much as I love him. But of all the things I've achieved in my life, a career in tech, running a record label, a Master's degree and two demanding kids, the achievement that I'm most proud of is keeping this relationship going for more than twenty years.

Katherine Vik is sometimes a writer, in between running digital projects, reading novellas and looking after kids, cats, turtles and a husband. Having spent many years putting on gigs, writing for zines and co-running a record label and record shop, Kat decided to get more serious about writing. She got involved in running a literary evening in London and editing an issue of the *Mechanics' Institute Review* after completing an MA in Creative Writing at Birkbeck, University of London. She feels lucky to have met so many fantastic women writers who continue to inspire.

THE POWER OF WHEELS

Isabelle Clement

My discovery of the power of wheels was a slow but significant one. I grew up as a little disabled girl in an able-bodied world. I was reliant on my mother for every journey till the age of eighteen: to and from school, to and from playmates' homes. Deciding to hang back after lessons and walk part of the way together with friends after college was never an option for me, as I could only walk safely or pain-free for a couple of hundred metres or so. It was never suggested I might benefit from using a wheelchair (other than during a few hospital stays, where I was medically unable to do otherwise). Walking was very much the thing everyone was fixated on, with the best of intentions, and growing up, I unwittingly internalised the strong message that wheelchairs were things you shouldn't get a taste for.

I was lucky to have a supportive extended family who, as soon as I passed my driving test, clubbed together to buy me my first 'set of wheels'. Getting my car let me set off on my own journey for the very first time and I'll forever be grateful to my family for giving me this crucial means to wave them goodbye.

I had no idea when I was setting off that I had inherited an incredibly reductive, ableist vision of mobility: one where walking

23

and driving are socially valued and therefore 'good', and where wheelchairs and other aids to mobility are equated with illness, failure and potentially faking, and are therefore seen and portrayed as 'sad', 'bad' and potentially 'mad'. I would only uncover this a few years later, having moved from my native France to the UK and becoming exposed to the Social Model of Disability.[1]

Crucially, while at university in Reading in the late eighties, through friends of my then boyfriend (now my husband), I met an amazing woman called Liz Crow, who opened my eyes to the existence of the Disability Rights Movement. In her mid-twenties, Liz was already a Disability Arts activist.[2] Through-the-night conversations with Liz resulted in what I can only describe as my *coming out* as a Disabled woman (Disabled, with a capital D). This was the moment I realised that my whole concept of myself until then had been that of a 'not quite good enough' able-bodied person; someone who needed to try harder; who should be grateful when non-Disabled people 'let' me be their friends or register on their course or enter their shops. This was the moment I stopped apologising for myself, to myself and to the rest of the world and instead started to embrace the fact that I was who I was, a Disabled woman, and that I was OK.

Liz took me to a few Disabled People's Direct-Action Network (DAN) demonstrations. There, I discovered the true bravery of Disabled activists, who were chaining themselves to buses outside Parliament, and were willing to be arrested so all Disabled people would one day have access to public transport. DAN's motto was 'To Boldly Go Where Everyone Else Has Gone Before'. I realised that things didn't have to be the way they were; that limited mobility choices for Disabled people weren't an inevitable result of our impairments but a direct consequence of decisions made by non-Disabled people, artificially keeping us from reaching our potential and our dreams – and, crucially, that change was possible, at both a personal and societal level. I'd understood the Social Model of Disability and my life was about to change.

Without this seismic shift in understanding, I likely would never have stood for president of my students' union (let alone been elected). The lid had been lifted on my life ambitions. It was no longer going to be about being grateful. I would take charge of my destiny; learn to reframe 'things I couldn't do because I couldn't walk very well' into areas where reasonable adjustments needed to be made or equipment needed to be acquired/provided to remove a particular barrier to my success in life.

Enter 'Pinkie', my first (fluorescent pink) wheelchair, as I started my year as president of Reading University Students' Union (RUSU). For Pinkie, I have the (Disabled) Welfare Manager at RUSU to thank. She suggested I apply for a wheelchair through the Access to Work scheme.[3] The power of Pinkie was that I never turned up at University Senate meetings panting and in discomfort, having dragged myself through campus, but rather arrived fresh and ready to fight the students' corner, as it was my job to do. Simple, really, but transformational.

Pinkie was my pride and joy, but after I had a child, and he got his first set of wheels – a bike – I needed something more all-terrain to keep up with him in the park. I was researching mobility scooters when I discovered handcycling. Until then I'd had no idea you could transform a wheelchair into a handcycle by adding a larger wheel to the front of it and handcranks to propel it. I still could only walk (increasingly) short distances, but suddenly I could cycle.

I'd loved family forest walks as a child but had had to give up on them when I became too scared and self-conscious to be carried on my dad's and uncles' shoulders, aged ten or so. Twenty-five years later, I'd finally become able to enjoy the pleasure of independent 'walks' along country lanes, but also the joy of not only keeping up with but outpacing my non-Disabled friends while feeling the wind in my hair! Twenty years after having acquired my first handcycle attachment, I routinely cycle-commute to work and have been crisscrossing London throughout the Covid-19 pandemic period; my car's hardly been used all year.

Discovering, acquiring and mastering each of these wheeled mobility options in turn (the car, the wheelchair, the handcycle) was for me like growing a new pair of wings each time. I sometimes wish my parents had realised cycling was an option for little disabled girl me, and my medical teams had encouraged them to get me to use a wheelchair for outdoor mobility, back in the day. Regardless, I will forever be grateful to Liz Crow and the many other Disabled activists I have since met or read about, who transformed my vision of the world and shaped my understanding of the power of wheels.

I'm now the director of Wheels for Wellbeing, a charity which exists to ensure that Disabled people realise they can cycle and campaigns to remove the multiple barriers to cycling which exist for Disabled people. Through cycling, Wheels for Wellbeing is changing Disabled people's lives. It is also changing the way society sees Disabled people and Disability. And that's why I'm proud to say I love my job quite so much.

Isabelle Clement MBE is director of Wheels for Wellbeing, an award-winning charity, based in London, which supports Disabled people to discover or rediscover cycling. Established in 2007, the charity provides cycling opportunities in south London; it has also become the UK-wide campaigning voice of Disabled people who cycle.

As an urban commuter handcyclist, Isabelle has extensive experience of what it takes to create the right environment so everyone can cycle. She works tirelessly to bring an understanding of cycling to Disability groups and of Disability to cycling groups. She co-created #BeyondTheBicycle, an alliance with parent cyclists and cargo cyclists who encounter many of the same issues as Disabled and older cyclists, and has become a leading influencer in the field of inclusive cycling. You can find out more about her work at www.wheelsforwellbeing.org.uk.

A note on the definitions

Isabelle uses a capital D in 'Disability' and 'Disabled' through most of this text. This is why:

Using a capital D for the word Disabled shows it is important to recognise that society continues to create barriers for people with impairments, and those barriers need to be removed. The capital D also shows that Disabled people have a shared identity and are part of a community that continues to fight for our rights and equality just like other groups in society like Black people or LGBT people.

See www.allfie.org.uk/definitions/use-capital-d/.

ENDNOTES

1   More about the Social Model of Disability: https://www.inclusionlondon.org.uk/disability-in-london/social-model/the-social-model-of-disability-and-the-cultural-model-of-deafness/

2   You can find out more about Liz Crow's work (and Isabelle would recommend it!) at http://www.roaring-girl.com

3   More about the Access to Work Scheme: https://www.gov.uk/government/publications/access-to-work-guide-for-employers/access-to-work-factsheet-for-employers

THE UNKEEPABLE KEY

Deborah Martin

Over the years, I've found my voice in various ways – in poems, in stories, in performances – and for a while afterwards the world and my place in it seemed to come into rich, glowing focus. I've worn my voice with pride at those times, a golden key on a chain at my throat. *Mine to keep*, I've thought.

And then something – a criticism, a rejection, a failure – will cause that chain to snap and the key to fall away. And then I'm down on my hands and knees again, patting the ground as I peer into every crack for the glint and glimmer of my own voice.

Because as a writer, as any kind of artist in fact (and especially, I think, as a woman), your whole life can sometimes feel like an on-going cycle of finding and losing that unkeepable key, the one that opens the door between you and the world.

True, as a child you might be given paints, a plastic trumpet or a pair of ballet shoes, and be told to make a mess, make a noise, make a show. But if your love for any of those objects should survive that first doubtful glance from a teacher, those sceptical words from a relative, and make it through the door marked 'Adulthood', then the attacks on your self-expression will not end there.

Naysayers might express doubts in your abilities, treat your dreams quizzically, talk about the tough, near-impossible road ahead of you. Eventually you'll realise that they are just hiding their own scarred-over artistic wounds, that they are in fact speaking directly from those wounds, and you'll learn to tune them out.

It's a whole lot harder to tune out the soothsayers of doom hiding in your own mind, the ones that promise you every single shade of artistic catastrophe should you dare to let loose your voice on the world. And if you manage to overcome those, you might still have to face the twin foes of criticism and indifference, their power to shrivel and shrink you. Before long, you may even feel the chilly fingers of lifelong invisibility brushing your shoulders. And all the while, the letterbox continues to spit out bills.

In the face of all this, is there a secret to keeping hold of that precious, unkeepable key known as your unique voice? 'Confidence', some might say and they might well be right, but we all know what an elusive beast that is, especially for women (the same goes for self-esteem).

Which is why I'm slowly aiming for self-kindness instead. By which I mean that I'm crafting – carefully and a little warily – an inner dialogue that turns towards compassion and away from self-attack. One that gives my dreams a seat of honour, one that encourages, one that even cheers me on. There are few more golden trophies than the belief in yourself that you can find after failure (in fact, it's worth remembering that swift and early artistic success might not bring this particular prize). And so I'll keep on writing, inviting Kindness to sit alongside me as I do.

And because Kindness is kind and does not like to show up in your life empty-handed, it always brings a gift. And that gift actually turns out to be confidence anyway, or at least its beginnings.

And because Kindness is kind, I know that if I lose my golden key again, it will get down on its knees alongside me to hunt for it. *Did you look in that corner over there?* it will say.

And of course, it was never the outside world that tore the key from its chain in the first place – it was always my own hand all along, itching with shame and self-hate. But nowadays, when I find myself reaching up to grab it, I hear Kindness say 'stop' in its fiercest voice and I try my best to listen.

Deborah Martin is a Glasgow-based writer whose stories, poems and essays have appeared in various collections. She was a finalist in the Fish Short Memoir Prize 2018, a co-winner of the FrightFest screenplay competition 2017, and a runner-up in both Poetry Rivals 2016 and the *Cadenza* magazine quarterly short story competition. She has also written and performed in two works for the stage. Deborah has an MA in Creative Writing from Birkbeck, University of London and is currently completing a short story collection.

BENGALI LESSONS

Susmita Bhattacharya

I'd always regretted not being able to read or write fluently in my mother tongue, Bengali. And when I got married, my husband promised that he would teach me to do so. Immediately after our wedding in July 2000, I joined him on a six-month voyage on an oil tanker and this was the perfect opportunity for me to begin my Bengali lessons.

A typical day for us would start at 3.45 a.m. for his morning watch-keeping shift. I'd make us some Darjeeling tea and we'd watch the sunrise together. (I was very enthusiastic as a newlywed! By the end of the six months, though, I gave up on those pre-dawn shifts and preferred to snuggle under the covers until breakfast time.) He would plot charts, do his watch-keeping duties and give me Bengali lessons. I'd take along my orange notebook and several coloured pens and dutifully listen to what he'd say. I made lists of vocabulary – all colour coded to help me learn the language more easily. Pink for nouns, green for verbs. Red for adjectives.

The only way of communication with the outside world was through letters and occasionally via satellite telephone. For me, it was important to document my life at sea, for which I kept a journal, in English. I also wrote hundreds of letters back home to my parents, my sister, my friends, and to my new in-laws. My husband's grandmother wrote to me in Bengali as that was her only language of communication. I found it difficult to understand her letters because I couldn't follow the cursive Bengali script very well. It was frustrating but slowly the words and the sentences unravelled, and I could read more easily. Writing took much longer as learning the complexities of Bengali grammar and structure needed more practice. I had a letter template that I used, written by my husband, and I tweaked it here and there to make it personal and up-to-date. There were often more English words scattered through the letters than Bengali and they never could convey how I really felt. The rich descriptions that I could create in English were not possible as my Bengali was very rudimentary. But I soldiered on.

By the end of around four months, I was reading my favourite detective stories, Satyajit Ray's *Feluda*. In Bengali. I cannot explain the sense of joy I felt in finishing my breakfast quickly to race back to my cabin and read, read and read.

Then, our ship sailed into the port at Shell Haven on the Thames Estuary. This was the perfect opportunity for me to visit London. To do a bit of sightseeing. And guess which story I had just read? *Feluda in London*. Imagine my absolute delight in discovering the city – with a map in one hand and my copy of *Feluda* in the other. I was also seeing London for the first time, just like the characters in the story. As they exclaimed, pushing through the crowds on Oxford Street – *A sea of humanity . . . a veritable ocean!* – I too negotiated the crowds and gaped at the shops mentioned in the story. Marks and

33

Spencer. Boots. Debenhams, John Lewis, Selfridges. I braved the Underground and stood in front of 221B Baker Street, I held the book in my hands and read aloud in Bengali what Feluda said in homage to the great detective – *Guru, you showed us the way. If I'm an investigator today, it is only because of you. Now I can say, coming to London was truly worthwhile.*

Those words resonated with me. Feluda, you showed me the way too. Your absolutely thrilling detective stories created the door I needed to step into Bengali literature. I was able to walk with confidence around London because I followed in your footsteps.

I returned to the ship, grabbed my letter pad and began writing furiously about my adventures in London. To Dida, my husband's grandmother . . . in Bengali.

Susmita Bhattacharya's debut novel *The Normal State of Mind* (Parthian, 2015) was longlisted for the Word to Screen Prize at the Mumbai Film Festival in 2018. Her short story collection *Table Manners* (Dahlia Publishing, 2018) won the Saboteur Award for Best Short Story Collection in 2019 and was a finalist for the Hall & Woodhouse DLF Prize in the same year.

Her short stories have been nominated for the Pushcart Prize and been featured on BBC Radio 4. She is a Creative Writing tutor and lecturer at Winchester University.

OH BABY BABY . . .

Joanna Howard

'Do you . . . feel any different from the first time round?' asks the sonographer. 'Like there might be . . . more than one in there?'

'How many?!'

'Oh, just two!' she laughs.

'Oh my Goooood! This is the end of our lives!' wails my husband.

Twins: a boy and a girl. My grandmother had a set of twins, the last of a brood of seven. They were a surprise, delivered at home by my grandad. My tiny nanny birthed seven- and eight-pound whoppers! My birth wasn't quite like that.

Thirty-four weeks into my pregnancy and I'm in hospital, laid on my back and strapped to a monitor. The medics are freaking, because they can't find Girl Twin's heartbeat. They bring a portable ultrasound and discover she's migrated to a transverse position. A male nurse with an unwholesome grin checks my progress and tells me I'm fully dilated. It's been a four-hour labour, a rollercoaster of pain.

'OK, Mum, we need to take you to the delivery suite. We might have to deliver Twin One vaginally and Twin Two by C-section.'

'I don't think so! Just get them both out by C-section!' I groan.

The room is full of people, manoeuvring machines. They are explaining some consent forms I have to sign.

'Just give me the pen!' I hiss.

I wake up at 4 a.m., my teeth chattering like an outboard engine. My husband hands me a pint of water. Our twins are OK, he says. They are in the ICU. I'm told to rest. My belly is like a marquee with the poles removed. I can actually see the coil of my intestine sitting on top of the weird cavity where my twins were.

The next afternoon I'm wheeled across to visit my babies. I hold them both at once; skin to skin and bone and I know they are going to be just fine. We are taught how to do their cares – changing, cleaning, feeding, negotiating wires and tubes – and it feels like a privilege to be able to do these small things for them.

I'm taught to hand express and manage to squeeze out one millilitre of colostrum. Soon I'm hooked up to a double breast pump, pumping every four hours.

'It's a pain in the arse!' says a young mum in the next cubicle. She's not wrong.

A week later I have mastitis. A happy side-effect is that I sweat out my water retention and wake up with normal-sized ankles for the first time in months!

Did I mention that we're moving house? Our twins are still in the ICU. We hired a man with a van and they've put a huge dent in our fridge, but we're in at least. There I am, among the boxes, expressing again.

After three weeks our twins have made good progress. I'm invited to spend a night in hospital with them. Premature twins are not good at breastfeeding. They get exhausted and fall asleep before they're full, then wake up screaming with hunger. So, here's how it went:

Boy Twin: 'Waa, waa! Suck, suck . . . snooore.'

Girl Twin: 'Waa, waa! Suck, suck . . . snooore.'

And so on. All. Night. Long. A nurse came and helped me swaddle them. It didn't work. I phoned her again and she said I'd have to get on with it. And so it goes! Babies cry, mothers go batty! I was seriously worried how I would cope with them at home.

And then along comes my Spanish mother-in-law. Angie is a baby-whisperer. She holds them like a sack of spuds and pats them on the bum, making a tutting noise.

'I bore them to sleep!' she says cheerfully. She is always cheerful. Recently retired, Angie stays for two years. Her dedication to her niños is boundless.

I give up breastfeeding and buy ready-mixed formula. I wean my babies on Cow & Gate jars, twelve for £6 at ASDA. (DON'T JUDGE!) My mum buys their clothes and my dad builds a ramp for their enormous buggy and Angie is there 24/7 giving the kids so much love.

So, we survive. The sleepless years. The scares when I'm carrying full bags of shopping and Boy Twin decides to balance on the edge of the pavement in front of a double decker bus. The super-quick trips to the toilet, only to discover my twin toddlers have pulled a chair to the sink and started spraying water all over the kitchen. The plane journeys to see Spanish family, when it was Russian roulette which twin would sleep and which would scream the entire journey. Now they are nine and so lovely!

It's true what they say, it does get easier. And I know I'm lucky. But I'm also going to give myself a massive pat on the back for surviving this far!

Jo Howard is a poet, singer, scriptwriter and writer of middle grade fiction. A regular on the Northern spoken word scene, her work has been published in Confingo, The Writer's Cafe and Funny Pearls online magazines. Jo is a mum of three and a producer at film and media production company Viva la Zoom, which she runs with her husband. Her work is inspired by funny incidents that show our human frailty and resilience.

THE WALK

Jo Martyn

A couple of years ago, I went through an episode of depression. My GP kept telling me that I needed to exercise, as it would definitely help me to feel better. The thing was, I had never been particularly sporty – I dreaded PE at school – and believed that I was largely no good at sport and exercise. At the time, I couldn't imagine being able to motivate myself enough to do any.

That winter, I looked after a friend's dog for three weeks. No matter how cold or dark it was, I had to walk the dog every day. I began to notice how much better I felt after walking, even on those dark January nights. At the same time, a group of my colleagues had signed up to walk 100 kilometres, about sixty miles, from London to Brighton, to raise money for our own charity. The challenge was to complete the walk in twenty-four hours. When the challenge was announced, I wasn't sure whether I could do it, yet after Bonnie the dog had gone home, I decided to sign up anyway.

I did training walks every Saturday, and increased my distances over time. Sometimes friends and family joined me, sometimes I walked alone. It was a great way of connecting with others, and with myself. I began to take more notice of what was going on around me, and what was going on within me. I started to process the grief that had triggered my depression in the first place. I began to see things more clearly, and to believe in myself again. And after each walk, I was high, buzzing on the positive energy that endorphins create. That positive energy spilled over into the rest of my life. I became more confident, more accepting and more present.

The big day arrived! The walk itself was fun, sociable, sunny, beautiful; and of course, challenging. After twenty hours of walking, at 5.30 a.m., with painful blisters, doubts crept in. I got slower and slower. At 8.30 a.m., twenty-four hours into the challenge and still seven miles away from the finish line, I cried with pain, exhaustion and frustration. I briefly considered stopping. But I just couldn't. I was going to get across that finish line, even if I had to crawl across it. It took me another six hours to walk the last seven miles, painfully slowly. I repeated to myself 'I can do this, I can do this' again and again, which has been my mantra ever since. Sometimes I just counted my steps, doggedly putting one blistered foot in front of the other. It was the ultimate endurance test, a metaphor for grief, depression, recovery, acceptance and moving on.

Crossing the finish line was one of the proudest moments of my life. I had endured, I had achieved my goal, and I made many unexpected discoveries along the way.

Jo Martyn is a trainer-facilitator from south London, who believes that stories are the foundation of learning, connection and community. Jo is more passionate than ever about the positive impact that walking has on mental health and wellbeing, and has founded Urban Hikes for Mental Health. Follow her adventures @urbanhikesformentalhealth on Instagram.

THE FEMALE ENTREPRENEUR

Charly Lester

In 2014 I set up my own company. I left a lucrative, secure job in banking to set out on my own and try to regulate an unregulated industry. The year beforehand I'd fallen into writing a dating blog. I wrote a Facebook status joking that I'd go on thirty blind dates before my thirtieth birthday if my friends selected the dates for me. At the request of those friends, I wrote a blog about the adventure and the blog ended up going viral. Soon people all over the world were asking me questions about dating, including the Big One – which apps or dating websites should they be using?

Rather than simply give my own opinion, I decided there needed to be a more democratic way to decide which dating apps were the best. I came up with the idea of the Dating Awards. I'd never run a company before, and at the time I can genuinely remember questioning myself about starting the company. My only friends who ran businesses were male. How could I convince other people that I knew what I was doing?

Now I look back on that reaction in shock. I've always been a confident and capable woman. I have a law degree from Cambridge and a Master's degree in journalism. Yet I doubted my own abilities for probably the first time in my life, because I had no female role models.

In spite of my fears, I set up the company and 270 top industry executives attended the first year of the awards in London. In the following years I expanded the awards from London to Amsterdam, to New York, also running conferences alongside the award ceremonies. I became recognised as a leading dating industry expert, often appearing on TV shows like *Watchdog*, *Newsnight* and on *Woman's Hour* on the radio. I was even asked to be a guest judge on the final of *The Apprentice*.

Running your own business can be really tough. Just starting out you have to be a general dogsbody, mucking in on every task and challenge. But it's so incredibly rewarding. I'm so proud that I managed to turn an idea I had one evening into a real thing, which has affected so many other people's lives. Winners of my awards use the company logo in adverts all over the world. Hundreds of people have attended my events, and winning one of my awards is the highlight of some people's year.

I'm proud to have started my own company, and since the awards gave me confidence in my own ideas, I have gone on to create many other businesses. Nowadays I try to encourage other women with a business idea to take the leap and trust their own capabilities. The key is acknowledging the doubts as fear, and stepping past it. You will never know how it can turn out unless you take those first steps.

Charly Lester is a serial entrepreneur and one of the world's leading dating industry experts. She launched her first business, The Dating Awards, at the age of thirty and went on to develop an online learning platform called A League of Her Own, to encourage more women to start their own businesses.

Most famously, Charly co-founded Lumen – the dating app for over-fifties – which was the fastest growing dating app in the world in 2019. She was profiled in *Forbes* in 2018. Charly is currently preparing to launch her fifth business, Peaches & Poppies – a plus-size activewear brand, inspired by her own struggles to find triathlon-specific clothing that accommodates her curves.

PUTTING MY CARDS ON THE TABLE

Lissa Berry

It's always been about voices for me, doing silly voices, copying other people's accents, reading other people's words and listening to their voices.

Nothing I like more than reading out loud. My mum taught me to read before I went to school and it was my greatest joy, reading stories to other people. I was lucky to become a voiceover artist and had quite a long successful time of it as the kids were growing up, and then the recession kind of put the kibosh on that.

I had always used my voice, but in a way that other people wanted it to sound, so finding my voice was becoming more important and I'd been thinking about writing a story for ages. I'd written stuff for years but had never been brave enough to show anyone.

There was something about turning fifty that felt significant. Being 'Mum' for so long, I felt lost, I felt kind of left behind. Don't get me wrong, I LOVE my kids. They're twenty-one and seventeen now, and they're flying out into the world. Don't want to get too emotional, but I gave up on my dreams of being an actor when they were little. The logistics were too hard. I think it's still mostly women who find that they're the ones who sacrifice their careers when they become parents.

I'd heard about a festival in Oxford that was looking for new writers and I found myself submitting an application the night before the deadline. I hadn't even written a whole piece, I'd written about maybe fifteen minutes' worth. I didn't honestly think the judges would go for the idea at all. I didn't think it'd be good enough, but they did, and so I had to write it. I had to write a play.

I'd been toying with an idea since meeting a wonderful Welsh director called Chelsey Gillard at a National Theatre Wales workshop. It was inspired by a previous story I'd written based on my great-grandmother who was a spiritualist and tarot card reader who passed on her witchy genes to me, so I wanted to explore themes of living a life outside the norm and the effects this can have. Luckily Chelsey agreed to be both dramaturge and director. Without her talent, belief and encouragement, I would never have been able to do it. It was a really tough process, though, suddenly having to find words and a story for a character instead of just speaking them. Really tight deadlines, a deck of tarot cards and a garden-shed floor with scraps of paper all over it helped me find my way – that, and handwriting the script.

Somehow with hardly any rehearsal, but with the help of amazing friends and family who made costumes, props and posters, it suddenly became real in the Burton Taylor Studio in Oxford on a Saturday afternoon in June. I still can't quite believe I did it and it was my voice, my words. Though I had never really thought of them as my words even when I was rehearsing. They belonged to the character. But it felt wonderful to be telling a story of my own in that space for forty-five minutes. People really liked it. Even my kids came and they were so proud. It wasn't perfect, but it meant the world to me. It felt like one of the best things I've ever done.

It still does.

Lissa Berry is an actor, narrator and voice artist. She has performed in many theatre productions and is a regular actor at the Berko Speakeasy where she had the privilege and joy of doing a duologue with Geoffrey Palmer.

Lissa wrote her first solo piece, *Though Lovers Be Lost*, in 2018 for the Oxford Offbeat Festival and this inspired her contribution to *100 Voices*. In 2019 she was a finalist in the BBC Radio Drama Norman Beaton Fellowship award. Her most recent audiobooks for Audible include *How to Belong* by Sarah Franklin and *Impossible Causes* by Julie Mayhew.

A CARTWHEEL STATE OF MIND

K. Lockwood Jefford

I'd always start by standing still, feet together, up on my toes, arms straight, stiff, and close to my sides, fists clenched, eyes on my nominated runway. I'd take a deep breath, feel my nostrils flare, my chest rise, my heart going like the clappers. Then: a short, rapid run-up – just five or six steps. I could feel when propulsion met muscular poise and momentum kicked in. Like finding the biting point on a car. I'd twist at my waist and spring off my left foot while swinging my arms up, down and out – wide as wings – and with a force that whipped my legs up and over in a cartwheel in mid-air. I'd see the grassy ground tilt, feel the wind rush on my skin, then, back on my feet, bouncing, beaming, breathless. Punching the air.

I did my first free-handed cartwheel one dinnertime on the school playing fields watched by my best friend, Siobhan.

I did it! I did it! I screamed.

You did it! You did it! she screamed.

We grabbed each other and jumped up and down and round and round.

We did the same when Siobhan did her first back somersault.

It was just after the 1972 Munich Olympics. I had posters of Olga

Korbut and Ludmilla Tourischeva Blu-tacked all over the wood-chipped wallpaper of the bedroom I shared with my sister Liz. I wrote a poem dedicated to them and my gym teacher had it printed up on A4-sized card and laminated. That went up on the bedroom wall too.

At that time, my mother worked most evenings as a waitress and had to leave before my father was back from work or me and my sisters were home from school. For our tea, she'd leave a pot of potatoes peeled ready for chipping to have with baked beans or a tin of Goblin beef burgers. (I still love crispy chips gone soggy with tomato sauce or gravy.) After my younger sisters had gone to bed, I'd stay up a while playing *Switch* with my father.

One night he said, Are you happy?

I paused. No one had ever asked me that before. I can do a cartwheel in mid-air, I thought, and felt a surge of something rise up from the middle of me and expand all ways, filling me with pace for all sorts of possibilities.

Yes, I said. I'm happy.

The swell of exhilaration I felt then, of pride and giddy joy, became a lifelong benchmark of unadulterated happiness.

Not long after the 2012 London Olympics, I entered a writing competition on the theme of *Flight*. I wrote a story about a young woman who sees a therapist at a low point in her life and finds herself recalling an experience as a young gymnast when she flew through the air performing a vault called the Yamashita. It won first prize and was my first ever published story.

I still turn cartwheels. Wide open spaces like beaches and fields and ballrooms bring them on. I have to stick to the ground now, use both hands, but my legs are always straight, my toes pointed.

The summer before last, leaving a restaurant with my husband Adam, Siobhan and her husband Roberto, we found ourselves on a wide, empty stretch of pavement. I stopped, placed my feet together, rose up on my toes, arms at my sides, fists clenched, and focused on the tarmac.

Oh yes, said Adam. She's going to do it.

I raised my arms and stepped into the cartwheel. A bit wobbly – what with wine and wedge sandals – but I did it.

And they all cheered.

K. Lockwood Jefford is from a Welsh working-class family full of strong, creative women. Growing up, her favourite things were books and cartwheels. She trained and worked as an NHS psychiatrist and psychotherapist in London and has an MA in Creative Writing from Birkbeck, University of London.

Her short fiction has won awards, most recently the Royal Society of Literature's 2020 V.S. Pritchett Prize. Her work is published in anthologies including *Brick Lane Bookshop Short Story Prize*, *Bristol Short Story Prize* and MIROnline, and she's completing a debut collection of stories. She is thrilled to feature in *100 Voices* alongside talented and treasured friends and writing peers.

TRAVELLING TROUPE

Miranda Keeling

It was the early 1980s. I was about seven years old and living in Montclair, New Jersey. We had moved a fair amount since I was born in Yorkshire, to London, the Netherlands and then America. I always threw myself into the change and suburban New Jersey was no different: I had *bangs*, not a fringe, thank you. The rest of my hair was *feathered*, not layered. When any English relatives pronounced the word 'stupid' as 'steeyoopid' rather than 'stoopid', I rolled my eyes like they had just crawled out from under a rock. Only a few years after this I would get out of a taxi in London and have to start again – lose the accent, the slang, the tan. Wherever my Anglo-American, Jewish-Christian-Atheist family went, I made it my mission to fit in. I listened hard to voices, studied clothes and practised ways of being until I could imitate them well enough to disappear.

School in the States was big. Wide steps to walk up. Endless corridors. During break times, the sound of kids' voices was a constant roar. When the bell rang, silence descended, lessons began and until the next bell you were captive. Only if a teacher agreed to give you a hall-pass to use the bathroom could you walk out of class once it had started and through the building alone – sneakers squeaking on the polished floors. I loved having a hall-pass and would always take longer than I needed to get back to class. It was a relief to be without the other kids, when I could let the American girl I was trying to become, drop.

On one of my trips to the bathroom, I saw a piece of paper thumb-tacked to the noticeboard. It read:

Want to join the Travelling Troupe? We are selecting a group of students to tour old folks' homes in New Jersey, doing a singing, dancing show for the residents. Each student will be given a pen friend – one of the elderly people who live in the final home they visit. At the end of the tour of old people's homes, they will get to meet their pen friend. Application by audition only.

I was not a confident singer. In fact, whenever I sang at home, my mum, who was a fantastic singer, used to wince. But something, I don't know what it was, made me sign up. Maybe the part of me that wanted to say, 'I am here.'

I told no one I was going to the audition. I said nothing about it. I couldn't read music. I really didn't know what I was doing. I tried at home, practising 'Somewhere Over the Rainbow', but it went up really high. You know the bit about the bluebirds? My voice would crack, and it was a disaster.

I had a little brother, Dylan. I still do. We're not so little any more. I used to make up songs to sing for him, just nonsense songs. I had this great idea: 'I'll audition with a song I made up for Dylan. Because they don't know it,' I thought, 'they won't know if I sing it wrong.' I didn't realise that anyone who had a musical ear could tell if I was flat.

There were so many children auditioning. The auditorium was vast, and dark, full of small faces waiting for me to fail. I got up from my seat and I walked up on stage to the microphone. I started singing a little song that I'd made up to help my brother fall asleep – about the stars in the night sky and stuff like that. They let me sing about five lines, and then they said, 'Thank you. Next!'

When the notice went up on the board that said that I had got into the Travelling Troupe, I was . . . I'll never forget that feeling. I told my mum that I'd got in and she said, 'It's OK, honey, you don't have to pretend to me,' and I was like, 'No, Mom! I *did* it! I got in.'

Oddly I don't remember the details. I don't recall the names of the other kids, or how many of us there were – maybe eight? I don't remember how we got to the homes – probably by coach.

What *do* I remember? Walking into the spaces. A part of the floor cleared of chairs, in a main room. Elderly folk sitting, facing our makeshift stage. Light coming in through the windows, often from behind us. On bright days, we were silhouetted for the audience – singing, dancing shadows. I remember my hair was in two bunches. My costume was simple, red and blue.

It was shocking at first. The people facing us were in all kinds of states. Some alert and smiling, some comatose – sliding into their chairs like warm play-dough. Others shouted or growled through the whole thing. We lost any expectation of reactions but performed our hearts out anyway. Moments stand out in my mind – a man's eyes blinking open at a particular song. Smiling, he starts dancing along with his hands – fingers floating in the air, his legs forgotten under a blanket. Two women making noises – almost words, nods of recognition at something. A sprightly woman standing up from her chair and coming to take my hands for a few steps of a routine before sitting down again – her memory of getting up fading immediately. The pieces we performed for them have faded for me now, too. What I am left with is a feeling, an image – of throwing a seed into a pond, not sure where it goes. Sometimes, a flower blooms in the water.

As promised in the audition notice, at the end of the tour, I met my pen friend. Her name was Pearl. She had short white hair. When she gave me a hug, she smelt of candy corn and talc. She told me about her children – all grown-up now. I told her that she had beautiful writing. I looked down at her hands that had written the letters to me. The veins were clearly visible. Raised spots covered her arms – darker than her skin. Her laugh was low and full of energy. We spoke about small things for maybe half an hour. She was seventy-three years older than me. It felt like nothing. She could have been seven too as far as I was concerned, or I, elderly. After that day I never saw her again. We didn't write. It was something complete.

In trying so hard to belong, I lost myself. As part of the Travelling Troupe, I put on a costume, practised words and steps given to me by someone else, and found myself. Everything about it from the audition onwards was the opposite of hiding. It was new and scary and brilliant. In that auditorium, singing my made-up song, I began to see a writer, a performer, and a kid who felt a bit different sometimes. And that was OK. In fact it was just right.

Miranda Keeling is a writer and performer whose writing credits include: METRO online, *Reader's Digest*, short story 'Alouette' in *Gains and Losses* by Barbican Press, miniature play *Bulldog* for Uncommon Nonsense upstairs at the Royal Court, *Panphobia* at the Stratford Circus Theatre, *The Carbon Footprint Detective Agency* at the Arcola, *Tweet-off on the Tyne* with Ian McMillan for Radio 3's *The Verb*. She is a winner of BBC Radio's Norman Beaton Fellowship award.

Miranda was delighted to contribute to this fantastic project. Her mother was an editor and writer who taught her to celebrate women's voices. Miranda writes observational vignettes on Twitter as @mirandakeeling.

THE BOOK

Amy Foster

It's really not the kind of book I, or you I'm sure, would buy a tweenage girl. For a start, Woody Allen seems far too prominently placed on its overwhelmingly male 'Sergeant Pepper'-style cover, and then there's the content; the inclusion of Dr Crippen's execution in the 'On This Day' section is somewhat distasteful, to say the least.

Yet, buy it, and what's more, gift it, my mother did. For me. And, somehow, this dodgy little number seems to have escaped the culls that other far worthier books have suffered at my hands.

I love it for the fact it has my real name, my birth name inscribed in it, written oh-so-neatly in black ink, back when I wrote with such things as fountain pens. In truth, what I really love it for is the section that has been relegated to the end, almost as an afterthought, but which to me is the *pièce de résistance*. The 'Your Star Sign' chapter.

There is something soothing in searching for the sentences that describe my life so neatly. Realising that I have indeed ended up in the profession predicted in this tiny tome's pages seems thrilling, despite the fact I'm (somewhat) certain that this is statistics rather than the stars.

Riding, it seems, is a good hobby for a Sagittarius. Though my blue-framed and -spoked steed is surely different from the one envisaged by my clairvoyant guide, it is undeniably true.

Despite my delight at these gems, I would generally say I have a healthy cynicism towards the influence of the zodiac. And yet, I have found myself starting to use my star sign as part of my identity.

Developing a project with an old, old friend, we relish the effervescence of our dreams. Our ideas carry us off on a tide of ambition, leaving us to helplessly hide behind our zodiac. We're both *Sagis*, we say, we just have ideas. We need to find a Virgo to rein us in, we say. Then we won't be so ridiculously ambitious.

Is this line easier than the truth? That we just are ambitious? That we want to do well, to make a change?

It was in this book that I first learned how I am 'inherently extroverted . . . have a clever mind . . . and . . . a great thirst to learn. Life is a marvellous adventure for [people like me]' as 'the excitement of risk runs strong in [our] veins'.

I may not be any of those things, but I knew, even twenty-five years ago, that I'd rather be a strong-minded, intelligent Sagi, having adventures and dancing 'til dawn, than anything else. I knew to use my voice, because it was expected of me, it was in my stars.

Years later, I know to 'lean in' and that if I feel like an imposter, I'm probably not the only one. And yet I can't help but wonder: would I have said *yes* or *why not?* to so many of the opportunities that have come my way, if I hadn't had this little book to help me voice my dreams?

Amy Foster is a primary school teacher from Croydon, south London. Her dream is to make Croydon proud of its wonderful green spaces and unique cultural legacy, and she co-founded Croydon Cycle Theatre in 2017 to help realise this dream. She lives in South Norwood with her husband and children where she enjoys cycling with her daughters on their family tandem.

MARATHONS

Peta Cornish

In 2014 I ran the London Marathon in aid of the RNLI, the Royal National Lifeboat Institution, with my dear friend Charlie. It's one of the best things I've ever done and we are proud to have raised over £10,000 between us. Running a marathon had been on my bucket list for a long time – definitely something I wanted to do before I was thirty – and it was tough. But it was Charlie and the RNLI that made it seem possible.

Charlie was six months old when I was born in the house next door. We grew up together. Our families were very much entwined and her father Robert played a huge part in my childhood. We holidayed together, shared nannies, alternated school runs, hosted joint barbecues in our adjacent gardens. Our mothers even worked for the same company at one point. She was my surrogate sister. And Robert was like a second father to me. He encouraged adventure, exploration, being outdoors as much as possible, getting the most out of each day and he *loved* a challenge. He was also deeply involved in sailing, working for the Merchant Navy for a long time. His energy and verve for life were always an inspiration and had a massive influence on my life.

In 2011 Robert died very suddenly in a tragic accident at sea. It was a devastating shock. To us all. More so because Charlie and I had fallen out of touch over the years. As teenagers we had perhaps lost sight of the foundations of our friendship, of 'us', getting sidelined by other friends, other hobbies, our studies, and the difficult distractions that hormones and puberty provoke. Having moved to different schools, we were naturally drawn apart. Charlie was pulled towards a group of friends that I didn't fit in with – I was never very 'cool' – and I started filming a TV series that took up all of my time and energy. These new priorities created a wall between us. I don't think we spoke more than a few sentences to each other for almost ten years.

When Robert drowned, it was like being woken up. All of our childhood memories came flooding back and I knew I had to reach out. The day I heard of his death was the day after the accident and Charlie was in so much shock she couldn't (and wouldn't) speak. To anyone. But she spoke to me.

I called her mum's house and said who it was and her aunt informed me that she wasn't available. But when Charlie heard my name being mentioned, she came to the phone. She had developed a stammer overnight from the shock and our first few words were not easily come by. What do you say? There are no words to comfort or explain.

We kept in touch gently over the next few weeks and I went to see her for coffee. The first time we'd met up in five or so years. She asked me to write something for Robert's funeral, which I read (with great difficulty) on the day. From then on – it's been ten years now – our friendship has grown into what it was meant to be. Based on what it once was. And the sense of perspective losing someone affords.

Running the marathon for the RNLI was a testament to Robert, to his love of the water and to everything the RNLI does to save lives at sea. It was also a way of paying testament to Charlie. To her immense courage, to a lifelong friendship, to our childhood and to the bond that we as women had built with each other over time. She continues to play a huge part in my life. After Robert's death Charlie trained as a yoga teacher, and her dedication spurred on my own practice and spirituality. We are always each other's sounding board. When you have shared that much together, there is a depth of understanding and love that is unmatchable, really. In my hardest moments of training, I thought of Robert and of what he taught us. And of our friendship.

Charlie is an incredible woman. A force of nature that I'm honoured and grateful to have as a friend. To have that sisterhood, those shared memories, that depth of knowledge, that cord of strength. Always. As we move through the different phases of our lives, forming our own families, forging careers, moving houses or countries, I will always know that she is there beside me. And her father's death and the marathon we ran for him was what reunited us in some way. Strange as that may sound.

Friendships aren't always easy or straightforward. Just like life, sometimes it's a bit of a marathon. A knotty, complicated, winding path. But friendship is always worth fighting for. The knowledge that someone is walking that path with you. Sometimes by your side, sometimes at a distance. But always there.

Peta Cornish is an actor, writer and voice coach. She trained at Bristol Old Vic Theatre School and the National Youth Theatre after gaining a first-class degree in English Literature. As a young actor she was part of the cast of the drama series *William and Mary* on ITV, referred to in the piece. More recent credits include *The Alienist: Angel of Darkness* (Netflix), *Cinderella* (CP Films), *Common* (National Theatre) and *Future Conditional* (Old Vic). She wrote for *100 Voices* after being connected to Miranda through a mutual friend and hopes her piece can remind us all of the importance of friendship and connection, even in the toughest of times.

LETTERS OF HOPE

Alison Hitchcock

If you thought a letter would put you scarily outside your comfort zone, would you write it?

When my friend Brian was diagnosed with stage IV bowel cancer, I made a bizarre offer. I offered to write letters throughout his treatment to cheer him up. I don't know what possessed me. Over the next two and a half years I wrote more than 100 letters. Brian told me the letters connected him to a world beyond his cancer; at his lowest points they distracted him from the reality of his life. I can't say my letters were particularly empathetic or profound; they were generally just about me! But they seemed to work.

To celebrate his recovery, Brian and I set up From Me to You, a charity to encourage people to write letters to friends and family living with cancer. People also donate anonymous letters which we distribute to cancer patients in hospitals. We run workshops and send out letter-writing kits to help the writers get started. But in running the charity the thing I have found the most challenging is the fundraising. I've learned to swim in open water for a triathlon, walked 100 kilometres in twenty-four hours and, hardest of all, taught my tone-deaf vocal cords to sing so I could busk in Carnaby Street.

I begin each challenge thinking I am invincible but at four weeks in I begin to doubt myself; I'm out of my comfort zone and I feel vulnerable. By three months I want to give in completely but I can't because people have already begun to sponsor me. On the morning of each challenge I visit the toilet many many times. During the challenges I feel my body has been possessed by a woman much braver than I. And then, when each challenge is done, I feel a little bit proud.

Each year the charity has thousands of anonymous letters posted from around the globe. The writers tell us the first letter is difficult to write – not only trying to connect with a stranger but one who is ill. But once it is written the second comes more easily. The patients tell us the letters brighten their day and make them feel less alone. Whenever I hear this I'm reminded of all the swimming, the walking, the singing and all those first letters and that the fear is always worth the discomfort of stepping outside your comfort zone. Time and time again.

Alison Hitchcock is co-founder of From Me to You, a national campaign encouraging us to write letters to friends and strangers suffering from cancer. She has a Master's in Creative Writing from Birkbeck, University of London, having left a City career in 2010 to pursue a love of writing. In 2017 she won a Point of Light Award for her work tackling the isolation experienced by cancer patients. She is currently compiling a book of letters donated to the charity. See www.frommetoyouletters.co.uk.

VOICES
THAT DIDN'T LISTEN TO 'NO'

IN THAT MOMENT

Melissa Fu

I lost and found my voice in the same moment.

At the start of 2016, I jumped into a challenging full-time job teaching Physics. Part of me believed that if I did well, I'd prove something. I'd catapult myself into some kind of redemption for all the ways I thought I had fallen short in my career.

My story went something like this:

I had been a good student.

I wanted to serve a need.

I had degrees in Physics.

I had enjoyed teaching Physics in the past.

I felt I should work in science, as there is a need for women in science.

The school's story went like this:

It was academically rigorous.

It had an incredibly accomplished staff.

Its students were motivated and talented.

It was equipped with amazing facilities.

It was very prestigious.

In the midst of such excellence, there was little room for error. Yet it seemed that once I started, all I could do was make mistakes: I made blunders while presenting, I couldn't manage practicals, I didn't mark papers quickly enough, I couldn't control the room, I didn't inspire, I couldn't motivate. My objectives weren't clear, my lesson plans didn't tick enough boxes, my methods were too imaginative. I was far from being an exemplar.

A few months in, after a disastrous classroom observation, I sat in a small room, behind a closed door, across from the administrator who had observed the circus that was meant to be my lesson. I was asked to reflect on what went well and what needed improvement. In short: nothing and everything. Then the conversation turned to his assessment of me.

'You need voice training,' he said.

'Yes, that's on my professional development plan,' I whispered.

'You need to learn how to stand up in front of a group.'

I nodded.

Then he cleared his throat, leaned forward and said, 'You will never have the kind of voice that can command respect in a room of people, let alone a classroom.'

I was shocked. He kept talking, but his words became a blur. That sentence kept echoing in my head. You will never have a voice that commands respect. You will never have a voice in a classroom. You will never have a voice anyone wants to listen to. You will never have a voice.

Shutters went down in my mind. You will never have a voice.

Shortly after that meeting, I lost the job. I lost my health. I lost my confidence.

That was years ago. Now, I can't imagine any educator in good conscience saying such a thing to a student, mentee or colleague. I can't think of a single reason to warrant such cruelty. But at the time, I thought he was right. And if I had no voice, then I should retreat into silence. I lost my voice.

Why, when asked about how I found my voice, do I return to this memory? Maybe it's because now I understand that those shutters going down in my mind marked a pivot, a turn inwards, a turn away from this man and the external validation he represented. Maybe it's because it was only after I left that job with my sense of self shattered, that I began to take my writing much more seriously.

That spring, the blank page became a territory of my own. A sacred space. My salvation. Its wide-open whiteness became a place to exist. To make marks, to summon half-remembered dreams, to ask questions without answers. Here was a place to be, without justifying decisions in terms of pedagogy, without fear of turning the page to find a chorus of shoulds lying in wait. That spring, I wrote. Not to demonstrate my worth, not to prove anything, but to hear myself. On the blank page, everyone else's chatter subsided. In the absence of outside agendas, I found my voice.

Since then, I have written most days. I write to hear my voice. I write to share my voice. I write because I have a voice and I respect it.

Melissa Fu is from New Mexico and lives in Cambridge. With backgrounds in physics and English, she has worked in education. Melissa was a 2017 Apprentice with the Word Factory and the regional winner of Words And Women's prose competition in 2016. Her debut poetry pamphlet *Falling Outside Eden* was published by Hedgehog Press in 2019. In 2018–19 Melissa was the David T.K. Wong Fellow at the University of East Anglia and received an Arts Council England grant to work on her first novel, *Peach Blossom Spring*, due to be published in 2022 in the UK (Wildfire) and the US (Little, Brown).

THE UNDERDOG

Sian Brett

From the age of seven, I knew I wanted to work in theatre. My gran would take me to see anything and everything at the local arts centre, from Andrew Lloyd Webber to Alan Ayckbourn. She loves to recount the time I turned to her, pre-show, tiny and excited, and said, 'I get so excited in the theatre, I feel like I'm going to be sick, Granny.'

So when it came to thinking about universities and career, I was sure. I was going to move to London and study Theatre. I was going to ace my A Levels, especially Drama, and go and live my clichéd dream.

But then, mid-Year 13, Dad got ill. And he got more and more ill, and we got told that he'd never get better. When you're told something like that, I think your whole world shifts. Everything you thought you knew to be certain falls away, and any concept of future plans, of a future at all, spirals away.

Dad was a journalist from the old days of writing about film. He took me to press screenings, and we walked around town together. We joked that he'd kip on the floor of my student flat when he was working in London. He was too ill, in the end, to come with me to university open days, so the job was passed on to his best friend and partner in crime, Quentin. We looked around a few, and I fell completely, head-over-heels in love with Goldsmiths. I applied, and spent the next few weeks routinely checking UCAS and my emails.

Amid the teenage, hormonal stress of A Levels and applications, Dad got increasingly unwell until, in a blitz of ambulances and paramedics, he died on the 24th of November. My very best friend in the world. My guide to London from day one.

Two days after he died, Goldsmiths offered me a place. I graduated in 2017, and I know that if he had been there he would have jokingly said, 'Wow, a Theatre degree, *so* useful' and advised me to do any job other than writing.

But he would definitely have been proud. He believed a lot in underdog stories, in coming back from the darkest of places. I think I did that. And more than him being proud of me for that, I'm proud of me.

Sian Brett is a writer based in south-east London, whose debut play *Heroes* had a sell-out run at the London Theatre, and was produced by award-winning theatre company Box Room Theatre. After graduating from Goldsmiths University in 2017 Sian produced comedy and cabaret gigs across south London.

Her theatre and comedy work has been performed at theatres including Summerhall, Pleasance Theatre and Old Red Lion Theatre, and she has performed comedy at venues including VAULT, Soho Theatre and Hastings Fringe.

Part of this piece is an extract from Sarah Frances Armstrong's The Physiology of Fear, *a memoir.*

THE ART OF FALLING

Sarah Frances Armstrong

Fresh out of military training, a novice officer and junior doctor, I had boots that shone bright and eyes that shone brighter. Armed with lever-arch files and chafe-proof underwear, I was embarking upon my first operational tour of duty with 2 Medical Regiment. Operation Herrick 10. Afghanistan. Apart from two years as a junior 'house' doctor, most of my life had been spent in learning (and drinking) establishments. Knowledge-rich and experience-poor, it is perhaps not possible to be a good doctor at twenty-six. Maybe it is possible to possess the building blocks that make a good doctor; I hope that I did. But if I did, they certainly hadn't stacked up yet.

However, one can be a lousy soldier at any age.

I joined the army with no military experience, and it showed. I joined because I was bored with medicine, and the sausage-factory system that was medical education. I joined because I wanted to travel to places outside the remit of gap-year students with henna tattoos and weed-infused dreadlocks. I joined because I saw myself morphed into Lara Croft, a pistol held in a garter around my thigh, bounding over a ditch of boiling lava as a rickety bridge fell from beneath my feet. But Lara Croft I was not. Doctors did a much shortened version of the course at Sandhurst Military Academy than the 'regular officers' did, but it was long enough.

I learned what it meant to pour lung-burning, vomit-in-mouth effort into an activity and just scrape below the finish line. To have my humiliating time on a run yelled out before the entire class by a Physical Training Instructor who was nothing short of a psychopath and not to care because I was too busy dry-retching on the sidelines. But fitness could be worked upon. I improved to a point where I was unremarkable. I was delighted with this new-found inconspicuousness. Some skills were more difficult to master; I remained dreadful with a rifle. A friend remarked that when I was on the firing range, the safest place was directly in front of the target.

After a few months of pre-deployment training, tourniquets tied around fake limbs spewing red paint and cardiopulmonary resuscitation performed while wearing a rubber gas mask, I was deemed trained. My combination of medical diligence and military disaster was perfectly honed. Finally, with lip balm stuffed into magazine pouches and baby wipes in my mess tins, I was ready.

I've been out of the army for ten years now, but look back with gratitude and fondness. Because that experience taught me so much. Not just where to smear Vaseline in the war against chafing, or just how useful dry shampoo can be. It taught me the art of being comfortable with not being good at something. And art is the word. A recent study by the Programme for International Student Assessment suggested that British girls ranked as fifth most afraid of failure, out of seventy-nine countries. Social media and persistent gender inequalities doubtless all play their part in this. There is a prevailing societal expectation of perfection in girls which leads to this fear of failure and inhibits growth.

By having an experience that was so far out of my comfort zone, I was forced to embrace the possibility of failure. During my army career, it wasn't acknowledgement of my strengths that built my confidence. It was painful, public exposure of my weaknesses, and the subsequent struggle to overcome them. In short, we need to give girls permission to fall (in my case quite literally) flat on their faces. Because it's in the picking themselves up again that they see who they can be.

Sarah Frances Armstrong (Fran) is a Birkbeck Creative Writing Master's graduate. Now a doctor in the NHS, her younger days were spent working as an army doctor, an experience that was exhilarating, rewarding and, at times, terrifying. Her writing draws on the unique window into the human psyche that being a doctor affords her. She is also a mother, wife, sister, daughter, friend and feminist. She proudly participated in *100 Voices for 100 Years* with this account of her experience in Afghanistan.

Sarah was shortlisted for *Wasafiri*'s New Writing Prize in 2017, and longlisted for the Bristol Short Story Prize in 2019.

THE WRITER AS MOTHER

Reshma Ruia

'There is no more sombre enemy of good art than the pram in the hall.'

—Cyril Connolly

My journey as a writer and as a mother began in Manchester. I was born in India and brought up in Italy, two countries steeped in history and tradition. There was beauty but corruption and chaos too. These were fertile pickings for a creative mind. Being newly settled in Manchester with a baby was challenging. The baby became the landscape of my days and nights, the moon and the stars by which I navigated the hours. Nothing prepares you for parenthood. The primeval joy of giving birth is accompanied by a slow-burning rage as you see your identity slip away. You become a footnote to your own life. Yet the power and pull of literature ticked away quietly, viscerally somewhere deep within. I could ignore its calling but not deny its existence. A male writer is seldom defined by his parenting role; a female writer who is a mother needs to create within the parameters of domesticity, child bearing and rearing.

Straddling so many identities and boundaries was a boon for a writer like me. The state of non-belonging is a privilege. I could observe the world around me with a sense of detachment and choose to immerse myself in it in order to recreate it. Once I grew used to the ubiquitous presence of rain and the challenges of motherhood, I found Manchester provided a rich source of inspiration and enquiry. The best thing that happened to me as a writer was enrolling in the graduate programme in Creative Writing at Manchester University. I did my Master's as well as my PhD with supervisors who encouraged me and provided support and a 'writerly' setting that was very different from domestic monotony. My first novel, *Something Black in the Lentil Soup*, took shape within these workshops and seminars. The novel portrays the nostalgic travails of its hapless main narrator, Kavi Naidu, a poet who travels between India and England, hungry for love and success. It is an irreverent portrayal of three parallel cultures – British, Indian and British-Indian.

After my Master's, with another child on the way, I was juggling competing demands of housekeeping, mothering and writing. Virginia Woolf extolled the virtues of having 'a room of one's own'. For a woman who has a growing family this can be elusive. Somehow, the writing was done in the margins of time. I submitted short stories and poetry, sending them to journals and anthologies. I did readings in bookshops and attended literary festivals. The publication of my first novel allowed me to experience a writer's life, albeit on a modest scale.

Male writers can engage with their craft with an ease and sense of entitlement that is not possible for a woman writer who is also a mother. The sheer exhaustion and noise of motherhood can drown inspiration and yet one must make space for it. Somehow, I found the strength and determination to start my next novel. I also had a supportive husband who backed my choices.

My second novel, *A Mouthful of Silence*, is set in Manchester. It is a story of betrayal, belonging and characters who lead translated lives. It describes the contemporary distrust of 'the outsider' and shows the arc of an entire lifetime, not just the constant tug of the past, but also the pull towards a better-imagined future. The novel was shortlisted for the SI Leeds Literary Prize.

My growth as a writer has developed in tandem with my children's growth as young adults who cheer me on. In 2011 I co-founded The Whole Kahani, a writers' collective of British South Asian writers. I have helped the collective in publishing two short story anthologies. A third is under way.

I have also returned to my first love, poetry. My debut collection *A Dinner Party in the Home Counties* won the 2019 Word Masala Award and my short story collection *Mrs Pinto Drives to Happiness* is published in September 2021. While I do not have a manifesto for mothers who write, my poem below articulates what I felt as a new mother.

EGG

I hear you at night.
A single cell, you keep sucking
my insides noisily. A parasite
slurping your way through.
Now a limb, an eye, a throat.

At times, you're a dead weight, not a crown.
Don't ask me to shut my eyes and breathe
your name out loud like a hymn.
It is too early to fall under your spell.
You are an accident of cells crowding the ultrasound.
There are no grudges against you. Not just yet.
Only this need persists to make you understand.
My blood will still roar though now it whimpers low.
You won't break me down, my unborn child,
with your love or your blows.

Reshma Ruia's first novel *Something Black in the Lentil Soup* was described in the *Sunday Times* as 'a gem of straight-faced comedy'. Her second novel *A Mouthful of Silence* was shortlisted for the SI Leeds Literary Award. Her short stories and poetry have been published in Britain and internationally, and broadcast on BBC Radio 4. Her debut poetry collection *A Dinner Party in the Home Counties* won the 2019 Word Masala Award. Lemn Sissay said of the poems, 'I feel I am reading someone whom everyone will be reading in future.'

Reshma's short story collection *Mrs Pinto Drives to Happiness* is published in September 2021. She is the co-founder of The Whole Kahani, a writers' collective of British South Asian writers, and passionately believes that women's voices need to be amplified and heard. Find her on www.reshmaruia.com.

SAY IT OUT LOUD

Branwen Davies

Say it out loud and it has to happen, right?

It's been my mistake in the past. Keeping it to myself. Allowing myself to just daydream. But if I say it out loud, I have to go through with it. Make it happen. I'm good at dawdling and, let's face it, excuses. Nothing will change unless, well, unless I change it, and I'm running out of excuses. Maybe running out of time.

So I choose my most sceptical friend. The one I think will laugh the loudest and convince me that I'm going insane. I drag her out for a drink. Only she doesn't laugh. She says go for it. So now not only have I said it out loud, I have validation and encouragement too!

I'm stuck. Agitated. Biting at the bit. Needing to do something. Go somewhere. Anywhere. Hell I'm bored and, even worse, feel boring. I need to shock my senses. Scare myself a little. Take a risk. I'm in my favourite Japanese restaurant and over a bowl of steaming ramen I think – Japan!

A week later a letter arrives and I recognise my sceptical friend's scribble. A postcard and a cutting from a newspaper. I spit out my coffee. Headline – *Do you want to live in Japan? Can you teach English? Be there by September!*

Is this real? I mean, I'd pulled out September from mid-air when I told her bold as brass after my third glass of wine that I was going to move to Japan and that I was going to be there in nine months and – oh my God – this is a sign! This is my green light!!

There's a small matter of an interview first but . . . I can pull that off, right?

Everyone is in suits. Grey suits. I don't own a suit. I'm in blue. Bright blue and purple. Purple with a splash of pink. Neon pink. And you know. Yellow shoes. With pink bows. I'm sweating. Squirming. He's frowning at me – the big boss guy – and he's asking me, in front of everyone, thirty of the suited ones – 'What possessed you – what possessed you to come dressed like that?'

The kids in ill-fitting suits snigger.

'Me? I don't own a suit. I'm an actor. I don't usually do interviews. I do auditions. I try to dress the part of the part I'm up for, you know. As this is a teacher position, teaching young children, I thought I'd dress the part.'

I'm offered the job on the spot.

And I'm here. Sat on a balcony in my new apartment in a strange city at night in my pants, a cold Asahi in my hand, feeling free in the warm Japanese air.

Say it out loud. I dare you.

Branwen Davies is a writer and theatre maker who occasionally directs and lectures and, when she can, travels. Branwen writes in Welsh and English and is a member of Dirty Protest Theatre Company and Os Nad Nawr Theatre Company. She recently co-wrote *A Night in the Clink* for Patertrail Theatre Company and directed the Welsh-language play *Adar Papur* for Theatr Genedlaethol Cymru. Branwen believes everyone has a story and that stories need to be shared. She believes it's important to create platforms, spaces and opportunities for the quieter voices not often able to say it out loud.

MO CHROI

Debbi Voisey

2012 was the worst year for me so far in my life. I lost my best friend to a car accident, and it's things like this that make you realise that we are only here for a short while, and that no matter what, we are travelling alone. However much you love someone, or however much you think you are joined to them, at some point you will be separated and you're flying solo.

Donna Bendistis Jubb was a beautiful soul. Sometimes troubled (as we all are) and sometimes unsure, and sometimes worrying about work, and money, and her children. But always optimistic, bright and alive. Even as she was cursing some spate of bad luck or frustrating work project, she was planning her next girls' night out or work trip, or visits with friends she had not seen for years, or trips to the beach in Delaware. That was her haven of peace and sanity, and the one place that always centred her, calmed her. She loved to tan (oh how she loved to tan!) and listen to the waves and the hubbub of families fishing and boogie boarding with their kids. She loved the boardwalk at night, the sweet smell of cotton candy and popcorn, the *ding ding* of the amusement arcades and the taste of King's homemade ice cream in Lewes.

Donna loved her friends and her family with a fierce passion. Passion was something she had in spades. Even though she was often called 'The Little One' because of her tiny stature, her personality was sassy and bold and often her volume made up for her lack of height.

She was generous to a fault; would hardly ever let you put your hand in your pocket to pay for anything. She could also accept kindness graciously when needed. Her smile was bright and white and BIG. Her husband Brian always said she could 'eat an apple through a picket fence!!' I like that.

I struggled through the last ten months of 2012 without her, and it was incredibly hard. It was our habit to email several times a day. Sometimes we 'talked' through emails for an entire work day (yeah, I know, that's bad! But we did do our work at the same time). We talked about things that you only tell to your soulmate. We spoke on the phone and of course we met as often as we could. We laughed and cried together. Now, when I have something I want to tell her, it takes a few moments to realise I can't.

So leaving 2012 behind was kind of bittersweet. I wanted to get away from it because it was the year I lost my soulmate. It was the year that hurt more than any other time in my life. But it was also the year in which she last existed — so how can I want to eliminate that, strip that memory away?

Donna was always my biggest champion as far as my writing was concerned. She loved and cared for me enough to be brutally honest about my work. She told me what didn't work as much as what did. She said she hated the parts she hated, and that she loved the parts she loved. Because of her, my writing is better.

After she died, I realised how short life is, and how you have to grab a hold and make things happen. As I moved into 2013, I actually became excited about the future of my writing, and wanted to move things along, to do something with the writing that she had so much faith in. I decided to reduce my working week to four days and to concentrate solely on writing on Mondays and, because of this, have made great leaps in my progress. I also set up a dedicated writing email address and added her initials after my name, so that she would always be a part of my writing journey. Now, whenever my .dbj email pings I think of her. And celebrate each success and near miss with her in my mind.

The flash fiction piece I have included here is called *Mo Chroi*, which is Gaelic for 'my heart'. It's the title Donna gave to her website. She wasn't the best at keeping it updated, but it had all the important things on there, and photos of all the people she loved. The flash is fiction, but she was very much on my mind of course, and her DNA runs all the way through it.

MO CHROI

The simple beauty of everyday things; that's what hurts the most. A bird landing in a puddle, a cherry blossom petal riding a breeze, a lamb bouncing on velvet green. The wind teasing a branch, prising its fingers loose and making it draw shapes in the air.

Seeing these things and knowing that she no longer can; that's pain.

And the sounds. You can't bear it; they cut into you. The mew of a kitten or the *dddddddrummmm* of a butterfly's wings. Even a gate banging against a post, or a child screeching; annoying but real.

She can no longer hear them.

And when you listen to the music she loved, it pulls something deep inside you. She will never again cry at the poetry of songs, or look at someone and feel the words like they were written from her heart to theirs. She will never again feel those human emotions that tie love and life together in aching chains.

You place the tulips – her favourite – in the vase next to her photo. Purple, for royalty apparently, although she was ordinary (yet extraordinary). Purple like the bruise on your heart whenever you picture her.

Beauty: it's what she had. It's what she was, despite all her fears and neuroses, the nervous tics and multiple apologies that were second nature. She had love; love for her girls and their dancing, for her job, for her family, for her friends. For life.

Love like that is passionate and raw and painful. It happens so rarely. And when it's taken, the loss is physical.

Mo Chroi – Gaelic for 'my heart' – was her mantra; her passion and love for all those in her life. She always gave her heart. She always had yours.

And she broke it when she left this place.

Debbi Voisey's short stories and flash fiction have been published in print and online. She has two novellas forthcoming for publication in 2021. She is seeking an agent for her novel, while running online writing workshops and courses, details of which can be found at www.debbivoisey.co.uk.

SMALL ACTS

Tamara Pollock

Whenever I think about what women have achieved in the last 100 years, I get a buzz. So I was excited to be contributing to this celebration of women's achievements. The first person I thought of in these terms was my mother, which led me to think about my seven siblings and the chaos of our childhood: the jumble of objects clogging the stairs, the wires hanging from the ceilings, the buckets of soaking nappies.

My mother gave birth to most of us in a room above the front door, a room we called The Boudoir. And it's only now that I'm writing this that I'm thinking, *What? We called a room in our house The Boudoir?* We should have called it the delivery room. When I was ten, I used to stand in the spot I was born in and think, if I stabbed myself now, I'd be one of the few people in history who had been born and died in exactly the same spot. Once she had had each baby, she was extremely casual about it. She would take it downstairs when it was a few days old and just leave it somewhere.

When we were all at secondary school, my parents bought the dilapidated house next door. To fund the renovation, my mother felt the wisest plan would be to accommodate twenty-four Italian students from a convent in Rome. When you're a child, you don't question your parents' decisions – you think everybody's doing that kind of thing. So, we prepped and painted all the bedrooms, and anything we couldn't decorate, we threw a blanket over.

Then there was the mystery of the extra guests at the table, fragile strangers with shaky hands whom we associated with nervous breakdowns. And for convenience, that's what we called them. When setting the table, for example, we'd ask if there were any Nervous Breakdowns coming. My mother would look up from peeling a potato, and instead of saying, how utterly callous and disrespectful, she'd say, no, not this evening. Though we learned not to trust her on this. It took us a while to understand she didn't know either.

When we reached our teens and early twenties, my mother started to look around her and discovered the house was absolutely disgusting. This was 1985, her elegant year. She bought wallpaper with peonies the size of dustbin lids. We hung it for her – and it did look strangely wonderful. She had the holes in the walls plastered over and acquired mirrors and vases. We began inviting friends over, and people to stay. It became very crowded and we began serving supper in two sittings.

When we grew up and moved away, she became a marriage guidance counsellor. She took in more students. She founded a catering company. Family supper became a weekly event: parents and siblings, paying guests and Nervous Breakdowns coming together on Sundays instead of weekdays.

In 2015 she died. At her funeral, a journalist friend told me she had written an article about her. In it were things we hadn't known;

that when a friend needed help she would drop everything and take them for a walk. That for all her fierce energy, there was, at her core, a unique stillness; that for years, by arrangement with the parish, on certain evenings of the week, she would place a lit candle in the window – a sign that her door was open to any friend or stranger who might want to join us.

Like other women of previous generations, she created opportunities for change from the world around her. I think this is why her friend wrote about her; because of the magnitude of small acts.

Tamara Pollock completed her MA in Creative Writing at Birkbeck, University of London, in 2010. Her stories have been published in the *Sunday Times Magazine* and broadcast on BBC Radio 4. Her story 'Elsa' was longlisted for the *Sunday Times* EFG Short Story Award.

Tamara runs Creative Writing groups for Kensington Libraries and is a member of Cathy Galvin's Word Factory team. She has just completed her debut novel.

RESULTS

Sarah Hegarty

In the spring of 2003, I was bringing up my family and trying to write. In my desk drawer, I had the beginnings of a novel. My writing needed a kickstart, but how? Was a Master's the answer? *Go for it!* said my husband.

I found a part-time Creative Writing MA, one evening a week, at the University of Chichester. I applied, and was thrilled to be offered a place. Each week, my sister drove miles out of her way to babysit our two young sons.

Suddenly I had assignments to write; deadlines to meet. I gorged on this new diet. I wasn't alone: here were others who shared my obsession. I was encouraged to find my voice, and was surprised that I wrote a lot about being a mum, which had changed my life in a way I couldn't have imagined. Too soon, the course was over. In May 2006 I handed in my dissertation, and set up a writing group to swap work with friends. We went our separate ways, and waited for our results.

That September, our eldest son found an ulcer in his mouth. Then there were two. Then there were too many to count. His eyes blistered. I dished out Calpol, and penicillin, and fought down panic. Nothing worked. He was admitted to hospital and put on a drip, while this nameless, terrifying thing – an allergy? An illness? – rampaged through his small body. My husband got leave from work, and we took turns to look after our younger son, and do shifts at the hospital.

Our world became our son's room, the bed, the tiny amount of food we were able to get into his ulcerated mouth. The doctors were puzzled. With medical students in tow they descended in packs, keen to get a look at this rare case.

They couldn't stop the ulcers spreading. The atmosphere changed from puzzlement to panic. One afternoon, a team of medics stood round our son's bed, talking about him as if he wasn't there. One of them explained: a blister was blocking the urethra, and our son couldn't empty his bladder. They would have to cut into it. His name was on the list for emergency surgery.

I've got no clue about science. I've never even Googled this thing, although I know its name now. But a bladder injury was serious. Our son was only twelve: invasive surgery could leave him with long-term problems.

He was too ill to speak for himself. But I knew how brave he was. He'd endured pain that would have floored an adult.

'No,' I heard myself saying. My face felt hot. I'd never argued with the doctors before. 'He'll do it by himself. Just give him time.'

Surprised, and cross, they agreed to wait until six that evening. We had three hours.

We watched TV – property makeovers, attic treasure hunts. I watched the clock, from the corner of my eye. We shuffled up and down the corridor, him leaning on me, his thin frame frail as an old man's. I felt the echo of my own slow walk, along different hospital corridors, years before, leaning on my husband, waiting for this boy to be born.

I stood outside the toilet cubicle, trying to give him privacy. Behind the flimsy door, I heard him crying. How could I do this to him? Was I risking his life? But I trusted him. At last, shouting with pain, he did it.

The operation was cancelled. We breathed again, and picked ourselves up off the floor. I went home, poured myself a glass of wine and switched on the PC. There were emails from friends and family, asking about our son's progress.

From the far-away world of writing, friends were emailing with their degree results. My degree. Where were my results? Had I submitted my dissertation wrongly? Could it have got lost? Fortified with alcohol, I emailed the course tutor to ask if I should have heard. I pressed 'Send', and went back to the hospital.

Next afternoon, back home, I wondered: had the uni replied? We'd already got the best result: our son was going to recover. But I wanted to do well.

Feeling sick, I switched on the PC. There was an email from my tutor. I clicked on it.

'Dear Sarah,' I read, 'I'm so sorry' – oh well. It didn't really matter.

– 'for the delay,' it went on. 'I typed in the wrong email address. I'm very pleased to tell you – you've achieved a Distinction.'

I stared at the screen, until I couldn't see the words.

It did matter. It did. It really did.

Sarah Hegarty's short fiction has been published online and in anthologies, most recently the *Mechanics' Institute Review*. Her novel-in-progress was shortlisted for the Exeter Novel Prize, and the 2019 *Mslexia* Novel Competition. She is represented by Annette Green at the Annette Green Authors' Agency. Sarah is writer-in-residence at George Abbot School, Guildford, and passionate about encouraging new writing voices.

Find her on Twitter @SarahHegarty1 and at www.sarahhegarty.co.uk.

ON THE NEW

Y. L. Huang

There is a photograph of me, aged eleven, perched atop a donkey in a touristy part of Mexico. There was a bright, colourful poncho draped around my shoulders, and a sombrero – too large – slumped on my head. It was supposed to be a standard holidaymaker's shot, with the child-me grinning excitedly for the camera. But the expression on my face, captured in print for posterity, was one of terror. I had one foot firmly anchored on the step that I'd climbed up on, terrified to let go. Scared of leaving my comfort zone.

Life went on. Changes happened, as they do. I switched schools. I moved to a different country. I became an adult. My comfort zone had relocated, but it hadn't expanded. It followed me around, like a large hula hoop that kept me confined within circles of familiarity.

I don't recall how this started, but many years ago, I decided to try four new things every month. I didn't have to like them, I just had to show up. I started small, a salsa-dancing class here, stargazing at a local observatory there. As time went on, I had to get more creative with my choices. If you've ever joked about joining the circus, I can confirm first-hand that you can take lessons in some of the requisite skills – trapeze, juggling and more.

Living in London gave me access to different types of dance classes. I wielded an Italian longsword; made a pair of shoes; baked bread. I ran a Race for Life. And, while I've never been on a donkey again, I did go horse riding, by choice. It was scary, but the panic wasn't pervasive. As the mare edged forward, I made a terse truce with the unknown, and was met by the rush of trying something new.

Once you get used to it, seeking new experiences (within reason) can seem like second nature. It's a humbling way to face fears, gain some perspective, and learn to deal with setbacks. Not everything works out. My first batch of bread was too dry, and the shoes I'd made pinched my toes. But that's the point of escaping your comfort zone – it gives you the chance to loosen the reins, to experiment and, hopefully, to grow.

Y. L. Huang is a content strategist, editor, writer and photographer who has spent some time seeking new experiences, from stargazing to sword-fighting. She photographs these whenever possible, and occasionally writes about them too.

Armed with an MA in Shakespeare from UCL, part of her career has included editing business publications, and ghost-writing corporate pieces that have been published or quoted in *Forbes*, the *Guardian* and other mainstream press. She has also penned art and film reviews in her own time (and in her own name). Her photography has appeared in media outlets including *Vogue* India and the *Daily Telegraph*.

VOICES THAT ARE
(NO LONGER) SILENT

THE WOMEN OF TROY

Jane Roberts

Growing up, I was enchanted by Ancient Greek and Latin texts, and I followed my dream to study Classics at Cambridge. But the majority of Ancient Greek and Latin texts were written by the patriarchy for the patriarchy. Studying in such depth increased my fascination not with the protagonists of the epics, but with some of the more unspoken stories.

It is an amazing realisation – whether you are on a train talking to a stranger or whether you are reading to a hundred or so people at a literary festival – that you as a woman, a writer, you now have the agency to pick some of those tacit, underwritten stories from history and give them new life, a new readership, new understanding.

At the festival where I read the piece featured below, 'The Women of Troy', a teenage girl came up to me and said that she was going to re-read Homer's *Iliad* and think about the importance of the unnamed women in the text.

I think that response is probably one of my highest achievements to date.

THE WOMEN OF TROY

When rosy-fingered Dawn dances over the rocky outcrops, the women of Troy are washing the undergarments and tunics of the Trojan soldiers in the river. They cleanse war from the wool fibres with practised fingers.

The women of Troy are given pathetic epithets by the Great Poet in his epic. Weeping and wailing, the women of Troy wash. Wretched wailing and weeping. Still the women of Troy wash the undergarments and tunics of the soldiers in the river.

Up in the palace there is weeping and wailing. Queen Hecuba. Cassandra. Andromache. The Woman of Troy – lovely-haired Helen – who is not from Troy, yet will define this city for eternity. None of these women have yet washed the undergarments and tunics of the men who fight this war. These women will be heard crying from the lofty battlements of Troy, beseeching both gods and enemy to spare their kith and kin. Down below, where the misfired pleas fall leaden onto the ever-death-hungry, blood-libated earth, the women of Troy are washing the undergarments and tunics of the soldiers in the river.

The god-like men of Troy let the city fall to the ground. The royal beauties are sorted in the Greek camps, most dispatched to the ships. The Greeks fight over these spoils of war like frenzied hounds picking at scraps of flesh on the mangy carcass of a once-prized horse.

Now the unnamed women of Troy are washing the undergarments and tunics of the Greek soldiers in the river, wailing and wondering: wondering if they would fare better at war than their menfolk; wondering why they are still washing and are not sent to the ships – as the blood and fragmented soil of their patriarchy escapes the river, weeping out into the wine-red sea.

Since she graduated from Cambridge University in Classics, **Jane Roberts**'s writing has featured in a variety of international publications, including Valley Press's *High Spirits: A Round of Drinking Stories* (Best Anthology, Saboteur Awards 2019; also highlighted by the Publishers Association in the 2019 Summer Recess Reading list for Parliamentarians).

Jane is a firm believer that the sharing of languages, experiences and education is crucial to furthering the empowerment of women.

Find her @JaneEHRoberts and
www.janeehroberts.wordpress.com.

THE RISE OF THE PHOENIX

Sharena Lee Satti

Poetry saved me, it was a lifeline. It allowed me to amplify my
voice.
To speak and be heard, to express through poetry and spoken
word.
Poetry became my oxygen, my fuel, my sweet escape from a life so
bitterly cruel.
Now my poems are inscribed into park benches and shared on city
screens,
Never would my younger self believe, when I say I'm living my
dream, no longer the little voice calling or the girl who is afraid
to unmask her vulnerability, poetry was the gift I was born with
and it actually saved me.
My message of hope and determination and never giving up.

It all changed starting with one summer evening,
I got this fluttering feeling, it was
Enchanting, my whole body felt full of light like a piece of heaven
was inserted into my
Body, into the depths of me. An experience I had never felt before.

I had another heart beating under my flesh and skin, embedded
   deep within my womb.
I didn't think I'd see this day, when I wasn't wishing my life away,
I waited and waited and gave up in the end but then God sent me
   this message.
This divine link to the heavens, when I heard her heart beating.

My life changed that day, and I never looked back
At the deep-rooted cracks that tried to attack
My footpath. Now I walk amongst mountains, and river banks,
   with flowing water that
Swirls in tune to my frequency.

It took me time to see clearly but once I started to see the good in
   me,
I no longer see the damaged me.
I see a lioness roaring, a wild flower growing
I could finally see that my past suppressed me and I was never
   going to be its victim, stuck in a repeated system.
I was destined for beautiful things.

I'm proud to have achieved all that I thought I never could.
To breathe without thinking, to think without hating, to love
   without worrying.
To be here alive, to say I've survived.
No longer the fragile girl that hides behind the shadows.
I am the dandelion that grows

Widely, unapologetically, my words are spilled onto paper pages of
poetic inspiration.

Standing on bookshelves, 'She' is the medicine that's good for your
health.

No longer seen as the weak one, the vulnerable one, the yes of
course one, to keep the peace one.

I am seen as me and all that I have achieved to be.

All that I have to contribute, too.

Not just changing my own life but through poetry changing other
lives

I am all that I thought I couldn't be.

Sharena Lee Satti is a poet and independent artist from Bradford,
West Yorkshire, whose inspiring words have been inscribed on park
benches in the city to uplift local residents on their lockdown
walks. Nominated for the British Indian Awards in 2020 and as
one of the '21 of 2021' creatives most likely to impact Bradford's
cultural scene, Sharena is a familiar voice on local and national
radio.

Sharena's work focuses on social and environmental issues.
Her poetry collection *She* was published by Verve Poetry Press in
2020. See www.vervepoetrypress.com/sharenaleesatti.

A BIT FUNNY IN THE HEAD

Stella Klein

I clearly remember thinking in images as a child, responding to the world via the mood and colour of things: the yellow of my boiled egg, the hard-baked blueness of an Australian winter sky, the mud-grey shimmer of the lizard outside my grandma's kitchen.

Alongside these image-recollections are the fiercer memories of my parents' vicious exchanges at the dinner table. My father the hot-tempered scientist, my mother the self-absorbed dreamer, look-ing for her own answers to the mysteries of the universe. And then there was my sister, fragile, artistic and clever too, who would say I was the lucky one, the one who came out bouncing, joyful, express-ing myself with a foot-stomp when I didn't get my way.

In truth, I rarely got my way, and was not expressing myself at all. Unlike my sister's artworks, my own attempts with crayons or paint left a hole or a splash in the middle of the paper, a sludge of mossy green, the colour of shame. As for words, oh, I could gabble all right. 'Loquacious', 'chatty', 'never stops talking', complained my teachers year after year. But with all my shaggy outpourings, it felt impossible to be heard.

Was I, perhaps, a bit funny in the head? A late-developer, I heard my mother sigh, as I turned the pages of *Janet and John*, reinventing the text as I went along. Thank you, Dr Seuss, I got there in the end. I eventually discovered the adventures of *Emil and the Detectives* too, the joys of *Pippi Longstocking* and *Clever Polly and the Stupid Wolf*. Though it wasn't until much later that I became an avid reader (my mind too often drifted from the small print on the page), words soon became not only a source of frustration but fascinating as well. I learned to love the look and sound and feel of them, how some denoted something rich or very particular, how others could shift or bend in meaning. In my earliest attempts at writing, I found my own misuses or bending of words could even be affecting. If I didn't bewilder my parents, I could sometimes make them laugh.

Aside from the stories, words and images, beyond the tensions at the dinner table, there were the rich encounters of the playground to contend with. Learning to read those assorted signals of anguish and desire, knowing who liked to play rough or use rude words, who was willing to share their skipping rope or ball, was, I discovered, as all animals do, my key to survival.

Now, much later, as I get down to the serious business of writing, of translating those memories, sensations, encounters into words, the dread of being unheard, the niggling old ache to be understood continues to hamper my advances. Though still I peck away, revising, replacing, reworking my gibberish into something round and true, growing in faith as I hop from branch to twig, as I build each nest of words, that the wings of a new story will ultimately unfold.

Stella Klein is a London-based writer and neurodiversity tutor in higher education. Her flash fiction has been published online by Flashback Fiction, Reflex Fiction, *Flash Fiction Magazine*, MIROnline, 101 Words and Otherstories.com.

Her work can also be found in the printed collections of Spread the Word's *City of Stories* (vol. 2), the *Mechanics' Institute Review* (vol. 13) and the 2020 *Fish Anthology* of stories, memoirs and poems.

A FLICKER

Louise Jensen

When I was little I was obsessed with Enid Blyton. Her characters were so real to me they became my friends. I'd often huddle under my covers, stifling my yawns and straining my eyes, as I read 'just one more page' by torchlight.

Mr Townsend, my primary school English teacher, always encouraged my love of literature, and it wasn't long before I'd read everything my school had to offer. The first book I created was six pages long, had stick-man illustrations and was sellotaped together. I was immensely proud of it. Writing was a huge part of my life, until one day it wasn't.

I can still vividly recall my excitement as I sat in front of the careers advisor at school, unwrapping my hope I would be an author, and the crushing disappointment as she told me it wasn't a 'proper job' and I'd be unable to make a career from writing. I followed her advice and went to work in an office and my dreams were tightly packed away, gathering dust for the next twenty years.

My thirties were a car crash. Literally. I sustained injuries which, when coupled with a pre-existing condition, resulted in me losing much of my mobility, forcing me to radically change my lifestyle. I felt utterly lost and utterly alone. Depression and anxiety tightened their claws and the future looked bleak.

Chronic pain kept me housebound for much of the time. Always an avid reader, I began to devour books at an alarming rate. 'You'll have read everything on the shelves soon,' my local librarian said. 'You'll have to write your novel.'

And there was a flicker, a shift, a rising of hope. I grasped that nugget of possibility and I wrote. I wrote when I was happy. I wrote when I was sad. I wrote when I was scared, and in between writing, I read, read and read some more. Words have the power to lift, to heal. They have illuminated my world, which for a time became very dark.

As Anne Frank said, 'I can shake off everything as I write; my sorrows disappear, my courage is reborn.'

After finishing my book I allowed myself to do something I hadn't done for years. I dared to dream. With shaking fingers, I typed a submission letter and sent my precious words out into the world. To my absolute delight I was offered a book deal. I'm now a full-time author, have published several novels, and my stories have been translated into twenty-five languages, have reached No. 1 in various charts in various countries and have sold more than a million copies.

Every day I think how lucky I am that such an awful situation has resulted in something so unexpected, so wonderful.

I love to visit schools and share my story, encouraging the children to reach for the stars, to never let anyone make them feel they aren't good enough or that their dreams are impossible, because you never know until you try.

Louise Jensen has sold over a million English-language copies of her psychological thrillers, which have also been translated into twenty-five languages. Her books have been featured on the *USA Today* and *Wall Street Journal* Bestseller Lists and have been optioned for TV.

Louise's books have been nominated for the Goodreads Debut Award, the *Guardian*'s 'Not The Booker' Prize, along with the best Polish thriller award. Louise has also been listed for two Crime Writers' Association Dagger Awards. When Louise isn't writing thrillers, she turns her hand to penning heart-wrenching contemporary fiction under the name Amelia Henley.

BOYS WILL BE BOYS

Grace Pilkington

Content warning: this piece contains references to sexual violence.

Ding-dong! Trump is gone,
the earth breathes a sign of relief,
while others storm the Capitol,
still in a deranged state of grief.
But how he managed to
get through the White House door
deserves continued uproar.
A tape was revealed,
'Grab them by the pussy' he said
women came forward,
stories of molestation
spilled over the press,
but to no avail.
It roused no response,
frustrated truths
further frustrated.
Shhhed back under the carpet,

where it's grey and dirty,

where rape accusations belong,

where no one can see them

and nothing looks wrong.

'Grab them by the pussy'

he said to the world

and 62,985,106 people of America

said 'Hey that's cool. What are you up to for the next four
    years?'

so when someone who has sexually assaulted women

is suddenly President of the United States,

you can no longer say 'Hi we're the western world,

and we're really tough on rape.'

And I refuse to hear how we've progressed,

while we continually repress the sexually aggressed

Sixteen years ago, 'my pussy' was grabbed,

And entered by a man I had not invited in.

I woke up, he was on top of me,

inside me.

The next time I woke,

I found my knickers on the floor,

I remembered a club, dancing, drinking his drinks,

And then.

Did I tell anyone?

No. I stayed silent,

My lips sealed

by all I knew

would happen

if I revealed:

Nothing.

Perhaps a long court case –

moments captured on CCTV

images of me

drinking his drinks

in mini, mini skirt,

giggling and having a flirt.

They would assess the situation,

go through it with

a fine-tooth comb.

'Hmm. It seems she was quite up for it'

They'd say.

'It was object vs object,

and now, how can she object?

She was leading him on

and lads – that's just what they're like,

you give them a taste and they'll want a bite.'

So I kept quiet.

I blocked it out,

buttoned it up,

pinned it down.

But when faced with attempts to silence us,

which they do, every single day,

with every rape accusation they hush and shhh away,

each time they try to tell us

'Oh no big deal, it's okay'
we have to say:
NO it's not.
It's not okay.
It's not okay.
It's not okay.

Grace Pilkington is a writer and poet who writes about taboo subjects such as mental illness and women's issues. She performs at literary nights across the UK, has recited her work on the BBC World Service and appeared at literary festivals including Hay and Port Eliot. She has an MA in Creative Writing from Birkbeck, University of London, and was longlisted for the Notting Hill Editions essay prize for her work 'Sugar-Coated' on the contraceptive pill and for the 2017 National Poetry Competition.

Grace shares poetry on her Instagram page @notatraceofgrace and her blog www.notatraceofgrace.com. With poetry collective Little Grape Jelly she published *Hell-p Me* (Eyewear, 2017). Her collection *I Have No Idea What I'm Doing: Poems on Pregnancy and Motherhood* is to be published in 2021 by Quartet Books. Grace also writes stories for children and lives in Hastings in East Sussex with her husband and son.

SURVIVAL IS PROTEST

Golnoosh Nour

'Achievement' can be a loaded term for someone who doesn't like to abide by capitalist rules and definitions. However, when I think about this word, I cannot help but think I have had an achievement in life, and that is my PhD. And it might be equally problematic to consider a PhD 'an achievement' too. Personally, I believe I am allowed to do so, because my PhD wasn't just about getting yet another useless higher education degree from an institution. I had two major traumas while studying for my PhD. So, to me, my doctorate is also a symbol of my survival.

I was in my twenties in a foreign country, the UK. I had already completed a Master's and was preparing to start my PhD, when my mother died in Tehran, completely out of the blue. The shock was so severe that after it happened I travelled back to Iran and decided to quit my studies and life in the UK, and live in Tehran with my grieving widowed father. I did stay in Tehran for a few months, but my father was also the one who encouraged me to carry on with my studies despite our loss and grief. I was lost, and I didn't know what I wanted to do or where to live, and my fear of loss had become intolerable. I was scared of losing my father. I didn't want to leave him, and I didn't want to be without him. My mother had such a powerful and, at times, formidable presence and role that it already felt like all our lives had come to an end without her.

I'm not sure whether or not I had come to terms with my mother's death when another trauma happened to me. It was only a year after my mother's abrupt death and I was still in my twenties. Long horrible story short, I ended up having a traumatic interaction with the UK police. Although as a leftist student I knew about the police being racist and queerphobic, I never truly believed they would bother with someone like me; as far as I knew they were obsessed with Black boys. Surely, I was too female, too light-skinned and too middle-class to fall prey to it. I was, of course, wrong. I still consider myself privileged and lucky for not having been treated worse, which I am certain would have been the case, had I been Black and poor. This interaction ended in the police officially apologising to me, but it has left such a scar on my sensitive temperament that, to this day, I consider not just my PhD (which I received two years after the incident), but my existence as an 'achievement'. In her seminal book *Living a Feminist Life*, Sara Ahmed states, 'Survival can be protest.' And I think as an Iranian queer woman, I am one of the many living proofs of this.

Golnoosh Nour studied English Literature at Shahid Beheshti University, Tehran, and completed a PhD in Literature and Creative Writing at Birkbeck, University of London. Her short story collection *The Ministry of Guidance* was published by Muswell Press in 2020. Her debut poetry collection *Sorrows of the Sun* was published in 2017 by Skyscraper. She has been widely published and platformed both in the UK and internationally, including on the BBC and in *Granta*. Golnoosh teaches Creative Writing at the University of Bedfordshire and designs and hosts a monthly radio show called *Queer Lit* on Soho Radio Culture. For more info, visit gnour.com.

HOW FAR I'VE COME

Stevie Tyler

I live with fourteen people in a warehouse. I'm thirty-four. I'm getting a divorce. I'm OK, though.

We all have our own rooms, but the distance from my bed to the bed next door is 30 millimetres of plasterboard. That's about the same length as the top half of your thumb. It is close enough that if someone turns over in the night, you hear their duvet rustle.

It's incredible what you can hear through the walls.

Sneezes

Snoring

The microwave door being shut

The switch being pushed down on the kettle

The bathroom light being turned on

Stirring tea if you clank the spoon on the edges of the cup

Things we all pretend you can't hear:

Shagging.

It was a slow afternoon working from home and I ended up in an internet black hole, which somehow culminated in me Amazon-

Priming a sex toy from Ann Summers. The first sex toy I've seen in about fifteen years.

Who even knew Ann Summers still existed? But as a child of my generation, I'm a loyal fan because of all the Ann Summers parties we used to go to in the early 2000s. The fond memories of being at a friend's house while their parents were away on holiday, drinking bottles of Lambrini while a forty-five-year-old woman from down the road made you hold a Rampant Rabbit under your nose, have stuck with me. As long as the person who booked the party was eighteen, it was *no questions asked* if their little sister and her mates came along.

We all hung out together and talked about masturbation, sex, what we liked and didn't like. No shame, no judgement, no talk of getting pregnant. Just our pleasure. There were no camera phones or TikToks. It was just us. And Sharon of course, but she was like a social worker, or the village witch. This is probably what sex education is like in Denmark. I bet everyone gets a free set of vibrating eggs to play with as part of their A Levels.

Do kids in their teens have a Community Sex Witch showing them what a strap-on is, or what crotchless knickers look like? Maybe they don't need one to buy a new sex toy. Maybe they won't forget who they were for the whole of their twenties.

The Amazon delivery man comes. I get it out and marvel at the 'real feel skin' thing, a new development from the Barbie doll plastic of the olden days. Fewer veins. More USB chargers. It lights up! Bright enough to cast a glow on my face in the low light of the bedroom.

The vibrations are . . . low? Not the high speed bzzzzzzzzzzzzzzzzz I remember, but the sort of deep resonating vibration you get from standing too near a speaker at a gig. I hold it under my nose, thinking of Sharon, and my eyes involuntarily rattle in my head. Maybe I should give it a road test.

I hear a cough from the room next door.

Can my housemate hear the vibrator? Surely not. SURELY not.

I sit there for a second, totally still, holding the vibrator with both hands like a weapon and listening really hard. I hatch a plan. I leave it vibrating on my bed while I head downstairs and out of my room to listen from the kitchen.

Just as I close the door, suddenly everything doubles in volume and there is a sound like a vintage wind-up toy being dropped on a tabletop. I realise that the vibrator has moved across the bed and bounced on to the MDF floor of my mezzanine.

I should run back and turn it off

I should be embarrassed

I should be as quiet as I can

Then I remember Sharon. I remember Ann Summers. I remember the joy of talking about wanking with friends.

I start cackling uncontrollably and call my housemate to come and have a look.

Stevie Tyler has been writing and performing poetry since she was seven and got told off in her primary school test for using exam time to write poems. She is a founding member of Rhymes with Orange, a standup poetry collective that champions new writing, and loves supporting people through the creative process.

INSPIRING WOMEN, INSURGENT WOMEN

Maureen Wright

I have always loved history and, like me, many historians of my generation grew up reading Jean Plaidy's brilliantly researched novels, interspersed with the odd 'Regency romance'! But I had not realised just how much women's lives had been 'reduced' in the telling of history – written, as it still was in the mid-twentieth century, by the victors, or those who told of the lives of the white, male, middle-class diplomats, politicians or military leaders so important to 'traditional' history-making.

I worked in the financial sector, in social services and in retail before commencing my university career in 2001, but I really had not appreciated the gendering of the workplace and the everyday sexism that I seemed to have (fortunately for me) mostly escaped. In researching and writing the past in the Noughties, and specifically the biography of the extraordinary Victorian suffrage campaigner Elizabeth Wolstenholme Elmy, who became the subject of my doctoral thesis, my eyes were opened to so much that the 100,000-word limit for my book was almost not enough to do justice to her story.

I began my own academic journey as a mature student in my

early forties and am always delighted when there are lifelong learners in my seminar groups today. Discussions always have a different dynamic; we share – at least it seems we do – more, and at greater depth, and younger scholars value their input, keen to highlight contrasts and differences of generational understanding. In my first week at uni I also took a class in Women's History, taught by the professor who would later go on to direct me in my research studies. And, from almost the first moment she started to speak, I knew that the topic would be somehow key to my future.

Of course, at the time, I didn't know how important it would be, or that I would go on to forge a new career path because of it. But that is what happened. Now, in the first week of my module – which centres on the Votes for Women campaign from 1865 to 1928 – I begin my lecture with a list: a list that I write in such a way as to provoke a response. First, I ask the students to imagine they were a woman living in 1868. I continue, deliberately slowly:

'You would,' I tell them, 'have no Parliamentary vote – no vote of any kind in fact, not for parish or town councils, local government in any form, or the House of Commons. And you certainly could never aspire to the offices of Member of Parliament or Prime Minister. There was little in the way of secondary education for girls. There was even less provision for Higher Education – and even when the first women's colleges were established in Cambridge in the 1870s, there were no degrees.

'If you married, you ceased to exist, legally that is. You could not own property as a married woman. Also, any money you earned through your employment could be collected and spent by your husband. If you and your children starved as a result, you had no recourse. You had no rights to your children over the age of seven. And you had no legal right to refuse sex with your husband – even if he was infected with venereal diseases.'

At this point the women (for usually it is women who choose this course – although some men have done so) look stunned. They have no notion just how hard it was for women, how little independence they had. Last autumn one person remarked:

'I had no idea, I thought this course was about Emmeline Pankhurst and the suffragettes.'

'So it is,' I replied, 'but we don't mention Mrs Pankhurst for another fortnight!'

That is the really wonderful thing about teaching Women's History. Each generation goes on to inspire the next: telling stories, making histories and narrating the extraordinary lives of those who sought to make a difference.

Dr Maureen Wright is a Visiting Fellow in the Institute of Humanities, University of Chichester. She retired from teaching in 2020, but continues to write and publish on the suffragette movement. Her latest work can be found in *The British Women's Suffrage Campaign: National and International Perspectives* (Routledge, 2021). As Patron of Elizabeth's Group, Maureen supports fund-raising efforts to erect a statue of Victorian suffragist Elizabeth Wolstenholme Elmy in her hometown of Congleton, Cheshire, which is scheduled for unveiling in March 2022.

TAKE THE STAGE

Sabrina Mahfouz

Speaking out loud in public was something that I had never, ever done until I was twenty-five. I'd been the prompt for some school plays, read sections of a book out in class – but being on stage and having a mic in front of me, that was completely new territory, and in the world that I had grown up in and seen, it was male territory. From raves, where everyone who took the mic to MC was a man, all the way to working in Government and seeing the people who were given a platform to speak at that time were, in the vast majority, men.

So to find myself standing on a small pub stage in front of a microphone with a piece of paper in my hand, shaking like it was connected to the core of the earth as its tectonic plates were shifting, was quite a surprise to myself. Although I had planned it, I never actually believed I would go through with it. The realisation of the plan was helped along, I guess, by a little bit of wine and by my brother, who I had bribed to come with me to a poetry night. In those days, poetry nights were once a week in London and not looked at as a fun way to spend a Friday evening. They've got a bit more of an interesting reputation now, thankfully.

I did it, shakes and all, and people clapped and laughed and I was floating. It led, in one way or another, to the career that I have now, as a writer. It really was that one stage that I stepped onto and didn't leave, that enabled me to take all the other risks and chances that I wouldn't have expected myself to take.

I would really encourage anybody who has that creative, artistic urge inside them to do something scary and unknowable to at least give it a go. You might enjoy it, you might hate it, but you'll never know unless you do it.

And it will never be as terrifying as that first step up.

Sabrina Mahfouz is a writer and performer, raised in London and Cairo. She is a Fellow of the Royal Society of Literature and resident writer at Shakespeare's Globe Theatre. Her most recent theatre show was *A History of Water in the Middle East* (Royal Court) and her most recent publications as editor include *Smashing It: Working Class Artists on Life, Art and Making it Happen* (Saqi, 2019) and *Poems from a Green and Blue Planet* (Hachette Children's, 2019).

Sabrina has received multiple awards for her writing and is also the editor of *The Things I Would Tell You: British Muslim Women Write* (Saqi), a 2017 *Guardian* Book of the Year, and selected by Emma Watson for her feminist book club, Our Shared Shelf. She's a regular on BBC Radio 4, recently presenting *Word of Mouth* and *Poetry Please* and writing fiction for *Short Works*.

WAKE UP

Angela Martin

I'm a singer-songwriter from the band Bugeye, so when I was asked to join the original *100 Voices for 100 Years* project, I chose to share one of our songs called 'Wake Up'.

The song itself is about the current political climate, from women's marches to the battle of saving our beloved grassroots music venues and our all-important creative spaces. It is a celebration of the coming together of communities in the continued pursuit to stand up for what we believe in and to fight for change.

I wrote this song at a time when it felt like more and more people were starting to wake up to the realities of inequality, racism, sexism and climate change. To stand up, speak out, march, petition and start asking questions and break the silence of just accepting things the way they are. I felt it was important to share this song, as music has always played a vital role in uniting people and inspiring them into action. From anti-establishment and protest songs to anti-war and visions of a better world; we express and share our ideas through music providing an important commentary on the world we live in today.

Now, it feels more important to speak up, and Wake Up, than ever.

'WAKE UP' BY BUGEYE

Pack another beer and pop another pill
Raising up the red flags
Noting all the press now
Stealing out the back door
Meeting up with friends
Feeling reminiscent
I'm feeling anecdotal
Wake up
It's time to wake up
They say wake up but do you wanna let it all out
I say let it all out

Clamber through the window
Crunching broken glass
Seeing cartoon mayhem
We're rising from the gutter
Waking from our slumber
Seeing all the stars yeah
Feeling agitated. I'm feeling motivated to wake up
It's time to wake up
They say wake up but do you wanna let it all out
I say let it all out
Hang up your red coat it's time to wake up
I say it's time to stand up together

Pack another beer and pop another pill and

Marching with our own flags

Noting no more press now

In it for the long haul

Try to shut us down yeah

Feeling reminiscent

I read it in a book somewhere

Wake up

It's time to wake up

They say wake up but do you wanna let it all out

I say let it all out

Hang up your red coat it's time to wake up

I say it's time to stand up together

Angela Martin is a singer-songwriter and guitarist for south London disco punk band Bugeye. She is also the host of the music podcast *Bugeye's Rock, Pop, Rambles* and the co-founder of arts and cultural blog the Croydonist and Cro Cro Land Music Festival with Julia Woollams.

YOU ARE ENOUGH

Natalie Twum-Barima

This poem is for those who are expected to attain certain
heights and always be focused,
Despite the invisible barriers surrounding their gender and
their colours

This is for those who are tired of depression deeply pressing
its two pence into everything that they try doing,
And to those who've ever been hurt by those that they once
trusted

This is for those who deposit so much into others, but the
returned interest is limited
And over time, only depreciation seems to be given

This is for every single mother, who never thought they'd be
a single mother,
But have a way of smothering their kids in love that fills the
void of absent fathers

YOU ARE ENOUGH

This is for those who get birthday blues, year-in-year-out,
And to those who are tired of explaining why they've not
    ticked certain boxes by now

You are enough!
And with the same measure of love that you show others,
    you deserve to be smothered,
Remember, it's your self worth, so don't leave it in the hands
    of others

See, I got tired of sticking with the status quo and not giving
    myself enough attention,
I got tired of living a life that seemed perfect but felt like I
    was just existing

I found my voice when I was reminded that those who settle
    for anything, stay at the bottom,
I found my voice when I accepted that everybody's journey is
    different,
I found my voice, when the voices of others disappeared
    through the path of forgiveness

Ladies, you're different because you're here to make a difference,
You're a blessing, an inspiration and uniquely the embodi-
    ment of a real woman,
So remember your voice matters too and doesn't deserve to
    be muted

Natalie Twum-Barima is a spoken word artist who centres her pieces around such issues as those faced by women and Black people. As an example, in 2020 Natalie featured in a *Forbes* article about how to ensure Black people are treated fairly in the work-place. Natalie has recently ventured into writing comedy pieces too and may be found on Instagram @natalietb1 and @natalietb_comedy.

FAILURE

Amy J. Kirkwood

Talking about my achievements has always made me uncomfortable. I subscribe to the whole 'work hard in silence, let success be your noise' philosophy – except actually, a lot of my successes are silent too, because I don't tend to dwell on them too much or allow myself to enjoy them. In a quiet way, for many years I was mainly driven by absolute terror of failure and a deep need to be perfect.

I think a lot of women – and men as well, of course – but a lot of sensitive, intelligent women are like that. I'm not afraid of calling myself intelligent now, although I used to squash it down inside.

I remember reading *The Bell Jar*, particularly the fig tree section where Esther stares at all her futures – the career, the family, the author, the Olympic champion – knowing that choosing one meant losing all the others. This book was published in 1963 and that fig tree image was still so vivid to me that I was physically swallowing back panic: the worry about which branch to pick, scared that while I wasted time picking, all those figs would dry up and I would lose everything, just because I was paralysed by the choice. I don't think that's just me; I think a lot of women my age feel that way, because we're still expected to have it all and be grateful for the opportunity.

I stood like one of the living statues that you see the tourists watching in Covent Garden: frozen, eyes moving back and forth watching the world pass by me, but held firmly in place. Holding myself there, really – too worried everyone was watching, waiting for me to mess up, to make even the tiniest movement.

So, perversely, the achievement I really want to talk about, if I have to talk about achievement, is actually all the times that I've failed. And I mean properly failed: the kind where you cry in the shower and it claws at you like a razor blade that's scraping away your stomach lining and you bleed it out through the pores in your skin – really *bleed* it.

I've failed that way over and over. And often I fail in silence just like I succeed in silence. It's rare for me to write so personally about anything, and if I didn't believe in this project so much, I never would have agreed to be so open about the thing that scares me the most. I've developed a hardness: a second skin, definitely, to cover the razor-damaged one. And it's difficult for anyone to get past that. I don't think I'm alone in that, either – in acting like I don't care.

But while I tend to fail and succeed in silence, it's definitely those failures that I'm proudest of. Because to fail in that gut-wrenching, soul-splintering way means that . . . I cared. It mattered. The job, the relationship, the submission, the friendship, whatever. It was something I really wanted – not something I thought I should have, but something I *wanted*.

I teach primary school kids. I have a quotation on my board that I discuss with them a lot: 'Only those who do nothing make no mistakes.' And a life without failure, to me, is a half-life, a half-happiness. It's when I fail that I feel closest to being me. The fortress that I've built myself crumbles just a little bit and I can peer out over the top, and I've learned that I am extraordinarily resilient. But I wouldn't know that if I hadn't lost everything on more than one occasion, if I hadn't sat on the floor of my shower and cried until my heart broke, holding onto all of my limbs in case I fell apart.

Failure has taught me to believe, and to forgive – myself, and others. It's given me humility and made me braver, kinder. I'm proud that I won't ever rely on anyone else for happiness, because I can and have created it for myself, from the ashes, over and over. Meticulously, I continue to piece together the jagged remnants of my losses like a patchwork quilt sewn with bright golden thread and make a beautiful, imperfect life for myself. One that doesn't paralyse me: one that I am excited by.

I think that's the only way to avoid staring, frozen, at that fig tree, or standing still for tourists in Covent Garden. Go for *something*, and keep trying until a loss knocks you off your feet – then get back up and start from there.

I had no idea what I actually wanted, until I started failing.

Amy J. Kirkwood writes middle-grade and young adult fiction. She has been highly commended for the Pageturner Prize and was longlisted for the Bath Novel Award, as well as the Write Mentor Children's Novel Award. Her prizewinning short fiction has been published online and in print, most recently in *The Real Jazz Baby* and Splash of Ink.

Amy is also on the Senior Leadership Team at a London primary school, where she teaches Year 6. She is represented by Thérèse Coen at Hardman & Swainson and can be found on Twitter at @amyjkirkwood.

VOICES THAT LEARNED

KNOW HOW

Amie Taylor

There was a time in my life when I very much felt I couldn't. Or I wasn't. Or I didn't know how. I worked in theatre and had always looked out to that world and saw people doing the things that I wanted to do, but felt that I wasn't clever or confident enough. Sometimes I felt I just wasn't male enough; by my mid-twenties it seemed to be all of my male friends were getting ahead in the business, and I just didn't know how to. I used to try and fail at things often, haphazardly chasing after my dreams, believing they would always stay out of my reach. I didn't know how to get ideas off the ground and I often felt quite intimidated by a male-led industry.

Then in 2012 I met this incredible group of people, mostly women, bold and mighty and vulnerable: indomitable women. I worked with them for two years on a theatre project called The Chaosbaby. It was my first experience of cross-generational friendship. Through working with them and alongside them I learned how to do things and they taught me that, yes, it was tough and unfair, but that hard work, resilience and a bit of confidence in yourself can go a long way. They spent time and love and wisdom on me, and they really didn't have to. It was in walking side by side with them that, for the first time ever, I started to understand feminism and how to challenge an industry and society that structurally holds not only women, but all minority groups back.

The more time I spent with this incredibly supportive group of people, the more I felt I learned how to become myself. I became more confident in my ideas and putting myself forward; that was a gift from them to me. To not be afraid of failing, but to try, to not give up and through trying things I found a part of me that had never quite fully revealed itself.

In 2014 I decided to launch my own website. It was called The LGBTQ Arts Review – a website that documented and examined LGBTQ+ theatre. I had recently come out myself and I realised I felt that I'd been really limited in the role models I'd had on TV and in theatre. I wanted to examine the lack of representation and then: try to change it. Through running my website I noticed that queer theatre was dominated by white, male, cis-gender, able-bodied voices and I wanted to do something that might shift that, even if only a tiny bit. So in 2017 I successfully applied for some Arts Council funding with the support of another friend and mentor and got given some money to run a scheme to support female, non-binary, trans and minoritised LGBTQ+ voices and writers. This was a really important moment for me, because it was proof that I could do something and I could achieve things and I wasn't powerless to try and change things. Five years before, I wouldn't have thought I was skilled enough to do something like this; I wouldn't have even bothered to fill in an Arts Council form, because I'd have doubted that I had an idea worth funding. But things had changed.

What I've learned in the last nine years is that the only way to know if you're the right person is to try. There will be many 'Nos'; some will sting, some will ache and lots will feel almost unbearably unfair. Some will be OK, because the person who got it definitely deserved it more than you, or needed that space more than you did. We don't live in a meritocracy and I have to acknowledge that I have privilege in lots of ways and we all have a responsibility to step aside when it's right to. However, the more you try, the harder you work, the more chances you take and the more audacious you are, the more 'Yesses' there will be.

Fundamentally, it was the support of this group of women that changed everything for me. From this I learned that supporting one another and building each other up is one of the most important things we can do. We should take some time to look out to the world, to the people around us who are doing cool things, whether they are friends, strangers or acquaintances. See them, offer words of encouragement; let's engage in one another's ventures and offer an impassioned boost, for no other reason than the fact that we can; it will make all the difference. I know, because it did for me.

Amie Taylor is a writer, theatre maker and storyteller. She teaches drama and shadow puppetry to children and adults and makes LGBTQ+ theatre shows for children aged four to eight. She has written two books: *The Big Book of LGBTQ+ Activities* and *The Monster Book of Feelings*, both published by Jessica Kingsley Publishers.

She founded and ran the LGBTQ+ Arts Review for six years; she cares a great deal about historically minoritised voices being platformed and listened to – which is why she loves the *100 Voices* book and is thrilled to be involved with the project. When she's not working she can be found growing things in pots in her small north London garden or wild swimming with her partner, Gemma.

LEARNING THE STEPS

Anne Carter-Roszkowski

I remember when I first came over to the UK from Sweden to study, I used to roll my eyes at those mums I saw taking the ferry boat; always loaded down with huge bags of nappies (the Swedish ones being more practical and so much cheaper) as they went back to their husbands in the UK. Of course, despite promising myself I would never be one of them, I became that person. I've been happily married to my British husband for forty-two years.

It wasn't always easy, especially being a new mum. Living in Bristol with two young daughters, husband at work, I didn't know any other women with small children and, like many new mothers, I felt lonely. I started to crave adult conversations. It was a godsend when I met several other young mums through the National Childbirth Trust. I made friends and joined the local committee – the start of what I would later call 'my committee phase'. I found it really interesting and enjoyed the camaraderie. Three of us took over the regular newsletter, which meant a lot of chasing people for contributions, deadlines to meet, as well as (in those days) sitting on the floor cutting and pasting the pieces together. I can still remember that glue paste smell . . .

Many cups of tea were drunk and, if we were lucky, there were even some biscuits.

A few of the mums and I discussed what we could do to put together some childcare after school as we were either working, or about to return to work. We established (another) small committee and, having set up a small playgroup for our younger toddlers, it felt natural for me to take a lead in this. We met up several times in each other's houses. Usually with teas, coffees and, if in my house, accompanied by a slice or two of Swedish ginger cake. These occasions were appreciated by the rest of my family – I did not bake often.

We all wanted an affordable and high quality after-school club. A club based in or near the school felt safe and right. Together with my friend Alison, one of the others on the committee, I set up a series of meetings with the head teacher, teachers, governors and parents. Using our best persuasion and presentation skills, we finally got the go-ahead. It was a sharp learning curve. There were times when we felt unsure and the two of us were sitting outside the meeting room, trying to hold ourselves together. We had to conjure up enough confidence to help us come across with some sense of professionalism and to seem as if we knew what we were talking about. Neither of us, nor the others on the committee, had any previous experience in managing a project like this, but somehow we found a way. I think the fact that we were so committed and convinced of the benefits helped enormously. We also had to overcome a lot of prejudice. We were asked pointedly whether there would be enough people interested in the club and if it was really necessary.

Some of the looks shot out in our direction were far from pleasant but we carried on undaunted. It seemed that not all parents and teachers were totally supportive of mothers working.

Initially, we were only able to set up the club in a church hall a short walk away from the school. This was far from ideal as we needed extra people to walk the children there. More meetings followed and after a few weeks, we eventually managed to convince the head and others that it made more sense from a health and safety point of view to have the club based in school. We worked hard to persuade them that the club would be careful with equipment and the room and generally be responsible. The idea that this would be something positive for the school itself took a little longer to bed in. We were eventually able to use the large nursery room adjacent to the main building. It was a good space as it had a large floor area with tables and chairs stacked around the walls. It had several large windows, so let in a lot of light and, importantly, it had toilets in the hallway. The committee of four of us fundraised, then advertised, held interviews and eventually employed three great staff members, whom we called play leaders. I ended up as staff liaison, having previously had some experience of organising and setting tasks for others when working as an occupational therapist in charge of a department at a London psychiatric hospital. I enjoyed the contact with the play leaders and spending time in the club but it was a bit of a mixed blessing. If there were any problems it was usually down to me to fix them.

One of the play leaders, Clare, also worked at another after-school club. This was set up for a very posh private school and she used to remark how lovely and polite our kids were compared to the ones at the other school who apparently could be quite wild and rude. That was really satisfying to hear. Even more so was that our after-school club became a real success. It was well used and eventually both of my daughters went to it, had lots of fun and were eager to go: an important tell. I really enjoyed entering the big room, met by the strong aroma from the large paint pots, and then hearing the happy sounds of children playing, painting and even seeing some of the older children in one area crouched over their homework. This club helped me hugely as I knew the girls would be in a safe place and have some fun – they might even at times do some homework. So often I would feel guilty about leaving our children for work and generally worry. However, this facility was great – I had a sense of achievement setting it up and it gave me a real confidence boost. It allowed me to go off to work relatively happily!

I don't usually think about my achievements, but given the work I do as an occupational therapist I know it is so important. Now, thinking back over the years, I can see the confidence I gained from these experiences carried over into my working life and gave me the self-belief I needed to eventually set up and run a project for teenagers with mental health problems in Swansea. I feel very proud of this too, though that came with plenty of its own challenges. But as in Bristol and throughout my life, persevering after initial setbacks has been a useful lesson. And as I have frequently told my husband and daughters – if your plan does not immediately work out, something better will turn up. Even if it means carting nappies across international waters.

Anne Carter-Roszkowski is an occupational therapist and also a trained cognitive behaviour therapist who until recently mentored university students with mental health problems. Originally from Sweden, she came over to the UK to study. During her studies she met her future husband Mark and stayed on despite her thoughts that she was never going to become one of those mums taking the ferry boat to and from Sweden. They have now been happily married for over forty years.

Anne is the proud mother of two very lovely, bright and independent daughters. One is, of course, Miranda who came up with the idea of *100 Voices for 100 Years* – and has been responsible for it becoming a book. Anne lives in Swansea with Mark and little dog Fidel. She is happily retired, trying to become proficient at golf and to stay fit and particularly loves spending time in their Italian house with her family.

MASTERING MY STEED

Alice Lipscombe-Southwell

I always wanted to ride motorbikes. Mum tells me that even as a child I said I wanted one. Dad, however, was not convinced. He'd had a serious accident on one as a teenager and told me I wasn't allowed. So I put it to the back of my mind. Nonetheless, over the years I managed to ride a friend's tiny, rocket-powered sewing machine of a scooter, and jumped on the back of a few bikes, relishing the feeling of speed and freedom. At twenty-two, I got my first car – an old Ford Fiesta – but the idea of a motorbike still played in the back of my head.

Years went by and a succession of low-paid jobs, a relocation and a wedding meant that I couldn't ever bite the bullet. Finally, a couple of years ago, I found a local training centre and signed up to the essential training that all bikers must undergo. I was shown to a battered 125cc motorbike – my steed for the day. It did not go well. By lunchtime, I was ready to pack it all in. I was finding it hard to control the bike. I felt completely useless. Everyone else on the course was a man, much taller than me and could throw the bikes around with no problem. But after lunch, we went out on the road and everything finally clicked into place – I was flying! At the end of the day my instructor signed me off.

I started trawling the internet for my own bike. Finally a bright red Honda CBF125 was mine – I christened her Ruby Rocket. The day of her arrival dawned. After climbing on, I nearly rode her straight into my neighbour's fence. Then I rode her up the road, stopped, and rather unceremoniously flumphed sideways onto some grass. With damaged pride, I rode into Bristol. The thing is, the gears were a bit twitchy. After an accidental few wheelies at the roundabout, I managed to reach the city centre, where I promptly pulled into a car park and cried. What the hell had I let myself in for? I couldn't do this. I had a rotten time on the way home as well – an older man on a motorbike saw me, then shook his head and rolled his eyes. This further cemented my conviction that I was wrong to even try.

Eventually, though, after much practising in a local car park, I was brave enough to start commuting. I was no longer at the mercy of Bristol's terrible bus service. And – with a good wind behind me – I could reach the heady speed of sixty-five miles per hour. My confidence soared. It reached a point where five gears just weren't enough. My foot was always searching for that non-existent sixth gear. I wanted more speed, more stability and more freedom.

I decided to go for a full licence, which would allow me to ride any bike I wanted and go on the motorway. So I presented myself at the training centre again and was offered a 600cc bike that tipped the scales at more than 200 kilograms – more than four times my weight. I climbed on and ended up with my feet frantically paddling away at thin air. After a few seat-lowering adjustments, though, I was ready.

After a day of far too many circuits around cones, lots of emergency stops and U-turns, I was ready for the first part of my test. I was on the verge of throwing up, sweating gently into my kit. I needn't have worried. I passed first time with no minors. And on a euphoric high, I signed up for the final part, which tested your riding on the road.

I once again arrived at the test centre, but had to wait my turn for forty minutes. I was dry-retching with nerves and dashing back and forth to the toilets. But I finally reasoned with myself. In the worst-case scenario I could pull over, wrench off my helmet and throw up in the gutter – as long as I did it safely, I couldn't possibly be failed, could I?

It was a freezing day, and I mounted the bike, trembling with cold and nerves. My hands were shaking so much that I hit the horn accidentally. I convinced myself I'd failed. But at the end of the test, I was presented with my pass certificate! Practically skipping out of the waiting room, I jumped on the bike and rode delightedly back – all too happy to follow the instructor's urge of 'Come on – let's open them up!'

I got back on my beloved Ruby Rocket. I found that now, well, she just felt like a tiny toy bike. I loved her so much, but it was time to move on. I've now welcomed the much larger Cherry Bomb into my life and I can't wait for the adventures that we'll have together.

Alice Lipscombe-Southwell is a managing editor, sub-editor and science journalist. She's from South Wales, but lives in Bristol with an assortment of animals. She is a keen climber and can often be found clinging to a boulder or a wall. She loves the outdoors, but is happiest at the beach, hunting in rockpools for tiny creatures, catching waves on a bodyboard or plunging beneath the water for a spot of snorkelling.

GRIT

Sarah Kosar

I'm Sarah Kosar and I'm a playwright.

So what have I achieved?

The default is to immediately begin censoring myself and feeling like 'well, that is a bit too much' or 'uh, do I sound a bit *too* proud if I say that thing?' and then 'well, what would others say?' I want to be low-key and not say anything too big.

But guess what? That's the problem and the achievement in one. I have achieved a lot and I'm proud of that. Why censor it? I need to stand in it, with two feet firmly on the ground, hands on hips and a slight smirk (which is my go-to photo stance).

I moved to the UK on my own in 2009 to try to make it as a playwright, and now in 2021 I'm doing it. Have I 'made it'? That depends how I define it but I am doing it. I am in the process, the journey. I am making it. Making it my way. Every day, every early morning writing, every long Sunday afternoon rewriting, every rejection I add to my list (I try to get as many as I can a year to reframe failure into achievement). It doesn't always work, but it's working the way it needs to for me.

So, both feet on the ground and staring at you, proud, here are some of my favourite achievements:

- I am on an Exceptional Promise in playwriting visa to be in the UK.
- I got a client into the *Spice Girls* musical when I was a musical theatre agent.
- I finally have a bath in my flat.
- I created a collective of playwrights called Playdate which includes my six favourite writers who are now also my best friends.
- I am in an incredible marriage that is truly feminist, equal, supportive and very very fun.
- I am an architect of the life I want to live and I'm living it – I'm a playwright, I work full time at a great company, I live in the city I always wanted to and I have fun.
- I've had my plays produced and published in both the UK and the USA.
- I work as head of talent at a music-tech startup called ROLI and genuinely love my job every day and the people I work with. It's such a joy to hire people and watch them thrive in a new role.
- I think twelve-year-old Sarah Kosar would think the life I'm living is pretty cool despite not spending as much time with the Spice Girls as she anticipated I would.
- I've learned how to properly ride a bicycle in the past few years.
- I love myself.

Overall my achievement is my confidence to believe that I belong here and I deserve it. And just like the tattoo of the word 'GRIT' on my wrist, I have grit to keep going for what I want every single day. And most importantly, that's to be happy and love myself.

Let's keep going.

Together.

Unafraid and unapologetic.

We deserve it.

Sarah Kosar is a writer for theatre, audio and TV. She has recently recorded her original audio drama *Bear Trap* for Audible and is developing an original TV series with NBCU. She was part of the Old Vic 12 (2017–18) and received a Tier 1 Exceptional Promise in playwriting visa.

Theatre includes: upcoming world premiere of *Our Name Is Not John* (Arcola Theatre); *Armadillo* (Yard Theatre); *Mumburger* (off the WALL – USA; Old Red Lion, The Archivist's Gallery – London); *Hot Dog* (The Last Refuge – London; Thinking Cap Theatre – USA); *Spaghetti Ocean* (Live Lunch Reading, Royal Court); *Butter Brain* (Broadway Barking Theatre, Theatre Royal Stratford East).

POWER/TRIP

Gaynor Jones

At school, I was allegedly gifted and talented for English. This was decided mostly on a four-page poem I'd written about Desperate Dan and the fact I wrote an edgy piece of fiction for my A Level coursework with a swear word in it.

So, I trotted off to uni excited to sign up for Creative Writing as part of my degree. Only my tutor there, it's fair to say, didn't quite get me.

It's just not very original.

It's not well thought out.

I don't think this is the right course for you.

I was gutted. I'd gone from cream of the crop in my little sixth form to bottom of the pile in the big wide world. And the worst part was, I believed him. I was eighteen when he told me these things and I didn't write again until I was thirty.

That time, it was more than a snide comment or a lack of confidence that stopped me, just as I was getting started. It was a crippling anxiety disorder. This was far more than the odd sleepless night, this was all-consuming, Earth-ending, life-shattering mental illness. And my writing was hit the worst. I withdrew pieces from competitions, I shredded my files, I deleted stories from hard drives and USB sticks. I couldn't believe I'd been so naïve, so reckless as to put my inner thoughts out there in the world, where people could see them. But in a way, I'm one of the lucky ones. I had a wonderful, supportive husband and a brilliant therapist who took the time to help me get better, and slowly, slowly, I improved. I stepped out into the world again, and I brought my writing back with me.

Anxiety is a funny thing, it knows exactly where your bad points are. It knows exactly where to get you. For me, sending a story out to a magazine is as terrifying as jumping out of a plane, or walking over hot coals. After I press send, I get palpitations, I get doubts, I get a major case of the what ifs, but I use my power and I shut it right down.

This time around, I thought about using a pen name, but to me that would mean a win for my anxiety and a loss for my creative self. In the past eighteen months I've written stories, articles, poems. Some I've had published, some are just for me, one's been nominated for an anthology. If I sound like I'm showing off, forgive me, but I don't care. I have overcome so much to get to this point. Each piece I write, each piece I put my name to represents a huge achievement for me. It's not too late, it's never too late. I'm forty in a couple of years and I'm finally doing what I've always wanted to do, I am a writer. And believe me, if I can get over my anxiety and say that, anything is possible.

Gaynor Jones is a writer and performer currently based in Oldham, Greater Manchester. She has won the Bath Flash Fiction Award, the Mairtín Crawford Short Story Award and a Northern Writers' Award and was named Northern Writer of the Year at the 2018 Northern Soul Awards.

Her short fiction has been published in various literary journals and anthologies. She has created bespoke spoken word pieces for the Not Quite Light Festival and the Words & Music Festival and performed at the 2019 Edinburgh Fringe with For Books Sake. Find her on www.jonzeywriter.com.

RUN, YOU MOTHER, RUN!

Elinor Johns

As I struggled to zip up my jeans my daughter said, 'You've got a lot of flesh, haven't you, Mummy?' My laughter was slightly bitter; it was true that motherhood had taken its toll on my waistline. I decided to get fit and after five months of stumbling through the lanes, I was able to run my first 5k. It was tough, but it was worth it. Running races didn't just help me get into my jeans; training for them was also extremely empowering. As Kathrine Switzer says, 'women say they run for their weight or their health but it is more than this; we run because running makes a woman feel like a hero.'

Since that first Race for Life, I have jogged my way along several half marathons, and a couple of marathons. The first time I ran the Reading Half I felt overwhelmed by the display of kindness; who were these strangers who cheered at the sight of my sweaty face, poised to refresh me in between official water stops? Children wanted to high five me, adults held out jelly babies in one hand and, a little beyond the call of duty, fingers caked in Vaseline in the other. I hadn't felt so cared for since the anaesthetist's lengthy apology for dropping morphine in my eye during my caesarean.

Sweeping down the ramp into the Madejski Stadium provided

such a great denouement: the curve of the track allows you to see the finish line, the crowd fizzes with excitement, the beat of the music vibrates with your final steps as you pummel your way across the finish line. Each time I run into the stadium I feel like an Olympic athlete, and even though footage shows me waddling like a demented duck, in my head I am elegant, powerful, invincible.

I have run several shorter races with my teenage daughters in the hope that running will give them the self-esteem they need to be assertive. I worry about the pressures of social media. My daughter shows me an app, Perfect365, which can change appearances in online photographs, altering features beyond recognition. Then she shows me a picture of a schoolgirl's cleavage posted on Instagram so that it can be marked out of ten by her followers. This is a 'game' called 'Can you rate me?' which my daughter scorns. I hope that instead of joining such degrading, objectifying fads on social media, my children will use running races as a way of rating their body's achievements for their own satisfaction, rather than anyone else's. I can't wait for the day when I follow them into the stadium at the end of the Reading Half, to share the ecstatic feeling, addictive as any drug without the ill effects. Most of all, I want them to cross the line loving their bodies for the strength, health and stamina that running races will give them. I want them for these reasons to believe that they are beautiful.

After a morning run out with my dog, I will rub him down while listening to the radio. Sometimes, I hear mothers call in to radio programmes to bemoan how invisible they feel as they get older; ageing has led to them experiencing a lack of femininity, and a sense of displacement. They lack empowerment, the very feeling runners get from the release of beta-endorphins. When I hear such lamentations I feel charged with the grandeur of this knowledge, a need to spread the word and let others see the light. The dog looks at me askance but I am on a mission; I grab the radio and yell, 'Run, you mother, run!'

Elinor Johns is a teacher and writer living in Hertfordshire with her family. She has had a short story published in the *Mechanics' Institute Review* and MIROnline and was shortlisted for the Myriad First Draft Competition and longlisted for the Bristol Short Story Prize 2021. In 2008 she took up running and discovered how inspiring this could be.

Elinor gained an MA with Distinction in Creative Writing at Birkbeck, University of London, where she was fortunate to meet Miranda Roszkowski. Having contributed to Miranda's spoken word evenings, she was delighted to get involved in a project to celebrate women's achievements; as a mother of teenage daughters, female empowerment is a subject close to her heart. Elinor can be contacted on Elinor@Johns.net.

THE RIGHT FIT

Farhana Khalique

When I was in my twenties, I was obsessed with bakerboy hats. You know, those poufy ones with a peak, roomy enough to stuff long hair into them. Having started wearing the hijab at eighteen, sometimes I just fancied a change. Cotton, corduroy, tweed, wool, in all the colours of the Accessorize rainbow. Whenever I wore one, I'd feel a little more glamorous. Other friends did high heels, red lipstick or cute handbags. I'd grab a hat.

I got rid of most of my bakerboys when we last moved house, but I kept my favourites. That was around the time I started writing more regularly, after I switched from being a full-time school teacher to part-time college lecturer. (Unlike my uni wardrobe, my teaching one had less need for hats, but my hijabs happily multiplied to match my work clothes.) Soon, I had my first short story published, in an anthology on the theme of Celebration. Appropriately, it was inspired by a friend's birthday. I even remember wearing a hat that day: a thick, electric-blue wool beanie. (Well, it was Southend in January.)

A decade later, I've had more short stories and flash fiction published, and I've performed my work in different places. I remember the first time I gave a reading, three years ago, at the Birmingham Literature Festival. *Don't hold the book in front of your face, make eye contact, don't read in a monotone, smile for goodness' sake* . . . So many things were rushing through my head, even faster than the train I took to get there, I don't even remember my reading. But I remember the smiles and applause when I finished, and my relief and joy. If I'd had a hat on me, I'd have thrown it up in the air.

Since then, I've also worked with two fantastic women writers as a mentee, via the WoMentoring Project and the Word Factory. The first introduced me to 500-word stories, and it was love at first flash. The second opened the door to a Tardis-like space of possibilities when it comes to short stories, and mine haven't been the same since. And, in the last twelve months, I've been trying on new hats; by accepting opportunities to teach Creative Writing, to edit, and to write new pieces. So, somewhere along the way, I guess I found my voice . . . Right? Well, to be honest, I'm still finding it.

Sometimes, it's like trying to pin down my own shadow, or catch a rainbow. 'Oh look, *there's* my voice – quick, bottle it up so I can pour it into my next piece!' Or, like trying to hold onto your writing hat before it's snatched by the winds of doubt, carried away and then dropped in the dirt.

Speaking of dirt, first drafts are messy. Rejections hurt. It's not a level playing field. The publishing world is not always welcoming to small, brown, hijab-wearing women with working-class immigrant roots. Imposter syndrome is real. However, the acceptances and achievements are priceless. But what does achievement mean to me?

Getting published? A 'proper' writer taking me under her mentoring wing? Getting paid?!

Maybe it was when I stopped giving my characters names like Jane, and started naming them Halima, Iram or Renu. Or, when I'd slip in a 'samosa', 'laddoo' or 'Salaam', instead of over-explaining or putting them into a Glossary. Or, when I remembered that sneering kid in primary school who asked loudly if my house smelled of curry, and I used the memory to depict a jealous bully in a short story. Or, when I mentioned that a character in another story wasn't just another girl about town, but happened to wear the hijab too.

Or, maybe it had nothing to do with me specifically. Maybe it was when I was so struck by the sight of a broken iceberg outside Tate Modern a couple of years ago, placed there by an artist to raise awareness of climate change, that it inspired a flash fiction about an unusual first date. Or, when I was so spellbound by images of moonbows at Yosemite National Park on a TV programme narrated by a physics professor who used to be in a pop band, that it inspired another story about a mother on a quest to see a moonbow for herself.

Maybe it was all of the above.

Either way, I'm glad that I didn't give up, and that I keep trying on different hats. English teacher, voiceover artist, writer, editor. Londoner, British-Asian, Muslim, hijabi. It's not always easy juggling everything, but it helps if you keep following your own curiosities, and honing your craft. In the end, you'll find the right fit.

Farhana Khalique is a writer, voiceover artist and teacher from London. Her writing has appeared in *Leicester Writes Short Story Prize Anthology 2020*, *The Brown Anthology*, *Reflex Fiction*, *Lighthouse Literary Journal*, *Litro*, *Popshot Quarterly*, *The Good Journal* and elsewhere. Farhana has been on TSS's BIFFY50 (best fifty British and Irish Flash Fiction) 2019–20 list, she has been longlisted for the Bath Flash Fiction Award, shortlisted for the Asian Writer Short Story Prize, and she has won a Word Factory Apprentice Award. She is also the editor of Desi Reads and a submissions editor at SmokeLong Quarterly. Find Farhana @HanaKhalique and www.farhanakhalique.com.

LA CRASSE

Kerri Smith

So it was really happening. I was eighteen; I was going to live away from home for the first time in this posh, snow-covered town in the French Alps. For four months! It was the ski trip of a lifetime, passed off as a formative linguistic experience. Until I got there, and discovered it was definitely more the formative experience than the ski-bunny fantasy.

I had naïvely thought that my newly minted A Level in French and my rudimentary cleaning skills would see me through as a chambermaid in a four-star hotel. But when I walked into the dining room on that first day in late December, I realised that in both of those assets I fell short.

I walked sheepishly over to where the other five chambermaids were sitting on an assemblage of dining chairs, chatting away in rapid-fire French. I understood almost nothing. I managed to introduce myself, at least.

'Bonjour, je m'appelle Kerri.'

'Kiri!' they cried. So delicious with a French accent. I learned later that Kiri is a cheap brand of cheese – the type that's pre-formed into triangles.

I also came to realise, when my French was better, that *les femmes de chambre* already knew each other – they'd worked several seasons at the Hôtel des Neiges. I learned that they only tolerated the snow and the ridiculous sport that everybody else was there for. They moved with the holiday season, working and living the rest of the year in the South of France, where they'd left family and lovers for the winter. They could earn more money in the joyless snow.

I didn't figure any of that out very quickly. My A Level had not taught me to handle colloquial French in a Dordogne accent; I could barely ask for a cup of tea.

But they took little 'Kiri Kiri' under their wing – this peculiar English girl who never really said anything, had a season pass to the lifts instead of a decent wage, and gorged herself on *pains au chocolat* at breakfast. Despite all the scrubbing and bed-making, I gained a good bit of pastry weight.

My roommate Agnès was one of the waitresses. She'd make instant coffee with three spoons of granules and three of sugar, and then zip off to serve breakfast in her neat black outfit and apron. On our first free night together we walked into the main resort.

She pointed at the cable-cars, still ferrying people up and down despite the fact it was dark. 'Ils bougent toujours!' I had no idea what she was saying to me. She gesticulated and repeated herself, slower and smilier. Eventually I clocked it. She meant that the cable-cars were still going at this hour, and wasn't that a surprise.

The proximity of our living quarters transcended our lack of language, and we quickly became friends. We'd sometimes pop out for a *petite coupe* of something bubbly. It was all very civilised. When

I went out with the other English-speaking staff from the hotel – Barry, the jovial Scottish snowboarder, who was one of the chefs, and Joe, the pale and lanky kitchen *plongeur* – there would be pints of lager and the Red Hot Chili Peppers on the bar speakers and once Barry lost a shoe in the snow on the way home.

My partner cleaning the rooms was Colette. Once again I found a patient and humorous companion. She gently repeated the necessary vocab until I could do my job without slowing her down. *Les oreillers*, *les draps*, *la crasse* – pillows, sheets and that greasy ring that's left behind by bathwater, in case you were wondering.

One day we were cleaning the room of a British couple who had made a complicated demand about the arrangement of the beds. They came into the room while we were working, and began disparaging our work in loud voices. Before I could stop myself, I was asking – in my best English accent – whether we could possibly help arrange the beds differently for them today? Any pleasure I felt from their surprise was offset by anger at being spoken about like I was of no consequence.

By the end of four months I'd learned so much more than colloquial French. I'd learned to be independent for the first time; I got a sense of how it feels to work long, physical hours. I skied, of course – but really, by the end, I'd come to look at sliding down the slopes through the eyes of the other chambermaids. It felt like the least important thing.

Kerri Smith is an award-winning science journalist with *Nature* magazine, where she commissions, edits and writes features on all strands of science. Her fiction has appeared on the short story website LabLit and she has completed three novel drafts – just for fun – as part of the annual National Novel Writing Month programme.

A MILLION TO ONE

Angela Wallis

Like the chance of anything coming from Mars, the chance of an Aston University Psychology graduate with no media experience whatsoever getting into the BBC were a million to one, they said. I had always been torn between training as a psychotherapist, becoming an actor, or working for the BBC. I had delusions of being a Freudian therapist with a chaise longue and all the essentials, but the training was all a bit too daunting and took far too much commitment: something I struggle with in all areas of my life. As for acting, I loved doing it but hated auditions; my fragile ego couldn't take the constant series of rejections which I understood would be part of the deal – hats off to all those brave actors out there. And everyone knew the BBC trainee scheme only took Oxbridge graduates. So I never applied to the BBC; instead I focused on being some sort of therapist and studied for a Master's in Social Work as a way in.

Unfortunately, I ended up being forced into the very hard end of child protection work and it nearly destroyed me. It happened to be at the time when the world decided to talk more openly about child sexual abuse, and social workers were trained with the police to enable criminal prosecutions of abusers. There was, however, very little support for the social workers dealing with these horrific situations, often blowing up families with inadequate solutions. I couldn't handle the frustration of having to offer children a least-damaging alternative, as all our solutions were damaging.

I decided I had to escape while I still could. I wanted to do some good and I needed something creative, so I explored selling my skills as a social worker to TV production companies. I started doing casual research jobs at weekends and during holidays and made my CV slightly more media-friendly; then I applied to every media company, job and production I could think of.

Eventually the big chance came: an interview with the BBC for a consumer show that covered child protection stories. I will never forget that interview day. Everyone else was called Tiffany or Torquil; I had never felt like such a redneck in my life. Tiffany told me she had pulled up old tapes of the show to prepare for the interview. I had no idea you could even do that, I was relying on my memories of old shows I had seen. I was ready to run. The interview was gruelling but I managed to not completely shame myself.

It took only two days to get one of the most important phone calls of my life. It was the HR lady from the BBC. They offered me a trainee researcher job, a one-year contract . . . I hardly heard the details but I was in. It had been a million-to-one shot, I had done it, and my life was never the same again.

Angela Wallis has always been an engaging raconteur and natural communicator. Born in Manchester to a very opinionated, noisy Jewish family, she really had no choice! After four years as a social worker in London, at the hard end of child protection work, she pulled off an impressive and unprecedented career change to re-invent herself as a BBC TV producer for the next eighteen years.

Angela now lives in sunny Tel Aviv where she writes stories – she has many – and teaches English. She was introduced to the *100 Voices* project by her close friend Kate Lockwood, and they're delighted to be published together.

REMEMBER THIS

Aliyah Kim Keshani

Five o'clock, your work is done. You're on a packed train, tucked under an armpit. Ignore the London damp creeping up your ankles. Salami breath hot in your ear. Turn your head. Make no eye contact. Sway through the tunnels till – suddenly! – open sky. *Reception!* Phone – unlock – Facebook!

There are weddings, concerts, meals. People hot-air ballooning over giraffes, eating macarons on Everest. Your jealousy throbs like toothache. Lol, you thumb, because you're a good sport. *Like.* Like like like like like like like like LIKE. LIKE.

Where are you in this? Head tilted in every picture, that same damn smile – everybody knows their best side. But the more you look, the more you can't help but see that this little pixelated face has no answers. Camera-ready, she says nothing about anything to anyone.

Hey, this is your stop. Get up. *Oh, no – after you*, you say. Polite nod. Polite all day. Every day. *Yes, I do see what you mean. No, I don't mind*. But it dogs you home, this . . . peace-keeping. You lie on your bed, face stiff, jaw aching, and wonder what you are in this world.

There is a drawer in your room. Sometimes, you remember this.

That second drawer, so full of notebooks it's hard to open. But do. Take one out. Have a read. And, there, you see? *There* you are.

That unreadable scrawl gives like a trap door and you fall into the rhythm of your thoughts, the familiarity of your voice and it is like breathing again. This media-res of you: twelve years old and finally wearing a bra. That first kiss. GCSEs and strawberry laces. Hangovers. Heartbreak. The baked potato you ate every day at work for a year. And that orange you saw last week, sat on the middle of the train tracks, and how it made your day. And you pause for a moment because you remember it now exactly – the round absurd beauty of that orange – and, hell, it makes your day still.

There are questions from your old selves, anxious requests to 'write me back and let me know how it goes'. So you do, sagely – a different pen, in the margins. 'It will be OK,' you print. 'Don't worry so much.' And that hand of compassion that is so rarely there in the moment stretches out through space and time and does the miraculous. It writes you back and completes the circle.

This is your other life. Your secret life. Your inner life. Where you are honest. And who knew you had so much honesty in you? Polite, funny, *yes*. But, here, uncompromising and difficult too. You *dis*like. You make trouble. You howl and rage. There are tops and tails of stories, jokes, wisdom and smut. And this, here, this *is* your best side. *Sides*. A kaleidoscope of selves, ever shifting and fluid. Spread through time, you find you are your own daughter, sister, mother, challenger, championer, friend.

Written or unwritten, it exists. This wonderful jumble of a life. There. Profoundly there. And yours. To the very end. Remember this.

Aliyah Kim Keshani is a London-based writer and editor who has had short stories and poetry published. In 2017 she was awarded a commended place in the life writing category for the *Wasafiri* New Writing Prize. She was also shortlisted for the Penguin WriteNow Novel Mentorship Programme.

In 2018 she was selected to feature in *My Lot Is a Sky*, a new international women's poetry anthology. She is thrilled to be published in *100 Voices* and cannot wait to delve into its many rich and splendid stories which, no doubt, will help her on the way to finishing her first novel.

DUSTY MEDALS

Stefanie Moore

Hobbies sit differently in your life when you're little. As a kid I was encouraged to fixate on a 'thing', be it gymkhanas, friendship bracelets or even New Kids on the Block. But the hobby that I eventually chose was quite different; it could be ruthless, it could hurt and it could involve a lot of lycra.

Every school night you'd find me training and rehearsing in a mouldy Scout hut. Then, every weekend, I'd be in draughty church halls up and down the north-east performing in dance competitions. Plastered with blue eyeshadow, hair gel and sequins, I'd be pushed out into the void to hurl my legs and arms around to bits of music – on cassette tape – by Procol Harum, Acker Bilk or the Gypsy Kings that were being forced out of a poorly maintained speaker system like cheap meat through a mincer.

I can still recall standing there, knees locked with impatience and excitement and frustration, as the adjudicator would read through the pros and cons of our performances. I'd be in a kind of grinning agony until my number was called out, and then I would feign shock, step forward, curtsey so deeply that it looked like my hip had just collapsed and accept the prize – a dusty medal in gold, preferably, with a picture of a dancing lady, a jazzy top hat or the Humber Bridge on it.

My sister likes to remind me (and often) that I was unbearable. She's right. I was precocious, self-important and vengeful if I didn't win, and so I look back on my talent with shame rather than pride. My knack at smiling and gyrating to Kenny G at the same time is not what I'm thinking about when I think about what I have achieved in my life.

What I've achieved, what I'm achieving after a long-fought battle, is the acceptance, nay the joy, in un-competing. Back then, I was so used to winning that I expected my entire life to follow that same pattern. That if I simply worked very hard at something, wore lots of makeup and had something or someone to compete against, that I would 'succeed'.

And that's not how it works, is it?

I went into acting. Of course. But after suffering countless casting rooms filled to the hilt with women who looked quite a lot like me, reading for the part of 'junkie' in *The Bill*, or 'footballer's wife' in *Hollyoaks*, I began to realise that I was not the only person with talent. Having brown hair and blue eyes which I could move around a lot on cue was not unique. I was not even the best at this particular brand of unique because I didn't get many parts. And here endeth my twenties, dear reader, a time of real crashing failure as I perceived it. I decided that the best way to handle these setbacks was to actively disappear in my thirties by making the most non-threatening choices that I could. I would drift between professions – you could name pretty much any job and I have spent at least a day on a training course to do it – but as soon as I felt any challenge, I would walk away.

So what changed? I recognise now that I let my thought patterns sit at the control seat for most of my twenties. I missed out on friendships, adventures and experiences because I was in a constant state of comparing myself to others, and ultimately finding myself lacking. What I have achieved over time is self-acceptance and the growing ability to be vulnerable, to fail, and to be happy when others do well, something that would have left me a snarling, blubbering mess in my twenties. Nowadays I teach, I look after my son and I write, sometimes badly and sometimes well, and these are things that make me happy. I still believe in the power of red lipstick and sequins but I also believe in the power of sharing good thoughts and laughing at myself when it doesn't go to plan. The dusty medals and Kenny G are safely in the attic.

Stefanie Moore trained and worked as an actor for ten years before retraining as a teacher. Her debut play won the Hive Award at Greater Manchester Fringe in 2019. She has also written monologues and a two-hander cabaret about a cartoon glamour girl and her sidekick, Oliver the dog. An alumnus of the Write Like A Grrrl course, her short stories have been published in Dear Damsels, The Cabinet of Heed and Funny Pearls. Her debut romance novel *The Long Game* will be published in 2021. She tweets @nefnywrites.

VOICES THAT TAUGHT

AN ARMY OF ARTISTS

Sharon Eckman

'So what do you do up there?'

This was the question my mother asked when I said I was off to North Wales to do more crazy stuff with Clwyd Theatr Cymru.

'We invade a school for a week,' I said. 'An army of artists.'

My first encounter with the company was when I played Beatrice in Arthur Miller's *A View from the Bridge*. It was also my first encounter with Tim Baker, one of the best directors I've ever worked with – one reason being that he entirely trusts his actors, which is rarer than you might think.

Tim rang me out of the blue, as usual. 'What are you doing for the next six weeks?' Given a little more than three days' notice, I might have been able to say 'whatever you want'. However, for the final fortnight I became a visiting artist and we did indeed invade a school. Two schools in fact, one for each week.

To quote Tim's press release: 'The team consisted of a core of five actors and a host of visiting artists including a street dancer, performance poets, musicians, visual artists, and events were created (as many as forty per day) all over the school. The Hub was always conceived as a creative "handshake" with young people and we consistently challenged students to respond to our interventions with their own creative work.'

The schools weren't necessarily Estyn (Welsh equivalent of Ofsted) five-starred. That was the point. We wanted to go to places that don't normally get a bunch of people coming into the classroom and performing an extract from *Lord of the Flies*. Tim gave us the freedom to wander round doing pretty much whatever we wanted. I'd patrol the corridors, peering into classrooms where students were immersed in Maths or French, and I felt like Puck or Anansi the trickster. We were anarchy; we were challenge, laughter and freedom.

A typical day: 8 a.m. in the corridor; singing to welcome the kids and staff. Lesson one, maybe a workshop, make a cup of tea, no time to drink it, oh I'm in English next, shall I do a poem or a song? Quick sandwich for lunch if you've got a spare fifteen minutes to eat it . . . more classrooms, workshops, singing, poems, tea gone cold again, then we wave them off until tomorrow.

Each day we handed out themed cards – friendship, fear, love and more – and the kids responded with lyrics, poems, monologues, scenes which we then performed back to them in their classes the following day.

So many highlights to this brilliant, wild project. Here are a few.

- Introducing the three (I know, JUST THREE??) A Level English Lit students to Primo Levi, shocking them as we spoke about how the doctor's pointing finger meant either the gas chambers or sort-of-life, and working on a modern poem about war. 'Ever done any acting?' I asked. They looked at me in horror, but half an hour later, performed it as though they were angry drunks at a bar, and loved every second.

- Touring the Maths classrooms with a song composed by Tim, based on a riddle written by one of the teachers. I still had no idea what it meant even after nine renditions (the median's the ... the mode is the ... oh whatever) but apparently I made Maths sexy.

- Singing a swiftly composed love song about a hedgehog – the girl who wrote the poem clasped her hands to her face, overjoyed, friends either side nudging her with glee. 'I'm in love with a hedgehog/I've never felt this way before.'

- Running lunchtime workshops on Sondheim's *Sweeney Todd*, watching a fifteen-year-old girl slide in and out and in and then stay to practise and perform with the group in the final concert. I was told by her SEN teacher that she'd never taken part in a school activity before. She came to thank me afterwards and it felt as good as any moment in my career. 'You've transformed the school this week,' a teacher told me. 'I've seen pupils who never join in or engage dancing, laughing, talking to the artists.'

The creative industries are worth £10.8 billion a year to the UK economy, £2.8 billion to the Treasury via taxation – but we're living in a time where arts in schools are cut to the bone or cut altogether. Working on this project and others, I've seen the transformational power of the arts in communities. The Hub was one of the craziest, most exciting, moving, exhausting and unforgettable things I've ever done and it – or something like it – should be in every school in the country.

Because every kid deserves to fight alongside an army of artists.

Sharon Eckman is a multi-tasking actor/singer/writer. She was *Time Out* Travel Writer of the Year, longlisted twice for the Fish Memoir Prize, shortlisted for the Words And Women prose competition and the Jerwood/Arvon Mentorship Scheme. Her short fiction has appeared in *Shooter Lit*, *Words & Women: Three* and New Flash Fiction Review.

Sharon is currently working on a novel and will never read anything where a dog dies. She is proud to be part of *100 Voices* and share her story in the company of so many brilliant writers because, 100 years on, women's voices need to be heard more than ever. Find her on www.sharoneckman.com.

BEHIND THE GREEN CURTAINS

Felicity Goodman

They hung high above. Sad and tragic, like the news delivered behind them.

'Let's give you some privacy.'

Privacy didn't count for much. No, you couldn't see my tummy. Bloated as if it would pop. Strapped in and hooked up. The quick *thumper thumper thumper* of my baby's heartbeat filled the room. My fears and tears would have to be silent.

We could hear the couple across from us. Although we could not see them or them us.

'I'm scared,' she said.

'What's there to be scared of?' he said.

'Imagine pushing a tennis ball out of your penis,' she said.

'I could do it,' he said. 'I wouldn't be scared.'

'You would be if you could. But you can't. So you're not,' she said.

My husband and I silently laugh behind the privacy of our green curtains. The monitor records every bounce, crack and giggle as my stomach muscles contract and tighten, stifling the laughter.

'You've done it before,' he said.

Our laughter evaporates. My deflection method. Find the funny. It now has a thick black line drawn through it. My baby might die.

We went into Asda and we parted ways. The gliding doors sliding with grace almost laughing in my face at the heavy pad plod pad plod of my swollen oversized feet. I'm keeping my head down avoiding eye contact. I pad plod, pad plod over to the checkout.

She's there. Pink cheeks, chiselled eyebrows, long fluttering eyelashes, neat fringe.

'Oh, you're big!' she says.

'Yep,' I say.

'Ready to go?' she says.

'Yep,' I say.

'Is it a boy?' she says.

'I don't know,' I say.

'Be bad to be born big if you're a girl,' she says.

The voice in my head yells, 'What the hell, your judgement rings as loud as a bell, as part of me thinks dear god don't be a girl. A girl born into this world of expected frills and bows and laces and lycra-blend T-shirts. Shoes you can't run in, your body held in skirts. Told by all you're not funny or clever or strong or silly or angry or gross. To be kept apart and held under the water, all because you were not a son but a daughter.' I don't say that out loud. I just say, 'Would it?'

'Dreadful,' she says.

I'm lost for words and stare at her blankly.

'Let's hope it's a boy, eh?'

'Yes. No,' I say.

When really in my head, all of my thoughts think, 'Let's hope it's not dead.'

She survived. Kicking and screaming into this world in a speedy delivery. I was sent home that night and after being in a week this did feel pretty sweet.

A healthy baby who suckled and grew. Time ticked on. Those green curtains had parted.

It was relentless. Never-ending stream of sour-smelling baby sick and drinking nappies nose wipes.

It was relentless. The squeezes, the sneezes, the sniffles, the snuffles, the shuffles, the huffles. The nit picking, back cracking, joint aching, bones shaking. The thumps and the knocks, the cuts and nicks, the picking up and throwing of sticks. The washing that piles high and the dishes in the sink that is blocked. The tap that is loose and the flannel that rots.

It was relentless. And the crying. To respond or not? What is needed now? The second guessing and the third and the fourth and the fifth and the sixth, seventh, eighth.

Nine green bottles hanging on the wall.
And if one green bottle should accidentally fall . . .

I'm falling. Who will catch me?

All the while I have a grey fuzz filtering in at the sides of the brain. A crickle and a crackle, I'm going insane. I would run a mile from myself but here I remain. Till I snap and the flood pours out. I'm mixed up in reality. I have lost my sanity. My sense of self is a cavity. I'm writing on the wardrobe. I'm packing a suitcase or so I was told. I'm asking about life jackets, escape routes, treasure to be sold.

I hear about this after. My brain went for a walk, and although I don't remember, I had someone else's life being played through my body. Fear piled on Fear. Smashing everything apart.

The journey was slow and is ongoing. There was who I was trying to be and then there is who I actually am. Each little act of sharing sets me free.

So I am stepping out from behind these green curtains. My tread may be slow and my path is uncertain. Yet every day I rewire and rebuild. The right way to live no longer resides in other people's ideals, but in myself as I start to become real.

Felicity Goodman is a storyteller, writer and community artist living in Warrington, Cheshire. She's an associate artist with Manchester Art Gallery and regularly runs writers' groups and story circles with her company, Stitch. It's in these spaces that she has seen the power of women telling their stories. She often hears from the female participants about the lack of visibility that they feel they have. Writing about her own maternal mental health provided her with order among chaos. Today her hair is greyer and her children are older, but they are all healthy and for that she is grateful.

MOTHERS AND DAUGHTERS

Tamara von Werthern

The first play I wrote that had a professional premiere was, at first glance, all about cycling. It's called *The White Bike* and it's set on a bike journey along an existing route. It was an incredibly ambitious production, which translated the experience of cycling through movement, sound and video installation and it was directed by Lily McLeish. I'm really proud of it. We were interviewed by the BBC, as the story of cycling fatalities in cities and the resulting ghost bikes is timely and awareness had not been raised through a theatre production before.

For me, the play is also a play about mothers and daughters. The protagonist, Isabelle, is the mother of a small child. When she is pinned under the wheel of a lorry, she in turn cries out for her mother. I am a cyclist in London and I care deeply about the issues the play raises and the need for safer streets. The fact that Isabelle is a wife, a mother and a daughter is important: she is not a statistic, she's a person. But for me, being a mother and a daughter also brings up the question of how you combine this with achieving your goals and spending time away from family to do so. As a woman who has always worked alongside raising a family, I ask myself: how are we perceived and how do we perceive ourselves? How much of a licence do we give ourselves to do the things we want to do? How can you balance having a family with achieving what you feel you need to achieve?

My mother was twenty-three when I was born. She had broken off her journalism degree a year before she got pregnant and had decided, against her parents' wishes, that she wanted to become a carpenter. At the time, it was unheard-of for a woman to enter into this entirely male-dominated domain. She went from one carpentry business to another, literally knocking on their doors and asking if they would take her in as an apprentice. She was laughed out of the door, time and again. Finally she struck gold and was taken on, as the first woman training as a carpenter, not just in her hometown, but in the entire county.

Half a year later, she found herself pregnant with me. It did not stop her; she worked until a few days before the birth, took maternity leave and then persuaded her bosses to let her finish the apprenticeship. The final piece she submitted was a bed for me, with integrated shelves and a wardrobe for my books and clothes and a sky with clouds and sun draped over the top for me to look at before I fell asleep.

Over the years, she built her own business, employed other carpenters (all of them women). Growing up, I was surrounded by wood shavings, sawdust and the smell of bone glue. I learned how to plug wormholes with beeswax, I had huge respect for the chainsaw. My mother is still working today, and has worked throughout the pandemic: for her it's been a lifeline to keep busy, to do what she loves doing.

My father took a year out to look after me when I was little, and my mother was working. That also had a really good effect on my relationship with him, and meant that I now see gender equality in relationships as really important for everyone involved. My husband and I have always shared looking after the children, and we each have one day a week when we are home with them on our own. That has played a huge part in me bringing the play to the stage, being given the freedom to work, and knowing that the children are equally fine with either parent. When the play was published, I was asked if there was someone I wanted to dedicate it to. And just as my mother before me built me a bed, I dedicated my first play to my daughter. This is partly because it is, among other things, a piece about the love between mothers and daughters, but also as an offering to her, as a thank you for allowing me to spend time away from her to do something I love.

Seeing my mother working as a natural part of me growing up has played such a big part in my own choices. I hope that my daughter will also learn from me that women are ambitious and that they want and need fulfilling work and that that's OK. That it's not an either/or when it comes to work or family. I think it's really important to pass this message to our daughters.

Tamara von Werthern is an award-winning writer across different genres, with a strong focus on stage and screen. She has had work performed at the Royal Court, Arcola and Southwark Playhouse, and recently won Best Screenplay 2019 for her work *I Don't Want to Set the World on Fire* at the Lift-Off Global Network Film Festival.

Tamara is a contributor to *Letters to the Earth* (Collins, 2019) and has written three German-language novels. She is also co-founder, producer and co-host of new all-female theatre podcast Fizzy Sherbet (www.fizzysherbetplays.com), which won a Sarah Award in New York in November 2020. Find her on www.tamaravonwerthern.com.

SUFFRAGETTES AND ME

Sakina Ballard

I was born in the 1980s into an Indian-descended Bahora community in East Africa, so the link between me and the middle-class white women who spearheaded the suffragette movement in the UK 100 years ago is not an obvious one. But when I consider what the vote meant for those women and the journey they went on to get it, I realise their actions had a resonance for all women, including me. It was a journey of overcoming societal obstacles, achieving a sense of agency and equality, of hearing their own voices and being heard, feeling empowered to be part of the change instead of having to suffer the status quo.

I wasn't told about feminism or patriarchy as a child yet I saw their influence all around me. I learned about male abandonment and power games by hearing about the lives of my female ancestors. To me, the injustice of it all was so clear. I wasn't educated into this realisation, it was an instinct.

Becoming British didn't give this to me. I felt it as a young girl when I asked why the women would sit hidden away from the men at prayers, or had to cover themselves. It made no sense to me that girls and women were being made responsible for the thoughts, feelings and actions of men. But living here gave me the space to develop my ideas of what it meant to be equal and to understand that I too had potential, a purpose I wanted to achieve. For a start, I was allowed to be ambitious, something the women before me hadn't ever been able to experience.

I moved to the UK from East Africa at the age of six, after my mum had met and married a British man, my stepdad. The shift in my life could not have been more profound, a different climate, culture, language, religion, expectations, society. I always spoke English but when I moved to London I lost the other three languages I had previously spoken fluently within a matter of months. A society that had not really seen young girls like me or families like mine before – an Indian girl raised in Africa living in a mixed-race step-family – left me in an identity 'no man's land'. Suddenly I didn't belong in any world, I had to adapt to survive, and adapt I did because as a girl I'd always been taught to be compliant, obedient and 'good'. I was now a good girl and a good immigrant.

Britain wasn't just the idyllic place of opportunities it is often presented as to immigrants; it presented barriers too. I wasn't white, and became deeply aware of that in 1980s London with its covert and overt racism. I was spat at and called a Paki as I walked to school. A family friend who was a prima ballerina kindly told me my dream of being a ballerina was unrealistic as I was tall and brown. 'There are no brown dancers,' she informed me and suggested I think about a different career, so I did. I shifted my dream to becoming an actress and achieved that alongside a Master's degree. The first woman in my lineage to hold a degree and the only Bahora girl in our community to have been an actress, as far as I'm aware.

Despite my ability to adapt and succeed outwardly, internally, the sense of not belonging, being an imposter, being an 'other' overshadowed my every success. I never spoke of these inadequacies to others and even hid them from myself for many years, yet they were always with me. That is what being seen as 'less than' by society does to us, it forces us to internalise the oppressions and rejection until we find we are not asking 'what is wrong with the environment?' but 'what is wrong with me, why am I not enough?'

This internalised pain led to mental and physical trauma for my ancestors and, as I entered motherhood, also for me. Following the experience of birth trauma and its fallout through my first birth, I went through another metamorphosis. I wanted to heal these fragmented parts of myself, and found the courage to try hypnobirthing in my second birth. It was the start of another new journey and, eventually, a new career. This time it was about finding my voice, my power and my authenticity and slowly building the confidence to know that in my entirety I am enough, without having to be perfect. This unravelling of self and being spurred on by wanting to provide something better for my children helped me start my own birth business and begin training as a coach, mentor and psychologist, where I have a particular interest in working with non-white women and women who have experienced previous trauma.

Millicent Fawcett said, 'Courage calls to courage everywhere, and its voice cannot be denied'. Courage can be defined as 'strength in the face of pain or grief'. This is where the suffragettes and I cross paths. It takes courage to live as women where we try to discover our own voice and potential in a society that diminishes it. To wish to amplify the voices of other women with little platform or support. To overcome the inner rage of injustice and see if we can create something better for the women and men who come after us.

The women in my family ran races they weren't allowed to be a part of, yet gave it their all, with no hope of succeeding in crossing the finish line of true equality, much like the suffragettes. It hurts us all to experience life without equality and justice, to grieve the loss of our dreams, potential and contributions. When we rise against those systems, politically, institutionally, culturally, religiously or individually, we call on others to do the same. Yet in their brilliance and courage to run anyway they made headway and passed the baton on to me and to us now to carry on.

That was the suffragettes' story and it is also mine as I take the baton and look to pass it on with some headway made.

Sakina Ballard is a women's coach and mentor specialising in the perinatal period. In 2020 she founded the Real Birth Project offering trauma-informed antenatal education to families. She's also the community lead at Make Birth Better, a collective of experts working to eliminate birth trauma. Her biggest role is as a proud mum to two lovely humans.

LAZY LEGS

Kate Smalley Ellis

About ten years ago I wrote a story and in many ways it became a marker in my fledgling writing career. I used to attend a writing group where the format was to read your work aloud and for everyone else to discuss it as if you weren't there. This was nerve-racking but very useful. When I finished reading this particular story, the group talked as if they'd enjoyed it and the characters were real. They seemed excited, invested. Something that had come out of my head had become worthy of discussion and disagreements – that was an achievement to me.

The story is about a young woman who goes to work and leaves her partner at home. Some people assumed the partner was male but others picked up on details that said she wasn't. When you write in the first or second person, writing groups often assume the 'I' is you, the writer, although they shouldn't, so by reading this story I had quietly outed myself. It wasn't an announcement but afterwards it was understood. I realised that was OK and that gay characters should be written without being remarked upon and that's exactly what I'd done. No one in the group reacted to this new information, which isn't my achievement, or theirs, but an achievement of the pioneers from generations before us. I thank them for creating a world, in London anyway, where this is easy and undramatic. Let's hope that achievement spreads. This was also the first story I had published, in *Open Pen*. It's called *Lazy Legs*.

LAZY LEGS

I love it when you walk me to the door with no top on. I kiss your lips and both your nipples goodbye. I walk to the tube with bounding steps, smiling. As I swipe my Oyster card, you feed the cat. I start down the escalator and you get back into bed. I push onto the tube. You rest your hand between your legs. I stumble into a briefcase and you close your eyes. You stretch your arms and point your toes. I get off the train, walk through crowds full of sleep and suits. You pad past the sink full of plates and last night's dinner. You scratch and yawn and stroke the cat, he weaves between your prickly legs. You fiddle with the fork lying in leftover korma, playing with the crispy edged rice. The sky above me is heavy and mauve, just about to split. You chew slowly on a chunk of Peshwari, pick at your belly button, skin still warm from bed.

You go to the toilet and stare at the cupboard we put everything in. I push through the revolving doors, you hear the kitchen window smash, stop your pee mid-flow. I say 'good morning' to the receptionist, turn to go upstairs. You stand and slowly pull up your pants, breathing as softly as possible, concentrating on a stray shoe visible through the open door. You hear footsteps, casual, confident footsteps strolling through our house like it's their house, peering into our bedroom, looking at our pile of duvet, jeans sprawled on the floor. I jog up the stairs and wander to my desk. You stand inert, leg muscles tense. A Post-it note nags me from the centre of my screen, I peel it off leaving a dustless strip. You look at the plug hole in the bathroom sink, to the world map shower curtain, at the spider in the corner, searching for an ally. I head to the kitchen. You hear rummaging through clothes and books, a squeaky cupboard. You're crouched over the toilet, sweat forms on your frown. I fill the kettle, spoon out coffee. You remember your phone is on the bed and pray nothing worth reporting has happened at work. I pour water, you scrunch your toes on the wooden floor. The spider abseils down the wall. A plug is unplugged, a wire is wrapped and shoved. There are footsteps made with heavy boots. You catch an unfamiliar smell, a new sweat. I think of you at the door this morning, pillow lines embossed on your face. You hear the kitchen tap, noisy gulping. I plunge the coffee, pick up my phone and begin to type. Your right leg wobbles, your nipples are cold and hard, you feel very small. The boiler rumbles into action and you jump, a cup clinks in the sink. A bag is zipped shut. Footsteps become heavier then silent. You hear a muffled text beep.

Get up lazy legs, meet me for lunch?

Kate Smalley Ellis is a writer and bookseller based in London. Her short fiction has been published in *Open Pen*, the *Mechanics' Institute Review* and *The London Short Story Prize Anthology* among others. In 2020 she was longlisted for the Deborah Rogers Foundation Award for her debut novel. She runs the Brick Lane Bookshop Short Story Prize. Find her @katesmalleyelli.

FORTY YEARS AND COUNTING

Vivienne Buckley

I turned forty last year. It was easier than turning thirty – I hated that! But, I think I like forty. It's made me more reflective.

I started my career as a Drama teacher at the age of twenty-three. Drama is my first love. Creating drama with young people, my first passion. In 2017 I was commissioned to create a piece of drama with a group of young people from the Batley and Spen area in memory of the MP Jo Cox. Together we created a work called #MoreIn-Common; a homage to Jo's maiden speech in Parliament. As part of this process, I was interviewed for a blog curated by a student on the project, called Deeds not Words. One of the questions was: 'If you had been alive 100 years ago would you have been a suffragette?' I wanted to shout 'yes, of course', but the question really made me think. If I was me 100 years ago, what would I have done?

One hundred years ago only unmarried women were allowed to work as teachers, so I tick that box and assume I would have been in the same profession. A good profession for political allegiance, once described as akin to National Service. A profession dominated by women at the turn of the twentieth century. A profession in which women could fight the existing norms of gender, rejecting a life of domesticity and freed from the shame of not marrying.

So, in my historical daydream, I am happy in this space. But, who would I have been?

Would I have been Isabel Cleghorn, the first woman president of the National Union for Teachers who fought for the union to get behind the suffragette movement and lost due to the male members' vote? I'm not sure I'm diplomatic enough for this hypocrisy.

Or, would I have been Mary Gawthorpe? I match some of her profile as a passionate socialist and a campaigner for disadvantaged students. After hearing Emmeline Pankhurst's speech, she became an activist addressing thousands in Heaton Park in Manchester. In 1909 she famously heckled Winston Churchill, was caught, beaten and suffered internal injuries. Arrested, chained, humiliated and force fed. I'm not sure I'm brave enough for this.

I salute both these heroes of feminism and education.

The truth is, I don't know what I would have done 100 years ago, but I do know what I do now. I'm the deputy principal at Bridgend College, an organisation with a culture and ethos unlike any other I have witnessed, rooted in equality and fairness. Earlier this year Sodexo published the results of a five-year, one-of-a-kind study that proves teams with gender diversity achieve better results. Bridgend College has a Curriculum Leadership Team with a seven-to-four gender balance in favour of women. At middle management this number grows to a 70 per cent bias. The governing body has a commitment to a 50/50 split by 2020; this strategy makes a difference, the organisation is better for it and I am very lucky to be part of it.

But I am reminded of the Channel 4 film *100 Years and Counting* in which the narrator says, 'A lot has changed in the 100 years since women got the vote, but we are not there yet.'

We are not there yet.

I need to do more to encourage young women to strive for better-paid jobs, to change the extraordinary numbers of boys still dominating the areas of construction, engineering and IT, to raise the aspirations of the brilliant girls I see in classrooms every day. To act as a role model to aspiring female leaders and arts practitioners. To stand up and say I am a Welsh woman from a working-class background, and I have got skills to share and stories to tell. Because if I don't, why should they? I need to let it be known that I am hopeful of the next generation, sure that they will be even stronger, even brighter and even better at creating a world which is fair and just and equal.

I hope I would have been brave enough 100 years ago.

I promise to be brave enough now.

Forty years and counting.

Following a fulfilling career as a drama teacher and theatre director, **Vivienne Buckley** now works in educational management as the deputy principal of a large further education college. Her current work centres around curriculum design, inclusion and wellbeing. Vivienne is also the artistic director of West Glamorgan Youth Theatre Company. She lives in South Wales with her dog Malcolm.

THE HAND THAT WIELDS THE PRIEST

Emily Devane

In June 2016, when the rest of the country was reeling from the EU Referendum result, I was reeling from news of my own. At the age of thirty-nine, I'd been diagnosed with breast cancer. Throughout my treatment – two lots of surgery, chemotherapy and radiotherapy – I continued to write.

The story I am sharing here was first scribbled in my notebook in the radiotherapy waiting room. Seeing a patient with a fly-fishing magazine transported me to a different time and, while my stories during treatment were laced with dark themes, and my brain was fuzzy from medication, here was a moment of clarity and light.

The story went on to win the Bath Flash Fiction Award and is published in its anthology, *Where the Lobsters Run Free*. Here it is:

THE HAND THAT WIELDS THE PRIEST

That evening, the fish left a strange taste in my mouth.

We'd gone together, Dad in his waxed jacket and waders, me in my parka and wellies. Flies hovered above the river, orange-tinged in the afternoon sun. He fastened together his rod and opened his box:

flies lined up like soldiers on parade. 'We'll try the March Brown,' he said, affixing one to the line.

I spied the metal hook; it glinted between his fingers.

'Can you see him?' he pointed to a pool of slow-moving water. 'There,' he said and I followed his finger to a set of tiny ripples where, seconds ago, a mouth had snapped.

While I sat on a long-rotten stump, he waded in. Shoulders stretched back then thrown forward, he cast the fly towards the pool to dance across the water's surface. He held his body still a while, then cast again. 'Patience is required,' he whispered. When I tried to speak, to ask if the fish had gone, he shushed me. A glimmer of something, more ripples.

The rod bent – and then jerked to and fro. Dad reeled him in, the fish fighting all the while to shake off the metal hook. On land, he thrashed and gasped for breath – the gills, Dad indicated with his fingertips.

One shiny eye gazed up from the bag. With his hand, the same one he used to stroke my head at night, Dad gave a firm whack with his metal priest. The thrashing stopped.

A priest, I wondered. Was that to save its soul?

Dad held the fish across his hands for me to see the tiny teeth that took the bite, the shimmering belly. 'Would you look at that,' he said.

That night, his hand felt different on my head.

Emily Devane is a writer, teacher and editor from Ilkley, West Yorkshire. She once taught a history module on women's rights and so leapt at the chance to be a part of this project honouring women's voices. Emily's short fiction has been widely published. Her writing has won prizes, including a Northern Writers' Award and a Word Factory apprenticeship, and her work was selected for the *Best Microfiction* anthology (2021).

Emily teaches Creative Writing courses and workshops. She is an editor at FlashBack Fiction, an online journal specialising in historical flash fiction. Emily tweets @DevaneEmily.

THE DEATH SLIDE

Freya Kelly

I still refer to it as the Death Slide in my head.

My grandparents had taken my little sister and me to an adventure park in a forest somewhere. We were young, no more than six or seven years old. She wanted to go on the swings. I wanted to go on the Death Slide.

If you didn't know, a Death Slide is three metres wide, about a mile high, and has a vertical drop almost all the way to the ground before it starts curving into a level surface. Therefore, you must drop yourself over the edge, free-fall for what feels like a split-second eternity and hope you don't bruise too badly when the bottom bit catches you.

It was a colossal thing, as tall as a skyscraper – or at least, that's how I remember it. For some reason, six-year-old me decided that it would be fun to join the children throwing themselves into oblivion one by one like raucous lemmings. So, my grandpa came with me and we trekked up the stairs to the platform. I sat myself on the lip of the slide, looked down at the vertical drop, and . . .

I couldn't move.

Now, I was known as the fearless daughter, too young and

beloved to have had my boldness knocked off-kilter just yet. Usually, I'd be the one encouraging my little sister to jump a gap, or wade across a river, or sleep without a nightlight – but I sat there, staring down at that drop. I was scared. I'd never done something like this before and I really wasn't sure whether I'd survive. It was the uncertainty, more than the height, that scared me.

My grandpa knew something was up as I sat there, silent and unmoving. I had never hesitated to do something stupid and dangerous before. He gently told me that I didn't have to do it, that we could go back down and find something else. There and then, sitting on the edge and staring down into the abyss, I knew that if I didn't do this, I would regret it.

It was a strange feeling. Though I'm familiar with it now, at the time I'd never felt it before. Maybe that's why I can still remember this experience so clearly. I just knew that if I didn't even try, I'd look back on this moment and wonder if I could have. I doubted I would find another Death Slide quite as terrifying and awesome as this one. This was my chance, and I wanted to do it.

The problem was, my muscles were all locked up. I couldn't bring myself to make that final push. So I looked back at my grandpa, and asked him to drop me. He laughed, deep from the belly as he was wont to do, then picked me up by the wrists and held me over the edge. I remember looking down at my feet dangling mid-air. Below me, I could see the Death Slide was a vivid shade of red. Thinking back on it, the colour was remarkably reminiscent of blood, and perhaps if I was a bit older, I would have taken it as a bad omen and rethought my decision.

But I was young and stubborn and determined to do this – determined to get over the fear that had crippled me for the first time. I took a deep breath and counted out loud. 3 . . . 2 . . . 1.

My grandpa let go of my wrists and I fell down. I think I might have been screaming, but I can't remember. I closed my eyes at some point, because when I opened them again, I was at the bottom, flat on my back. I sat up, feeling strangely breathless. My grandpa called down to me, 'You still in one piece?' I checked myself over. All my limbs were attached. My head was spinning a little, but I actually felt great. I whooped in victory, and got to my feet.

I must have gone down the Death Slide 100 times that day, never getting tired of throwing myself from the precipice that had almost defeated me, conquering it again, and again, and again. Proving to myself I was still brave. Even now, in my twenties, if given the chance I would hurl myself down that thrilling slope once more.

I was so proud at the time. Am proud, still. I like to think it helped shape me as a person, a keystone part of the woman I became. Am becoming, still.

So, if you ever come across a Death Slide – literal or otherwise – and you can't bring yourself to jump off from the brink, don't be afraid. Get someone you trust to drop you over the edge, and you'll be fine. I promise.

Freya Kelly is a Languages student and a writer; words are her world. She has many stories 'in progress' and if she had a superpower, she'd like the ability to finish one, please. In the meantime, she'll settle for writing nonsensical, self-indulgent poetry and starting new story ideas with no concept of plot or character development. She likes to think she'll get there one day.

Writing for *100 Voices* is the first of hopefully more published works. And what an amazing beginning it is.

THE DAY I STOPPED HATING MY FACE

Robyn Addison

When I was little my mum and dad had an affectionate nickname for me: 'Funny Face'. I think because I make silly expressions, or can't hide my feelings on my face, or because my face looks funny at times, or because my face simply is funny at times.

When I was about eight, I was a 'bonny wee lassie' as my auntie put it and I remember I desperately wanted to be pretty so I could be a pop star or an actress, or Prime Minister of the world when I grew up. How I looked was important to me. When I was ten I had a bad haircut and was nicknamed 'Nora Batty' by the boys in my class. It knocked my confidence. The year after, my hair now grown out, my budding breasts attracting some notice, they dubbed me 'Pamela Anderson'. It was a quick turnaround in the fortunes of my public persona. I was secretly pleased.

I've always had a funny relationship with my face. I know it's there on the front of my head, looking out at people, but if you asked me to describe it to you in detail I would most likely struggle. I'd pause and say . . . Well, it's big. I've got a big face. It's busy. I mean, I don't wear earrings because my face has got 'a lot going on'. Big eyes, bug eyes. Half a nose, like it's unfinished. If pushed, I'd probably say that I like my eyelashes. They're good. They're long. I like them.

My face tells people things at times that I don't want them to know. It betrays me. I blush readily, my eyes water easily and sometimes I forget that if there's a smell under my nose, people can guess it with just one glance at my expression. I've been told at times, 'Be more aware of what your face is doing.' As if it doesn't belong to me. It does and it doesn't.

And now, I work in a profession where my face is my currency, I'm constantly being judged on how I look, what my face says about a character, about the world. So I'm constantly assessing and reassessing my attributes. Am I beautiful enough, quirky enough, 'me' enough?

A few years ago I started agonising over ageing and about what it meant to be a success or a failure. I lost confidence, my anxiety rose and I gathered up all that negativity and I took it out on my face.

I dislike having my photo taken because when I see the results I think . . . that can't be how I look, that isn't it, that's not the face I want. It's not me. In my head I look one way but to others I look different. In September last year it was my friend's birthday, and as the five of us were going out for dinner we took a quick snap before we left the house.

It's a lovely photo, my friends are all happy and smiling and it looks like that's what I'm doing too. Laughing. And I was. Except I was also hiding my face, because twenty minutes before I had burst into tears after looking at myself in the mirror. So, there's me, in the middle of the photo, head down and hair covering my features. I'm there and not there.

I know the pressures young girls, young women and older women face daily from images splashed across the media and social media. And I realise that as a cis-gendered white woman, I'm privileged to see myself reflected, to have faces that look like mine stare back at me on stage and screen. But looking at that photo, which is the image on our WhatsApp group, I thought, I'm a grown woman, I don't want to do this to myself any more.

So I decided to take my mum's advice and only look at myself once in the mirror before I left the house and try not to look again. To accept that was how I was for that day and carry on. It felt liberating, to not have to check in all the time with my reflection, to just be.

Of course, I had a relapse. I was unkind to myself and to my face. Then my life changed forever. I was twenty weeks pregnant when I found out I was expecting a girl and I was elated. I had always wanted a daughter, but try as I might, I couldn't picture her, I couldn't see her face. I hoped she would look like my husband. Never like me. Please, not like me.

Then she was born and it was impossible not to see that she looked so much like me, she had my face. The face I had struggled to be kind to for years, the one I have always wanted to change, to pick at, to destroy.

My daughter is beautiful. I want her to grow up loving and appreciating who she is on the inside and out. So, I've reached a level of acceptance of things I cannot change and I'm finally at peace with my appearance. And as my husband pointed out, how can I hate my face, if I love hers?

Robyn Addison grew up in Belper, Derbyshire and has lived in London since graduating from Cambridge University over ten years ago. She is an actor and voiceover artist who works in television, theatre, video games and film. She is also a writer, longlisted for the Bruntwood Prize in 2019, and was previously a member of the Bush Theatre Emerging Writers' Group. She is a current member of the writers' collective The Defectors.

LITTLE BLACK GIRL

Lucy Thatcher

There's a little Black girl
Reading a book in the corner
She stops
She turns to her father
She says when I grow older
I am going to be prime minister
He smiles
Then he sighs
He decides not to ask her why
Instead he says
'You know, I think you would be a great Nurse'
She agrees but it hurts

Daddy thought he was doing the right thing
By reining her dreams and her aspirations in
Years of institutional racisms
Had made him develop a slightly thicker skin
He has managed to stop the pain getting in

But he doesn't hear his heart shout
'How will your dreams get out?'

One day that little girl will say
I understand why you are afraid
You taught me that I would have to try harder
Work longer
Be ten times better
Just to rank second place
Sometimes I think I am not the right gender or race
And I consider my blackness in every decision I make
And I am sure that I will get called racist names
I've seen Black female MPs threatened with violence and rape
But still, I am not dismayed
'Coz you see Daddy
Daughters of immigrants have managed to carve out spaces
Despite their beautiful black faces
In this white British men's politics

Despite isolation and alienation
We have rallied Church groups
And organised troops
In Hairdressers
And in other women's living rooms

We have always been active activists
Responding to our community

Promoting unity
And Equality
For the masses
From the fairest to the blackest
And not just for the few

And when I read
That a white woman said
I would rather be a rebel than a Slave
I wish I could explain
How I laughed at that phrase
How I would laugh in her face
The total disregard for those enslaved
When we are rebel by nature
And not just by name

We possess that genetic rebel spirit
That traditional resistance
That has helped us to ensure our existence
Despite the opposition

Like Queen Mother of the Ashanti
Or Nzinga who fought the Portuguese
They are both in me

From Africa to Britain
Across the whole of America and the Caribbeans

We have always fought hostility
Ideas of white superiority
We established our priorities
Raising the voices of our communities
And in some cases, all whilst taking care of families

You see, until the lion tells his story
The hunter will always have the glory
The brave policeman
Versus racist police brutality
Olive Morris was beaten so badly
Because she stepped in to help a Black man
Arrested unfairly
Because he had the audacity
To drive an expensive Mercedes

This fearlessness
Shows that we are well placed
To enter into this political race
And yeah,
It's hard to be what you cannot see
But one day
A little Black girl might look back and see me
And know that she has the ability
To ensure change and reform
And not just be forced into her black uniform
And she could inspire Black people to the ballots

And elect MPs like Diane Abbott
And Black female politicians like King
I hope you hear me Daddy, I hope you are taking this in!

Claudia Jones the mother of Notting Hill
Inspired generations of women who still
Take to the streets with pride
Who dance and cast oppression aside,
Who take strength in their femininity and difference,
Although many cannot see the sense in it
Notting Hill still belongs to us
Even though they put the gentry in it.
And I wonder how many Black women
Were feminists
Before the idea of feminism even existed
How many of them resisted
The idea that women were submissive?

Sarah Parker Remond
Has all my appreciation
Without her there might not have been emancipation
And she has shown exactly where we fit in this equation
Whether black or white, as a female she
Highlighted your plight and strengthened your
Fight for equal rights.

Do you know her name like Emmeline Pankhurst?

A simple action can speak a thousand words

Like a million biographies erased from history

A million victories won by minorities

But you see

I do not need your permission to take my place in history

And even if they try to erase me

I will still fight

Because one day

A future little Black girl might

Just come looking for me

So she knows she can be

Exactly who and what she wants to be

Lucy Thatcher, author of *Small Thoughts and Poetry* and self-proclaimed goddess, is an Instagram poet, blog writer, host and performance poet. She has been involved with several events including: Vote 100: Black Women, Parliament and Power, Croydon Council's International Women's Day Celebrations and 'The Village' event exploring maternal mental health.

From Brixton, south London, Lucy still lives and works within the community as a sexual health advisor for the NHS and is committed to the empowerment of women and the uplifting of Black female voices.

FREE

Christabel Johanson

What does freedom mean to you?

A few years ago I bumped into a girl who went to my old school. She was eighteen and told me she was bisexual, nonchalantly like she was revealing her star sign. She recalled how all the girls would snog each other in the park. Well, this sounded much freer than my experience of school. What a great feeling to be so open, not just with others but with yourself. After all, isn't that where your first healthy relationship should start?

Free was how I felt on 30 June 2017 when Melissa and I tied the knot. Seeing her in her wedding dress was unforgettable. Surrounded by friends and family, I walked in to 'Colourblind' playing on the cello and violin.

The gathering was small and the venue was cosy but it was a day that left us spellbound. That was when I knew I was free to follow Love, and Love led me to this woman. This is not just our story but one in a growing narrative of people choosing freedom over captivity.

Nowadays sexuality might be an easier conversation to have but it doesn't mean there won't be hurdles. It doesn't mean there won't be tears. Healing the wounds of judgement and rejection through loving yourself unconditionally. It isn't easy, none of it is, but it is worth it.

What does freedom mean to you? For me it meant saying 'I do'.

Christabel Johanson graduated from University College London with a BA in English Literature and an MA in Film Studies. Since then she's been interested in storytelling and capturing the narratives of everyday life. This has led to her editing two magazines, shooting documentaries and publishing poetry. She is currently working on her writing, freelance ventures and continuing her path to freedom.

NEPHEWS

Melangell Dolma

It was just before Christmas. I was sitting in Madame Fromage's café when my sister rang. I was in my first term at drama school and in my experimental phase. I'd been to dye my hair platinum blonde that morning and kept turning to catch glimpses of myself in a mirror as my sister let me natter on excitedly about my new hair. Eventually she said she had a bit of news for me too. And then she told me one of the best things anybody has ever told me. 'I'm pregnant,' she said.

A few weeks later she emailed me. 'Thought you'd like to see this,' attaching a file called JumpingBean.jpg. I stared at the black and white scan. I already loved that teeny, tiny little bean-shaped form more than I could put into words – though I did try. I wrote a piece about it as homework for sight-reading class. My year group sat in a circle and stood up one by one to read our pieces aloud. In mine, I vowed to be the best aunty the world had ever seen.

I loved what I'd written for that class, and I was proud of it. That was probably one of the last times I felt like that about my writing. Soon after, writing started to make me feel vulnerable and exposed. It happened gradually, but I remember the final straw vividly. Our year group was sitting in a circle, again. You do a lot of sitting in circles at drama school. It was a feedback session for our end-of-year assessment. We'd each had to write our own half-hour piece of theatre and perform it in front of the college. The tutors gave us our feedback, one by one. Mine was not as glowing as I'd hoped. My stomach sank. Heat rushed up the back of my neck. I felt embarrassed and ashamed. I stopped writing.

My nephew, the bean, was born. He was Elis, and he was wonderful. People would say he looked like me when I was his age, all blond ringlets and chubby cheeks. As he grew, he reminded me more and more of myself as a child. When he couldn't hit the ball with the paddle bat, he'd become enraged, throw a tantrum and walk away sulking. That instinct to reject anything he wasn't instantly good at was one I recognised all too well. He was a perfectionist, just like me.

Slowly I'd try to coax him back to whatever activity he'd abandoned. To encourage him to be patient with himself. Tell him that it was all right to not always be very good at something, as long as he enjoyed doing it.

Through all this, a voice in the back of my head wouldn't let me be. It whispered that I should write; I tried to ignore it. It got louder; I tried harder to block it out. One day, five years after that dreaded feedback session, a friend encouraged me to contribute to a project that was looking for writers. The voice screamed that I should write something for it. I screamed back: No way! I couldn't. It was too scary. I knew what lay down that path – sitting in circles and humiliation.

I suddenly realised that this perfectionism I recognised in Elis wasn't just something from my childhood. I was still a perfectionist, and it was still paralysing me, holding me back. I was still rejecting things that made me feel vulnerable. The voice softened. It reminded me of sitting in a different circle. Of reading my piece about my beloved little bean. Of feeling proud of what I'd written.

Elis is now nine years old. Elis, my kind, creative, talkative nephew, who loves swimming in the sea whatever the temperature. Who is also now a big brother to Idris. Idris is four. He's mischievous and wild and has started collecting animal bones he spots on walks through the fields. Elis still has tantrums sometimes, so does Idris. And I still feel the urge to reject things that make me feel vulnerable, but these days I try to push my way through it.

Because by now, as well as being an aunty, I am a writer. It took me a long time to build up the courage to write again. But in the end the voice won, and I did write a piece for that project. And then I wrote some more, and some more again. I'm proud that I kept going even though it terrified me. I've achieved so many things that seemed impossible to me once. I've sat in the audience for a play I've written and produced, with Elis sitting beside me watching, taking it all in, and laughing at jokes I wrote.

Being the best aunty in the world isn't always easy. Sometimes aunties are tired, distracted and impatient. Sometimes aunties snap at their nephews, or don't have as much time as they'd like, or have to change their plans last minute. Letting my nephews down is painful. I beat myself up about it and feel guilty a lot of the time. But when

I am with them, joking and laughing and listening to their stories, that guilt falls away. Being the 'best' aunty in the world isn't even important. What matters is that I love them. And I know that they love me. And that means more to me than anything else I've achieved.

Melangell Dolma is a writer and actor from Gwynedd, now based in Cardiff. She trained at the Royal Welsh College of Music and Drama and works in theatre, TV and radio in both Welsh and English. She is a member of Theatr Genedlaethol Cymru's New Playwrights' Group and has been a writer in residence at Theatr Clwyd. She produced her first play *Bachu* as a co-production with Theatr Genedlaethol Cymru and Theatr Clwyd at the National Eisteddfod in 2019. It took a few years for her to find the courage to write, and this project definitely helped her get there.

VOICES THAT WENT
THE DISTANCE

A FUTURE IN MID-FLIGHT

Louise Taylor

A classified ad in *The Times* in the early 1980s kickstarted my writing career. A Girl Scout group in Ohio was looking for British Brownie pen friends.

I'm not sure why my pen friend and I were matched – but it didn't matter. The writing was enough; the rest came from there. By the time we eventually met, I knew her better than anyone I'd ever called a best friend.

The arrival of email gave our writing relationship a new immediacy. It was also, we agreed, rather like keeping a diary that wrote back.

We were also both writing other things. Poetry mostly. She sent me carefully illustrated copies of some of hers, and I did the same, minus the illustrations. I never have been able to draw. One, which she wrote while flailing in the backwash of the ending of her first serious relationship, contained the line, 'And futures have a way of falling down in mid-flight'. The line stuck in my head.

We made plans, separately and together. I moved 200 miles to London, to take the first tentative steps in a legal career. She moved almost 2,000 miles to Phoenix, to work as a third-grade teacher.

And, the following February, I was to visit her in Arizona. She sent me photos of some of the places we'd see, and even a smear of red dust on the back of a postcard.

I never made that trip. One day I received an email from her mentioning some awful headaches she'd been having. The next day, the headache worse, she came home early and collapsed. One of America's best neurological hospitals couldn't save her – and she died two weeks later, her brain peppered with aneurysms she hadn't known were there.

I wrote her a last letter, one she'd never read, and packed it away with all the others. I even packed away her poem. Was I scared by its prescience or, at twenty-three, was I not old enough to appreciate that it was a prediction that could just as easily be mine?

I missed her all right. One bright Saturday afternoon, dozing on my bed, it seemed as if she came to sit beside me. I heard her voice, felt her hand on my shoulder.

Unless it involved statutes and case law, there wasn't much writing for me over the next few years. I was a lawyer now, not a writer. Then, six years later, my phone rang. My father, at only sixty, had had a heart attack – the sort medics call a 'widow-maker' – and he was dead before the taxi from my Fleet Street office reached Euston station.

Even at the time, I was surprised at how effectively adrenaline carried me through that dark aftermath. My father's business needed winding up and then there was my mother, alone now.

I think it was during this period of parenting a parent that the cold cloak of my own mortality settled around my shoulders. I thought a lot about my American friend and how her future had indeed fallen down in mid-flight. And I thought about my father, whose belief in his own future was evident in the tiniest of things: the note about a dental appointment he'd made for the month after his death, and a new shirt hanging unworn in his wardrobe.

I tried hard to think less about what he'd lost out on and more about what he'd done. Forty years earlier he'd eschewed Oxford for Liverpool University. It was the tail end of the 1960s and there can't have been many more exciting places to be young. As Ents Secretary at the Students' Union, he booked many of the era's musical greats. No surprise, really, that he ended up ditching his teaching career in favour of opening his own record shop.

In my head, a clock started to tick. The arrival of two babies in just under two years muffled it for a while but it emerged, stronger than ever, in those unfriendly pre-dawn hours when I tried to persuade my toddler back to sleep or fed my baby.

The final catalyst was a redundancy exercise. An employment lawyer, I was more used to being on the other side of the table. Although I kept my job, my enthusiasm was gone – and that clock was ticking louder than ever.

And so, with the support of my long-suffering husband, I did what everyone always tells would-be writers not to do: I gave up my job to write. Several years on, I'm still here, still writing – and just about earning a living from it. I've done it for myself but I've also done it for my long-dead friend and for my father too. I'll fly with my future for as long as I can.

Louise Taylor is a freelance writer specialising in the legal and travel sectors. She also writes poetry, fiction and nature essays, and is co-founder and occasional editor of Words for the Wild (www.wordsforthewild.co.uk), an online platform for nature writing. A Scouser by birth, she lives in Hampshire with her husband and two children. She tweets @SariskaTiger.

3,000 DAYS

Ciara McVeigh

I came from a small town in Ireland, of around 7,000 people. My friend Chris got a job in Manchester. He said, 'Join me. Try it.' I'd never been before but I had nothing to lose, and he was my number one.

I moved to Manchester on 30 April 2009. I was twenty-five.

I loved the tall buildings. There were no tall buildings where I came from. I remember walking down Ducie Street with the buildings rising up either side of me. I was in love with the sight of city lights in darkness, thousands of bulbs lifting the night.

I got my first real job in Manchester, writing for the internet. I started earning properly for the first time. Welcome zeroes. Later that year, I met a man, Jon. We met on a friend date outside Piccadilly station. Three years later we were married. I was twenty-eight. We're still friends.

Chris moved on to London but I stayed here. We learned, we worked, we grew together, me and Manchester. More tall buildings. More restaurants. More people. Momentum.

I worked in Ardwick. I worked in the City Tower. I worked near the universities. I danced on Canal Street. I lived in Ancoats, and in

Castlefield. I drank everywhere. Three years ago, we moved to Sale. My family life began. We bought our wonderful Victorian terrace, with true Manchester red brick. Two up, two down. I went to Wythenshawe hospital when the first baby went away. Only nine weeks. I went to Wythenshawe hospital when the second baby arrived. Over nine pounds.

Some of the most important things in my life have happened to me here. Some of the most important things in my life happened because I came here. It's been over 3,000 days since I first came to Manchester. I left home to come home.

Manchester gave me freedom, love and work. I owe her everything.

Ciara McVeigh is a freelance writer, creative, sometime journalist, and curator of newsletter community The Primordial Scoop, sharing stories and thoughts about the bigger things that bring us all together – connection, joy, purpose. Find more info at ciaramcveigh.com.

THIS IS WHY

Anne Summerfield

I don't much like thinking about how long I've been writing – and when would I say I started? The so-called book I scribbled down at eight? When I wrote technical manuals for a living? Or when I started writing poetry in my spare time? Maybe around then. About thirty-five years ago. I'm that old.

After a few years of poetry and computer manuals, I'd started producing little paragraphs of something that I could see wasn't a poem, though I didn't know what it *would* be, at my desk in between sections of 'press this button' and 'use the return key to enter data'. Then I went on an Arvon course – to Lumb Bank – armed with a title and these scraps of something. My tutors were Barbara Machin, a TV writer – now most famous for being the creator of *Waking the Dead* – and Kathy Page, whose first novel *Back in the First Person* was a favourite of mine. Both were kind and encouraging, as were the other people in the group, and it was a lovely week.

On the last evening, we all had the chance to read our work to the group. The reading was held in a small crowded sitting room with everyone perched on baggy sofas or squashed uncomfortably on rugs on the floor. The reading chair in the corner was an old wooden carver with arms like something from a farm kitchen. We took it in turns to scramble to the chair clutching notebooks and papers and read for about five minutes each. I was one of the last to go. I had a little piece from my story in my hand. There were still only little pieces. I climbed over everyone and was shaking and glad of the chair's hard embrace. But as I read, something happened, something wonderful. I stopped feeling self-conscious or aware of my trembling hands or awkward about my unlovely accent. Because the story stopped being mine and the words just seemed to come from somewhere else, and I felt like I was listening, listening to the story for the first time. There were only the words, the character telling her story, and I disappeared. Only when I stopped reading, breathless, stunned, not quite in the room any more, did I come back to being me. It was magic. Not mystical exactly, but pretty darn close.

It was years – literally – before that story from the fragments was finished after many false starts and revisions. In the meantime I gave up technical writing, did an MA, got married, had children. When the story from the fragments, *The Velvet Maid*, was read on Radio 4 my second child was a three-month-old baby – he's in his twenties now and six foot three! But still that feeling, that chance to conjure with words has kept me going, has made me try different things in writing, and always want to learn more. It seems odd to say I found my voice by disappearing, but that is the why of writing fiction for me – to create an imaginary world that's strong and real enough so that I – the writer – can disappear.

Anne Summerfield gave up working as a technical writer in the computer industry to study for an MA in Modern Fiction at Exeter University. She taught Creative Writing at the Open University. Last century she won an Asham Award and a Jerwood/Arvon New Writing bursary, had stories in Virago and Serpent's Tail anthologies and broadcast on BBC Radio 4.

Most recently, she has been writing flash fiction with work shortlisted in the Bath Flash Fiction Award and published in print and online. She is married with two grown-up children and lives in Hampshire. She tweets infrequently as @Summerwriter.

ANNE MEETS JEFFREY

Emma Miriam Berentsen

Content warning: this piece contains strong references to sexual abuse.

'It's difficult you know to find words now to say you know like it's difficult because you know like she is the victim you know and I am the one who did it, so it is already been done you know. I can't really say sorry you know because that would be too easy.'

Seven years after *Jeffrey* had raped me he said this.

Anne was the name of my first doll, my first guinea pig and the name of my friend from kindergarten. The night that *Jeffrey* dragged me from my bike, raped me and took my freedom for hours, he had asked me what my name was. As I was sure he would find me if I told him my real name I made up a name and told him that my name was Anne. After the horror of that night, I was found by policemen and a long process started to find *Jeffrey*. Months later he was found and the trials in court started. In court, I found out his name wasn't Jeffrey either – just like my made-up name he had made up his name. It almost felt as if that night nothing had happened to either me or him, but to these characters we had made up.

Seven years after the rape had happened I got in touch with a

238

mediation organisation to set up a meeting with *Jeffrey*. At the time I just finished my MA in Performance Making in London and was sure that this meeting would not only be a personal achievement of facing him but would be part of something bigger, a piece of art, most likely. With a recorder secretly hidden in my bag, my hands shaking and my heart pounding in my chest I stepped into the meeting room and talked to him for almost three hours. No miracles happened, he did not say sorry, I told him I didn't even want him to say sorry. I asked him questions, he asked me questions and most of all he spoke a lot about his difficulties. Instead of feeling any better I felt worse after this meeting; the trauma started getting back into my body and mind and I started to have nightmares and flashbacks all over again.

A few months after the meeting, I decided that, with this experience of rape, meeting my rapist and living in a time where rape culture was in lots of public discussions, I had to make a piece of art about it. I tried to make a solo – I performed a small work-in-progress in a theatre – but I didn't feel as if this was the way to tell the story. It needed something else, maybe even someone else, and I asked Tiffany (Murphy, my co-performer) to join me in the creation of this piece. It became a long process spread over almost two years where we started with a recording of me sharing the full story with Tiffany, where I dived into rape definitions, artworks about rape, artists working with these thematics, researching rape culture, filming the places where my rape happened, transcribing the recording I had of the meeting with *Jeffrey* and slowly the documentary/live-art style performance *Anne Meets Jeffrey* was born. A performance not with self-pity or being over-sentimental, but a piece I can be proud of, a raw documentary work that had gone far beyond the sole experience of my rape.

Anne Meets Jeffrey premiered its first work-in-progress in December 2017 at Camden People's Theatre in London and was followed by a full-length version at Veem – House for Performance in Amsterdam (2018), Battersea Arts Centre in London (2019) and Theater aan Zee festival in Oostende (2019).

Being able to perform this work has been difficult, but it has also been a very important way for me to tell such a personal story in an artistic way. The importance of the piece was not solely for me, it was also of great value to the friends, family and professionals who came to see it. I believe that in the current discourse within our society on these subject matters *Anne Meets Jeffrey* is a piece that could contribute to several discussions and should be performed and talked about.

Emma Miriam Berentsen is a performance artist, theatre maker and facilitator. Most of her work is based on autobiographical material, transformed into theatre, performances, texts and installations. She is interested in working on the edge of non-fiction and fiction as well as the connection between the art, the artist and the audience.

Emma uses conversation as a performative tool to talk about subjects we normally avoid talking about, such as mental health, death, mortality and sexual violence. She has presented work across the globe including at the Venice Biennale, Marieta, São Paulo, Glasshouse Project, New York, and in venues across her native Netherlands and the UK. You can find out more about Emma at www.emmaberentsen.nl.

BECOMING A STRONG WOMAN

Maya Kay

Five years ago, I formally set off on a journey I never thought
I'd take.

Searching for my purpose.

Not on society's terms, on my terms.

'Where do you see yourself in five years?' they'd say.

Back then, I knew what I wanted and I knew who I wanted
to be.

Yet, little did I know what it would take to get there.

Well . . .

Perhaps not there.

Rather, here.

Laying the foundations, building high walls, allowing them to
come tumbling down, and rebuilding.

Shaking the roots of the tree I thought I'd planted.

Nature versus nurture.

This is the story of how to be a strong woman, something I
have achieved after facing the weird and wonderful and
there's still a long way to go.

I use words quite loosely.

Carefree, without a thought.

Words such as I don't know, I can't recall, I forgot.

I ought to remember really, as I'm not a robot

And I ought to remember I am not a robot.

I am designed to shine bright and live my best life.

That's what they tell us to do on social media, right?

It is vital

To consider the words I choose to use.

The power of I am.

I am powerful.

I am strong.

Unwavering.

I must remember who I used to be.

Who I am.

Who I am going to be.

Support . . . no, actually, uphold each other.

Together.

Us.

We.

As many previously held me.

A diamond in the rough, a true gem, tough stuff.

A gemstone is made after millions and billions of years of
    pressure.

Rarely flawless.

At times marked with inclusions.

Invisible.

BECOMING A STRONG WOMAN

To the naked eye.

Laid bare and

Upon closer inspection it is clear to see,

Je pense donc je suis.

The only way I know who to be, is me.

Beautiful beyond the facets,

Beautiful beyond all those language classes.

Beauty that runs deep.

Beauty I ought to keep,

Hold onto it, whilst I sleep.

As well as when I am awake.

Or is it woke? Hashtag, who knows.

I must always remember, for goodness' sake

To see how things unfold, and to go with the flow.

A strong woman is made after a few woes, foes and lows.

All of the above, I have had plenty of those.

Yet, I carry love and strength wherever I go.

My dear friends, in fact I call them soul sisters,

We maintain close bonds despite the distance

Surrounded and clothed and cloaked and bathed,

In unity, standing together, unscathed.

Forget networking events,

Focus on my own network instead.

In real life, not online.

Stiff upper lip, I'll be just fine.

My resolute attitude

Helps me stay away from the lewd

People and places.

My intuitive personality keeps me in the best spaces,

And allows the stars to align

Which helps to be in the right place at the right time.

Be conscious, be cautious and mindful, rather than sudden
  jerks

Of movement from one place to another, to find who I need
  to be.

The threads of women that make my whole tapestry.

Woven and weaving at times threadbare,

Wandering and wondering across the globe without a care.

In the world we see what we want to see,

Acting on obligations of society.

'We must catch up and chat over coffee darling!'

Another faux friend I just can't wait to flee.

Running away won't solve anything,

'Buy a house, white picket fence, engagement ring.'

According to Mohs Mineral Scale of Hardness

Diamonds are the hardest.

Ten.

I have the strength of ten women.

I am a strong woman.

Maya Kay is an author. Her writing includes essays, poetry and short fiction, for print, social and digital media. Since 2009, Maya has also led initiatives to elevate women in her industry. In 2015 she launched The Carat Soup, which catapulted her career. It is a website about gemstones, jewels and the arts, in which she interviews various individuals, ranging from rural southern Africa, to industry leaders in London, Geneva and Monaco. When she was approached to be a contributor to this book, Maya wrote and hosted *Hidden Gems with Maya* on Women's Radio Station. Connect with Maya Kay via Instagram @TheCaratSoup.

NAILING IT

Laura Windley

When I first started writing, *I* was going to rock. I was going to nail it.

In fact, I *was* nailing it, or at least I'd begun to. Deciding to take writing 'seriously', oblivious to any rules, real or imaginary, I had some early writing successes. 'Hah!' I thought. 'Hold my beer, folks. This is it!'

Turned out it wasn't 'it' at all, but in the years that followed, I endeavoured to build on those achievements. In many ways I did. But instead of an upward trajectory as I centred writing more and more in my life, I instead experienced a kind of reversal. Wondering about permission. Frustration that my work didn't seem to be improving and didn't flow the way it had at the start. I had some wonderful egalitarian writer support around me, but as time went on I began to feel increasingly fraudulent and found myself hurtling into the most enormous crisis of confidence. All the naturalness and joy I'd had in the sheer act of creation seemed to disappear. The 'writing thing', my supposed great passion that I'd given up so much for, began to feel like a mountain I'd grown and that I'd failed to climb.

Losing my trust in myself and my creative and writing abilities after those early successes, my focus for so many years – and importantly admitting to myself that that's what happened and it wasn't going to improve just by making myself try even harder – was a tough experience. I'd taken a huge leap of faith, invested a huge amount of energy, and concluded I'd let myself fail. Worse, this was topped by a number of convergent events in my last year or so in London which were almost comic in their negative synchronicity. Much wasn't writing-related, but if a thing was absurdly awful and *could* happen, you can bet it did. Banking errors, lost keys, micromanaging bosses, grudge-filled exes, wrong turnings, knotted-stomach mornings, domestic woes. Personally, professionally *and* writing-wise, the rest of my life seemed to be going backwards, with any achievements I'd ever had seemingly wiped from the map. At that time, I felt like living proof of the Very Worst occurring: 'Now, let her be a warning to you all!'

So what can be done when a big dream seems to bite the dust? When a leap of faith you took has you falling flat on your face with a bunch of people watching? In wanting to 'prove myself' as a Writer and that I could do my own thing, all I felt I'd proved was the exact opposite. 'This is Not For The Likes Of You, And What Were You Thinking, You Insane Fantasist?' Who was I to claim that birthright? Who on earth did I think I was? Although I was still writing and although it was all So Important – the clue was in the making it So Important – I wasn't submitting work. I froze whenever the prospect loomed of doing so. The whole thing became a vicious circle. I hadn't measured up.

Getting 'it' back, or making a new 'it', began by ditching the load. No to anything unimportant. No to taking writing Terribly Seriously. No to a method or route that might work for you but I know doesn't work for me. No to having an ego overinvested. No to a One True Path. No to focusing on Out There, Maybe instead of Right Here, Now. No to 'It has to be *this* one and perfect.' No to external drivers, or supposed boxes to tick. No, too, sadly, to certain people in my life, but that's another story, unrelated to my work.

Instead, I took a long breather and then crafted rules anew. Yes to doing what feels right. Yes to choosing freedom over lifestyle and building up from there. Yes to keeping work to yourself until you're ready to share it. Yes to creating your own thing. Yes to humour and personal writing, and Very Bad Writing, and particularly the yearly Very Bad Novel I now task myself to write. Yes to writing in multiple forms. Yes to experimentation. I started some non-fiction blogs to see what happened. I started making regular money from that writing, and although it's nothing to do with fiction, the act of writing regularly, for an audience, under a pen name and with far less ego investment, has been immensely freeing. Doing so seemed to unlock a great deal in my continued fiction writing. A degree of permission, something my old rules could not provide.

And it's true that if you never take any risk ever, you guarantee failure. Success may require a number of those, even disaster. But even most disasters aren't forever. Make it through some and you might nail it too.

After careers in teaching and book publishing with a sideline in script reading, **Laura Windley** is currently a freelance writer and blogger and no stranger to ups and downs. Her ups include being runner-up in the Bristol Short Story Prize, shortlistings in competitions such as the Fish Short Story Prize and the London Short Story Prize and publication in various journals.

She runs two non-writing-related non-fiction websites and (horror of horrors!) self-publishes non-fiction with some success under pen names. She is finishing off some new short stories, as well as working on her latest Very Bad Novel. She also writes reviews for Cambridge-based short story website TSS.

THINGS

Sharon Kanolik

This piece contains strong language.

These are some things I am proud of:
Standing in the playground aged 9
When I realised
I'd stopped falling over all the time

Learning to cycle without stabilisers

Giving up my lying problem aged 8,
My stealing habit aged 7
Still having the same friends I had when I was 6

Learning to read,
and when it fell into place
Realising I wasn't stupid
But sometimes I'm just

A slow learner,
A slow burner

Singing from the torah in a power suit
Aged 13

I passed my cycling proficiency test
The second time
My driving test
the 6th

I can say hello in 17 different languages

I have watched *Neighbours* for 33 years.

I learnt to be like my parents
And to be **different** from my parents
To follow my own path

I have worked
As a builder, in a factory, in a pub, in a supermarket, in a
    school
I have made connections
On coaches, on trains, in refugee camps, on council estates
With people from places I never thought I would meet

Those moments have made me richer
Than any possessions
ever could

I have fucked up
And tried to repair the fuck ups
Papering over actions
I don't want to repeat,
Learnt the hard way

Hand in hand with my ego,

I am part way to realising
How much I don't know

I have climbed mountains
I have holidayed in Prague alone

I am proud of my heritage
That my Nana was also my friend
That I'm trying to use my privilege

To do
some good things

I'm proud
That I look like Groucho Marx when I wear glasses

That I'm fucking good at playing Streetfighter

That I am a woman
With strong biceps
And strong opinions

That I'm learning
not
To give a fuck

Because life is too short

I'm proud to be still learning
And proud to be open

To love
and to be loved

Sharon Kanolik studied Creative Writing at the University of
East Anglia and Playwriting at the Royal Court as part of its
Young Writers Programme. Her plays include *Pioneers*, an audio
play made in 2020 with the Bush Theatre and White City Youth
Theatre, *Things to Do in a Blackout*, audio plays for Bounce Theatre,
and *Empires*, which was performed at the Bush Theatre in 2014.

Sharon also writes performance poetry, spoken word and occasional song lyrics. When not writing, she works in theatre and par-
ticipation and loves hanging out with her two-year-old son Noah.

An earlier version of this piece was originally published on the Books By Women site in November 2016.

HOW I BECAME A WRITER

Emma Flint

I became a writer when I was ten years old.

It was the same year that I discovered Agatha Christie – and therefore crime fiction. On Christmas Day 1984, I unwrapped a notebook and a box of pens, and after lunch I made a nest in the corner of the dining room and began to write my own murder mystery.

By Boxing Day, I'd filled my notebook with a story about a series of country house murders, a French detective with an enormous moustache and his bumbling English sidekick. There was a victim who wore tweeds, and a murderer 'with greasy hair the colour of egg yolk', who I named after me.

I became a writer when I was twenty-two and started a novel without a plot, about a twenty-two-year-old girl who was lost in the world.

I became a writer when I was thirty-five and made myself do something I'd always been afraid to do: I booked a place on a writing course.

Our first exercise was to take a walk and find a place to sit, to observe. And then to write five sentences, describing what we were experiencing through each of our senses. I sat in a pub garden, my notebook open on a splintered sun-blistered table, and found I was looking at the world differently. It was as though something fundamental had shifted in me. Two of those sentences became my first short stories. Another exercise we did in the classroom became my third. I began to hear the first weak cries of what would become my writing voice.

I read my work aloud. I listened to the feedback from my classmates and tutor. And on the last night of the course, the tutor (Julia Bell) told me I must keep going, must keep writing. She said I was a writer – and with that, she held up my wildest, biggest, scariest dream, and she told me it could be real. She took me seriously.

I hugged her words to me all the way home and through the following winter. I wrote more. I read more – more widely, more deeply. I thought more about what makes a book work: what makes a character walk off the page and into your mind? What makes a sentence or a paragraph or a metaphor sing to you?

I kept writing. I made friends with other writers, joined a critique group, stood naked and tense and terrified in front of them when they gave me feedback.

I cried. I made mistakes. I couldn't do it. I got back up. I kept going.

I had the germ of an idea about a woman called Ruth. I wrote about her waking up one hot morning, about the mask she put on to face the world. I didn't know where the idea might go, but I couldn't forget her. I spent time with her. I watched her. I learned how she walked and danced and ate and cursed. And I realised that my idea was more than a story about a single character. It wouldn't be contained.

In 2013 I started a course at Faber & Faber, and told my classmates about the novel I was writing. I began to try out the words 'I am a writer' – on paper at first, then inside my head. And one day I said them out loud. At the end of the Faber course, we were offered the opportunity to read aloud from our work for two minutes. I couldn't imagine anything would make me more nervous than I was already, so I chose the rawest and bravest and most visceral part of my book, and read it loud and slow to a room of agents and publishers. If I only had 300 words, I wanted to make them count.

That reading was like walking into a white winter's day: exhilarating, shocking, breathtaking. Two weeks later, I had offers of representation from nine agents and a publisher. I chose the agent I felt most affinity with, and who I felt understood me and Ruth Malone best. Jo Unwin wasn't just enthusiastic about *Little Deaths*, she believed in it, and saw how good it could be. She was interested in my other ideas, she wanted me to have a career as a writer. And she was the person I knew would be there on the days I felt I couldn't do it.

In the spring of 2014, I sent her what I'd written of *Little Deaths* so far. It took us eighteen months to polish my raw rough material into something that hinted at the novel it could be. In September 2015, we sent it out, and within two weeks I had six offers of publication.

At forty-one, I became a writer.

Emma Flint's first novel *Little Deaths* (Picador, 2017) was long-listed for the Baileys Women's Prize for Fiction, for the Crime Writers' Association Gold Dagger Award for best crime novel of the year, and for the Desmond Elliott Prize. Set in 1960s suburban New York, the novel retells a horrifying true story with a modern feminist slant.

Emma is currently working on her second novel, which is also a retelling of a true story, this time about a love triangle that ends in murder. Set in 1920s London, it explores shame, guilt, and the power of fantasy and obsession.

AUNTIE MIN

Ros Ball

In front of me is a picture of a woman I always knew as 'Auntie Min'. She's clearly not my auntie. The grainy photo shows a woman in the early twentieth century with a floor-length skirt, a high-necked white lace shirt and hair teased out to the sides and piled neatly on top of her head. She's not smiling. She wears small round spectacles and looks like a governess or a teacher. She's holding a fine ladies' bike.

Auntie Min was my grandpa's auntie, making her my great-great-aunt. Despite her being ninety-two when I was born, I remember her, just, and have always felt a kinship with her, particularly through cycling. A picture of me on my bike in 2016 shows a woman of similar age, 100 years later. The bikes are so similar and they helped us both to have careers.

Born in 1885, Minnie was from a 'good' family in Biggleswade in Bedfordshire. She was bright and energetic and became a teacher. She cycled to teacher training college from Biggleswade to Bedford, about ten miles each way. I'm pretty sure she was unusual in doing this at the start of the twentieth century. Some people believed women shouldn't be riding bicycles at all. The photo of her with her bike is a postcard; she writes on the back to her sister, 'Em, how do you like this? I got them done for 2d each.'

Last year my mother and I sat down to read through Minnie's postcards and letters. Minnie loved her job as a teacher and she loved children. That's why I found one of the letters to her so tragic. Being a middle-class woman, when she decided to marry at thirty that was the end of her career (working-class women have always had to work). Women like Min who got married couldn't stay in the workplace, they had husbands and inevitable children to devote their lives to. The head teacher of Langford School writes, 'I am very sorry indeed to lose her from the staff of the school.' But lose her, he did. Teaching or marriage, there was no doing both, but most sad was that Auntie Min wasn't able to have children. I wonder what she did all day while her husband was at work. Her brother became a prominent town councillor and was active in every area of public life. Women didn't even have the vote, so this role could never have been an option for the equally intelligent Min. Only in 1944 was she able to teach again. It was needed for the war effort; suddenly her skills were in demand outside the home.

Jump to 2008 and this thirty-year-old is co-habiting with her long-term partner. We're not married and don't intend to marry, and we've got a ten-month-old daughter. All things Min wasn't able to do.

I am ill. I have endless breastfeeding and other health problems. I have undiagnosed post-natal depression. I'm due to go back to work after maternity leave and I buy a bike. A bike makes my complicated life work. I can come and go as I please. I can get back from work in time to pick up my child. I am stressed and tired and miserable but I ride with something in my mind that I heard once: 'Cycling has done more to emancipate women than anything else in the world.'

I have another child and I tell myself everything will be different this time. Depression engulfs me again and worse. This time when I go back to work I buy an electric bike and I love it like another child. Riding it makes me feel like a stingray gliding under water. In these busy years I write a Twitter diary about how my son and daughter are treated differently because one is a girl and one is a boy. I'm angry. I'm angry for them and I'm angry for me. My career stalls because I work part time. I see my friends with husbands who don't share the work of looking after the kids. And I'm furious.

But it lifts slowly. Slowly. My Twitter diary is a place where I meet like-minded people and we share ways to challenge gender stereotypes that put our kids in boxes. My partner starts to work part time and do all the childcare while I go full time and revive my career.

What would Min have thought of that? A publisher offers us a contract for our diary to become a book, *The Gender Agenda*. I am filled with a sense of achievement, that these difficult years have actually been my greatest accomplishment. What would Min have done if she had been born when I was born? What will my great-great-niece achieve that I can't? So much, I hope.

Ros Ball is an author, former journalist and equalities specialist. After many years at BBC Parliament she now works in Whitehall on policy that supports disadvantaged women. Her first book, *The Gender Agenda*, a two-year diary of the way the world treated her daughter and son differently, was published in 2017 by Jessica Kingsley Publishers. The book is an eye-opening account of the everyday gender stereotyping that affects children everywhere, with tips on how to fight back.

Ros is currently writing the book *Women Who Won*, an illustrated anthology profiling seventy extraordinary elected women who have changed the world of politics: unbound.com/books/women-who-won/.

FIVE-YEAR PLANS

Rebecca Root

When I was in school in the 1980s, we learned about Stalin's Five-Year agricultural plans in the early Soviet Union. I was a bit rubbish at History, but something clearly stuck, and I seem to have internalised this notion of half-decades being a thing, and have adopted a similar approach to planning out my career.

After school, I was offered a place at Mountview Theatre School in London, and on graduating from the three-year acting course in 1990, I set out my goals for my career plan ahead. Within five years I wanted to have had a job on TV, and to have worked with a big theatre company. After a couple of years working on various UK theatre tours as an assistant stage manager and acting understudy, and a lot of unpaid fringe theatre, I eventually landed a role as member of ensemble (AKA Sailor/Courtier/Spear Carrier) on the Peter Hall Company production of *Hamlet*, which opened the newly renamed Gielgud Theatre on Shaftesbury Avenue. Around the same time I got my first tiny role on TV in an episode of the hit BBC sitcom *Keeping Up Appearances*. Within the next five years I worked hard to build on these small beginnings. More TV parts and additional theatre roles followed. But it was difficult, and all the time I was wrestling with my gender dysphoria. I resolved that within the next five years I would transition. I achieved this goal, with the love and support of my family and friends.

After transition, the work became scarce. This was the reality facing a female actor (and a trans female actor at that) in a male-dominated industry, there were fewer parts and more competition. In my subsequent five-year plan I decided to focus on teaching. I went back to university and did my MA in Voice Studies at Central School of Speech and Drama. My career as a voice teacher began.

Of course, even with the best agricultural plans, you can't predict whether it will rain or shine. My career plans have been the same. But to me it seems that things come in cycles and you have to work within that and be ready.

A turning point for my career was getting the part of Judy in the BBC's comedy series *Boy Meets Girl*. The show is a romantic comedy about a younger man and an older woman (me). The show came into my life almost exactly ten years after I had transitioned. At the time, I was making most of my living through voice teaching, and getting smaller roles here and there. It changed everything. It took three years from being in that first table read, to making the pilot and finally getting the show on air. It ran for two seasons, so nearly five years all in all. A five-year plan all to itself, the show opened many doors for me.

The script, by Elliott Kerrigan, was discovered through the Trans Comedy Award, a talent search for scripts with positive portrayals of transgender characters. It was unique at the time, because it showed that trans people were (shock!) just like everyone else. I'm thrilled that things have changed; there are more and more parts for trans actors. And moreover, parts where in fact gender identity doesn't matter, it's more about the character. Now I can be a police officer, a doctor, a teacher. And show that a trans person can be all of those things. *Boy Meets Girl* paved a way for others.

What I'm really proud of, though, is that I have built, over many years, a career. I've gone on to play not just trans characters but cis characters and gender-non-specific characters. I have played characters where gender really doesn't matter. I have continued to expand and learn. For me it's all about the person I'm playing; I was always very clear that I wouldn't just want trans parts. Speaking up isn't always easy. Because of my training and experience, I know my abilities and skills and that gives me confidence when talking about voice training or acting. That's by no means true in every area of my life.

Finding your voice is really about how you feel, your voice reflects your identity. When I'm working as a voice teacher, I never tell anyone what their voice is or should be. With drama students, we talk about finding clarity, and finding the truth to convey the text. When working with a non-actor, perhaps a business-person or someone who is trans, I ask, what do you need your voice to do? It always comes from them – I just help them to channel that.

My partner and I are starting to think about our own five-year plan, too. We'd like to buy a little doer-upper. As a pair of inveterate renters it'll be a big step, but if all goes well with our careers, we're hoping we'll get a place to call ours. Maybe one day even some land! Acting, like farming, I suppose, is an uncertain business.

But I'm constantly building, keeping the avenue open to the next break (hopefully). I've been fortunate to play some amazing roles in the past five years, and have appeared opposite some extraordinary actors, such as Eddie Redmayne, Emma Thompson and Joaquin Phoenix, to name but a few. *The Queen's Gambit* in 2020 (thirty years, or six cycles of the plan, after I graduated from drama school) was a real gift. When I was a child there were two things that I was absolutely sure I wanted:

- to be someone who made their living through acting and performing;
- to be a girl.

So far, my plans have taken me to where I want to be, and for that I feel incredibly lucky. Now for the next seven plans!

Rebecca Root is an actor whose TV and film credits include *Sex Education*, *The Queen's Gambit*, *Finding Alice*, *Last Christmas*, *Creation Stories*, *The Sisters Brothers*, *Colette*, *The Danish Girl*, *Flack*, *The Romanoffs*, *Moominvalley*, *Hank Zipzer*, *Boy Meets Girl* and *Keeping Up Appearances*. Her theatre work includes *Rathmines Road* at the Abbey Theatre, *Trans Scripts* at Edinburgh Festival Fringe and American Repertory Theater in Cambridge, USA, *The Bear/ The Proposal* at the Young Vic and *Hamlet* at the Gielgud Theatre. For radio she has appeared in *Clare in the Community*, *Life Lines*, *The Hotel* and *1977* for BBC Radio 4. Rebecca is also a voice teacher, chiefly working with trans clients.

WE CAN MAKE IT

Sophie Olivia Ali

Content warning: this piece contains references to domestic abuse.

Sometimes I hear them. Those not in my creative world. 'But she's not published yet. She's never even been on *EastEnders*. She hasn't made it.'

I made it. All those years when I thought I wouldn't. But I did. I made it. All those nights and days of hiding. Self-destructing. Standing by the Thames.

All the doubt and self-hatred. Holding pills. All the depression. Temporary and clinical. Hormonal and self-induced. All the voices, mine and his. All the abuse, physical and emotional. All the anger. Mine and his. The anger that still rises. In waves. In storms. The anger that is fear. The anger that is sadness. I made it. Despite him. And it isn't perfect. Life. I am not perfect.

I make. I create. I lactate. Stories. Characters. And babies. I made babies. I was never going to. EVER. I didn't want to. But when I thought maybe I did I wasn't good enough. I couldn't because didn't history repeat itself? Wouldn't I royally fuck it up? But then I did it. And it made me ill. But somehow it also made me stronger. And I do fuck up, daily. But that's OK. Because I can admit it and say sorry. Because I won't use silence or violence like he did. Because, I made it.

I think of other women's struggles often. I think of past generations. I think of my grandma and her strength and I am proud. I think of women and girls all over the world daily and I know we are resourceful and amazing. We are amazing. We can make it.

I have three little girls. THEY are amazing. They inspire me. Infuriate me. Overwhelm me. Frustrate me. Annoy me. God they annoy me. Because, they are so like me. But, they are so not like me. I made it. I fought it. I still have to fight it. For some, like me, it takes a long time. But that's OK. Because I know that I have made it. Because I am here. And there were days when I nearly left.

It's not always easy. I still have doubts, failures (a few successes). Love helps. Being loved and loving others. Loving life! Listening.

But mostly, friendship. Never underestimate it. Female solidarity. Female protection. Female fierceness. Female softness. Women, girls fighting. Standing side by side. Saying come on, you can make it. We can make it.

Sophie Olivia Ali is an actor and playwright living in south London with her three daughters and partner. Her first play *A Town Without Pity* (about abuse within a family) was performed at the Arena Theatre when she was twenty-one. Since then her writing has been performed sporadically throughout her acting career and motherhood. She was longlisted for the Papatango New Writing Award 2017 for her play *Block of Seagulls*, and her play *The Tequila Mocking Birds* was shortlisted for the Kenneth Branagh Theatre Award.

As a writer, she has had plays performed at the Bush Theatre, Theatre Royal Stratford East, Rialto Theatre, White Bear, ORL and Southwark Playhouse. As an actor Sophie has worked at many venues in the UK including the Criterion Theatre, Wiltons Music Hall, TRSE, Park Theatre, Theatre 503, Nuffield, Arcola and Jermyn Street Theatre. Find her @SophieOliviaAli and www.spotlight.com/0615-5646-1821.

VOICES IN THE DARK
(AND OUT OF IT)

THE C WORD

Sarah Burnett

It was a fairly quiet afternoon in the X-ray department, so I took the opportunity to have my annual mammogram. I had been screened from the age of thirty-eight, as my mother had perimenopausal breast cancer.

The previous year, in October 2004, I had undergone stereotactic biopsies for changing microcalcification. The histology was benign, so when my digital mammogram popped up on the screen, I was shocked. I turned to the radiographer. 'Oh f★★★, that wasn't there last year.'

I went back to the main department, and wasn't surprised to be told that the breast radiologist wanted me back upstairs for an ultrasound. My right breast had always looked like an accident waiting to happen, and now it had. I went back up – 'I'm only on the meter 'til half four.' The response was, 'Don't worry we'll get someone to feed it.' By now I had figured out this much – I had breast cancer, but to me the lesion looked quite small. I was scanned by the man who had taught me all the breast imaging I knew. He went very quiet, so I asked him what was up; by way of a response he simply turned the screen towards me. There were at least three tumours on that image alone. That's when I cracked.

As a doctor, I knew that I would have to have a mastectomy, and chemotherapy, so I was denied the opportunity to assimilate each piece of information before moving on to the next. However, there may be a school of thought that says if you're going to have bad news, you might as well have it in one downpour, rather than a recurrent toxic drip. Since the diagnosis I have often been asked whether it was better or worse for me, being a doctor. I think the simple answer is both. I was well aware of the potential complications of surgery and chemotherapy, I had a pretty clear idea of what could go wrong; but worse than that was the inevitable blurring of the doctor/patient boundaries.

The day after the diagnosis I went to do a shift; it was full of old blokes moaning about having to get up to pee at night, and telling me, 'You don't know how awful it is.' So much of me wanted to batter them with the ultrasound probe, shouting, 'You have no idea what I'm going through,' that I decided it was safer not to see any patients prior to the surgery. Safer for the patients, that is. The rest of the week was filled with tests, needles, biopsies and yet more needles. I am terrified of needles, unless I am on the plunger end. Many staff I encountered during my treatment seemed to find this hard to believe at best, and risible at worst.

Doctors make lousy patients at the best of times. We think we know it all, even when we're miles out of our specialty area, and colleagues collude in this by not treating you like any other patient. For example, a year after the original surgery, I needed bilateral prosthetic revision. In my wisdom I decided not to spend the night in hospital afterwards. I insisted that I didn't need drains. I walked down to theatre at 3 p.m., and by 8 p.m. I was home. The wound oozed so much the steristrips fell off within two days. Ten days later I was readmitted with a periprosthetic collection and septicaemia. We doctors are very bad at giving ourselves the time and space that we need to recover.

On the positive side, at least I'm not frightened of hospital smells, anaesthetics, jargon, or any of the myriad tiny fears that confront a lay-patient. I was able to source the best care, and to make highly informed decisions. I worked throughout my chemotherapy, and the response from my patients was amazing. Alerted by my bald head, they were supportive and empathetic, many relieved to see that doctors are not immune to disease. We swapped tips on dealing with hair loss, and the dreadful early chemical menopause. I learned a lot.

That was back in 2005. Ten years on and I was looking forward to the date of my being able to say I was cured. That was until I found a lump in the other breast. The most terrifying Groundhog Day ever. Another mastectomy and chemotherapy that has left me with no feeling in my fingers or toes, and disabled through complete lack of balance. But I'm still here when so many friends are not. It's a difficult daily tightrope wobbling between gratitude and survivor's guilt. I try to make the most of every day I've been gifted.

My tip to any doctors who find they are diagnosed with a life-threatening illness would be this: leave the medical degree at home, metaphorically speaking. Don't just listen to the advice that your specialist is giving you – take it. Above all, remember: it's OK to be scared, and it's OK to feel exhausted and it's OK to take painkillers. Contrary to what we would have people believe, under the white coat, we're human.

Sarah Burnett is a consultant radiologist who diagnosed her own breast cancer from a mammogram in 2005, and again in 2015 — just at the point where she should have been celebrating being 'all clear'.

At the beginning of 2020 she decided to work from home, reporting scans online, in the blissful ignorance that the entire country would soon follow suit. The time saved commuting has enabled her to spend more time on her visual arts, and in January 2021 she started an MA in Illustration at Falmouth School of Art.

FORK AND KNIFE

Usha Rowan

November 1972

I was sitting with my sister having lunch in the refugee camp when our *bhai* [brother] approached.

'Look at what *Dhootali* [mischief maker] is up to now,' he said to his standing refugee friends. '*Jaldikar* [hurry up], fetch Ba!' and my sister ran. 'You've hardly touched English soil and already you've become one of them!'

The soldiers at the Heathfield Army Barracks had emptied their bunks for us. My bedding was so much cosier than at home. It smelt of England and fresh snow; this was my new home now. Ba had taken to the English kitchen with vigour, ordering women about as if they were her staff. Within a day she was ladling dhal, rice and turning piping hot chapatis to make way for the refugees to adapt. Her discovery of washing-up liquid, gas hobs and tea towels was a prize for taking care of the kitchen.

Outside, the hills and ground were white and picturesque. Inside, sitting opposite us, were three fanciable blond soldiers. Until now, I had not seen a fair-haired person or snow. They could've been brothers; athletes, with hair as fine as straw and drop-dead gorgeous.

One of them had been glancing at me and I returned an impetuous cheeky smile, noticing my breasts had a mind of their own. His sky-blue eyes, his white eyelashes camouflaging his perfect moon face; I was hypnotised. I was sure he had winked at me to stop me staring at him. I wanted to feel his long lashes. How is it fair that God made him so pure? Gave him manners to eat with fork and knife instead of hands? He tasted his food with his eyes, moving his Adam's apple like the chicken next door which was broiled the day before we left for England. The servicemen were sprinkling salt and brown sauce over chips instead of chilli and sour sauce over cassava chips when Ba came and stood next to me.

'Look at your *Dhootali* with a fork and a knife,' my brother bemoaned.

'I am only copying them,' I said, pointing at the trio, and Ba sighed hard at my brother. There and then, I had the idea that an arranged marriage with the moon face would be most suited instead of Ramesh from India who, by the way, did not speak a word of English. I know Ba found me to be a handful at times, and was even disappointed when I refused to marry Ramesh – 'I would be awfully miserable.' Instead, I had made her more miserable. Besides, I thought, who wants all the hassle of a lousy dowry, the purpose of which I never understood when Ba had always toiled at selling cassava chips and popadoms to pay for her flight to India to visit *nanima*.

But today, I could see that Ba was on my side for a change.

'Don't make a scene here, *dikla*,' she said, tucking her purple toes inside her open sandals. 'We are indebted to these kind people.

Without them, where would we've gone? Who was going to feed or house us?' she said, controlling herself from welling up. She pulled her yellow *sadlow* over her head while clasping her hands and turned to my idols as if thanking them for saving me and my sister from being raped. She told us later that she had hidden my little sister under her *sadlow* between her legs when a gang of thugs had kicked the door open. Thank God that my little sister had the sense not to squeal or stir!

I was gloating inside but my brother gave me an ugly frown when Ba left for the kitchen again. Suddenly, I was left on my own eating potato chips with the fork and knife. It was then, when my blue-eyed soldier came and sat close to me. He smelled of perfume like Johnson's Baby Powder.

'My name is Lieutenant Hendricks,' he said. Suddenly, I was transfixed and speechless like I was melting in front of him. My heart became molten, liquefied, when the hairs on his arm brushed the skin on my naked arm. It tingled as he leaned over and man-oeuvred my fork from the right to the left, and then the knife from the left to the right.

'This is *knife* and *fork*,' he said slowly.

I looked at him vacantly, repeating the words after him, 'Hendricks, this is knife and fork,' imitating his words, and I giggled like a little girl.

'Very good,' said Hendricks, his eyes set on mine as he left to join his friends who had been making fun of him along the way.

Usha Rowan completed her MA in Creative Writing at Birkbeck, University of London, in 2017. *Fork and Knife* is an extract from Usha's first novel *The Milkman's Son*, based in Uganda, where she was born, and is in its final stages of being edited.

Usha has written published articles about British cultural history for The Culture Trip, an online magazine. You can find Usha on Twitter and Instagram @usharowan.

BLUE

Sarah Rayment

The sea is where I find myself; where my cells come alive and signal that I am whole. I can't imagine a life without water now, but I've not always been comfortable with the blue stuff.

Four years old, by the steps of the baby pool. I jumped in, head-first, and the rubber ring around my waist pinned me upside down while water swooshed around my head until adult hands tipped me back upright.

School swimming lessons. The pyjama test: treading water wearing heavy, baggy, flannel pyjamas. A nearby swimmer grabbed my head and pushed me down. I resurfaced with lungs full of chlorine and failed the test.

My teen years. A Cornish surfing trip. I was on a roll of catching short gentle waves, pretending to onlookers that I was in my element, and then I caught a not-so-gentle-wave which spat me out on jagged rocks. There was a lot of blood: a close call.

Yet the water kept beckoning – the sensation of waves washing over my skin, creatures navigating an otherworld, even the murky shadows tens of metres down. I didn't want to be so afraid.

So I learned to dive – in the beautiful Indian Ocean, of course.

Scuba diving, freediving, board diving, duck diving. It didn't come naturally — I was panicky, indecisive and exhausting for those around me. But finally, I emerged from an endurance swim and thought I might just nail this.

Then an unimaginable encounter with Mother Nature. Boxing Day, 2004. A three-metre wave. Me inside it, tumbling, gasping, drowning. I knew my time was up, that this time I wouldn't survive.

And yet. I did.

Someone, a man in a red T-shirt, who I later found out goes by the name of Mr Blue, risked their life to save mine.

Physically, I healed and went back to help — at first on dry land clearing debris, rebuilding houses, and eventually into the water to retrieve plastic bags from the sea floor — I needed to give back, to save others. I continued pursuing diving and sea rescue qualifications. Passing those exams should have been a celebration — not only had I overcome my fear of water, I'd done so despite great adversity, and now had the skills to save others.

I did not feel amazing. Aware of my Western privilege, survivor's guilt kicked in and there it stayed like a slug in the back of my throat. I berated myself for thinking that learning to dive was courageous and mourned those who lost their lives and would never have had such opportunities. Another kind of blue took hold. How could I rescue others when I couldn't save myself from my own misery, even though I survived? I didn't deserve to feel good.

Years later, my anticipated moment of 'redemption' finally came. By the water's edge in another tropical location, I looked up after hearing splashing, and saw terror in a woman's eyes as she desperately tried to cling to the whipped-up surface. Without a beat, fully clothed, I waded in and hauled her back to safety. I can still hear her breathless thank yous as we collapsed on the shore and looked up at a different, never-ending blue.

It's nothing, I told her. But it wasn't true. It was everything – for her, for me.

For her, in the same way as Mr Blue for me. For me, because I realised that I didn't need rescue skills in order to be in the right place at the right time.

The sea is where I find myself; where my cells come alive and signal that I am whole . . . The underwater world gives me hours of uninterrupted reflection time. And in this space, I notice that my experience has given me a useful skill after all. A way of relating to someone going through something difficult.

I don't go around risking my life to save others, but in my everyday conversations, I've helped some people a little bit, and that is certainly something to be proud of.

PS Mr Blue, thank you, and I still have your red T-shirt.

Sarah Rayment grew up in London with dreams of exploring the world and writing stories. After spending several years wandering the globe and getting into all sorts of scrapes, she returned to London and started writing stories.

Her young adult novel *The Art of Not Breathing* (written under the name of Sarah Alexander; Usborne, 2016) won the Sheffield Children's Book Award. She also works as a coach helping creative folks bring their brilliant ideas into the world.

RIDING THE WAVES

Lucy Arden

I lie here under the bright lights of theatre, no jazz hands in sight, numb from the waist down. Powerless to hold the baby I've wanted, hoped and wished for. My voice, muffled by the chatter of the sea of blue people. 'I want to hold MY BABY.' I've waited nine years . . . don't let me wait any longer. Wanting, longing, hoping, praying, wishing, heartache, grieving . . . and finally joy.

Are you pregnant yet? Four simple words that struck fear into my heart and a lurch inside my tummy. Those little glances from my eyes to my belly, looking for signs of new life. Weighty expectations, from the outside world. We got married and planned to have a baby. Simple. Or so we thought. What we didn't conceive of was the road that lay ahead of us. The rocky road of infertility.

Two years on from our wedding day we found out for certain there were no sperm. There, I've said it out loud. Egg + Sperm = Baby. We were missing one vital ingredient in the baby-making cocktail. Our plans for a rosy future were ripped apart. We were grieving 'nothing' and everything. An indescribable loss. Nobody had died but it felt like death. A silent grief that goes unnoticed, unheard and is not understood. The shock of finding out we couldn't conceive a child has shaped me as a person beyond recognition of my old self. The colour drained out of my life. For any woman who desperately wants to have children, it's like a knife to the heart. I carried this cloak of sadness and crumbled under its weight. I now realise it festered inside me and my body shut down with debilitating chronic fatigue syndrome (CFS).

During the early days of our fertility investigations, to save our fears, we joked that if we couldn't have a child, we'd get a dog. That was our backup plan and what a wonderful plan it turned out to be. When CFS hit me like a freight train, I had to build myself back up from ground zero. We adopted Levi the rescue dog and without intention he became my therapy dog. He helped me to deal with not being able to have a child because I could mother him the way I so desperately wanted to mother a child. He became our firstborn. He led me to people I had never met, places I had never seen and helped me to heal.

When the overriding urge to have a baby could no longer be suppressed by the unconditional love of our dog, we explored our options and finally agreed to use a donor. It took years of work and a strength in our marriage to be open to this idea. By publicly writing this for the first time, I hope to shine a light on infertility and the often-hidden struggles that some couples endure. It can drive you apart or bring you together. Or both. Each visit to the assisted conception clinic was met with trepidation. We sat on the strange wipe-clean, high-backed chairs. Sensing painful unspoken stories, hidden behind blank faces. A strange stifled silence filtered through the air.

Pregnancy was the dream I had clung to, so when it finally

happened after eight years, I embraced it with every ounce of my being. I was now one of the lucky ones. My creativity resurfaced and exploded like a firework. My sacral chakra and creative brain went into overdrive. Our son was born and he brought a rainbow of colour into our lives. Despite adversity I had created a living and breathing human being . . . so what next?!

Serendipity landed at my door when the opportunity arose to share a studio. Having the support of three creative mothers gave me the confidence in both my creativity and my mothering abilities. I heard about an amazing initiative called Mothers Who Make, a growing international movement supporting creative mothers to do both jobs which are undervalued in society. I went on to set up a hub in my local town. Women supporting women, mothers supporting mothers, artists supporting artists . . . it's what I'm passionate about. Spurred on by this support, I gained the confidence to build my own business.

Behind the scenes I was preparing to make a baby . . . again. A second child. A sibling. Like an athlete training for the Olympics, four years on from the birth of our son, I invested my heart, body and soul. We only had one chance for a donor sibling match, but I was ready. Devastatingly, it didn't work. I was here again. Rocked to my core. The grief of our entire exhausting fifteen-year fertility journey finally landed at my door. I have had to manage my son's grief, of never having the human sibling he so desperately wanted, alongside my own permeable sadness.

I have learned more about grief in the last few years than in my lifetime. I have learned to allow myself to step into the darkness and not be scared by it. To feel the feelings, the heartbreak, the pain, and accept that nothing is ever permanent. I can find that glimmer of light and step towards it. When Levi sadly passed away recently, after twelve years together, I felt bereft. He was always so much more than a dog; he was our firstborn, a wonderful big brother to our son and helped us through some dark times. 'It's just the circle of life, Mummy,' my son the animal lover said. This miracle child is wise beyond his years. People say you should never work with children or animals, but I believe they have been my greatest ever teachers.

Lucy Arden is an artist, crafter, writer, wife, mother, daughter, creative activist, feminist, home maker, and much more.

She is passionate about women supporting women. She founded her local Mothers Who Make hub and represented the organisation on BBC Radio 4's *Woman's Hour*. Feminism, mental health and women's place(s) in the world are important influences on her life and work. Lucy's writing has been published on the Dwell Time and Sheroes in Quarantine websites and The Mum Poem Press. You can find Lucy as LucyArdenMotherArtist on Facebook and Instagram.

INVENTORY

Ceri Ashcroft

A brief confession: I am an inveterate list maker. I make lists daily, weekly, monthly, yearly. Continuously. Lists of things to do. Lists of things done. Lists of things not done (that one's pretty long . . .). Lists of the lists of things to do once the first list of things to do have been done. Lists of aims. Lists of goals. Lists of places to go, people to see, things to make, shows to write, books to read and films to watch.

This used to be a leisurely activity . . . on a Sunday afternoon I might put on a wash, read the papers, make a list of things to do that week in a specific notepad, colour coded into days of the week or genre of task with illustrations or notes as needed. I am decidedly not this neat and tidy in the other aspects of my life. It was elaborate and deeply satisfying.

But . . . things have changed.

10 June 2016. 9 p.m. My waters broke. A watershed for the era of the list.

They're still useful. More so. Now, they're essential. My life-blood. With an eighteen-month-old in tow, and touring as an actor with a family, lists help us get our shoes on, teeth brushed and lines learned before we get out of the door on a daily basis. But they've changed – they're written at 2 a.m. in the bathroom, or while breast-feeding on a train to Sheffield. Colour coding is limited to the nearest available writing implement (pens are a luxury now and invite written additions to walls or faces by small people. Crayons are an excellent substitution). The notepad is liberally daubed with remnants of snacks, scribbles and handprints. The lists persist.

The lists are the reason I can record a podcast in a closet in central Texas while my daughter naps in the room next door. The lists helped me write this piece while on the road in California. They keep me on top of acting, writing, producing, mumming. A friend with children told me, when I was pregnant, that with a small child you need to change your expectations for what you'll achieve in a day. Your lists of things to do might need to be more succinct. Pithier. More to the point. I mean, sure, you'll get stuff done. But it might be at odd times, or in a closet. Sometimes having a shower and brushing your teeth will be an achievement, something to tick off the list. Sometimes writing about an achievement in the back of a car and then recording it really quietly under some coats will be the achievement itself.

Ceri Ashcroft is an actor, puppeteer, clown and theatre maker. She has performed around the world at venues including the Sydney Opera House, Hampstead Theatre, a fjord in Norway, and dangling 40 feet off the ground from a crane. She still tours with her four-year-old daughter. Based in Oxford, she also runs Tiny Light Theatre making shows for babies and children and recently developed a show in Northern Iceland. Ceri writes short films with fellow *100 Voices* writer Miranda Keeling, and is passionate about supporting female, BIPOC and LGBTQIA voices. She can be found at www.tinylight.co.uk.

WALNUT WAY

Livvy Brinson

I started to take my writing ambitions seriously in 2012. I enrolled on my MA, became part of a brilliant writers' group, and started on a novel. In 2016, however, I hit a wall.

People who suffer from anxiety experience it in different ways. For some, it can feel like there's a rubber band around your chest. Every day it gets a little bit tighter, and tighter, until you can't move at all. My first reaction was to take control. I compartmentalised my life and isolated myself. Growing unhappiness, alongside daunting feelings of self-doubt and worthlessness, set in. I stopped contributing to writing groups, put aside my novel, and slipped away.

Finally, in 2018, things began to change. I started to write again, slowly redrafting old short stories.

It took me a long time to realise I had to snap the band, and even longer to find the courage to do so. Most importantly, I gave myself *time*. As the words came back, everything else began to lift, and I started to become myself again.

Walnut Way is the first piece I rewrote. It's not the most polished, but each word was hard fought for.

WALNUT WAY

Three chimes and I'm back. This old faded armchair is the only piece of furniture that's not covered up. I listen to the clock. Its dull ticking fills the sitting room. The spell breaks as the cuckoo cuts through the vacuum.

There's nothing left to do. I get up and head towards the music room.

Along the corridor light magnolia squares scar the slightly darker wallpaper, the ghostly shapes sitting in memoriam to the missing framed faces that were once there. I catch my own reflection in the window opposite, the curve of my features mirrors those that had occupied this hallway for so many years. There's a flash near the floor. I pull back the dust sheet covering the hall table and find an old picture frame, dropped and forgotten, yet still intact.

I wipe away the dust from the glass, and my mother's smile is revealed with each streak of my finger. She's laughing, her hair done up in rolls, and I hear her words lift into song – *it's the tops, darling! Just you wait and see* – before she's lost to me again.

I forget all the previous worry, the dread and anxiety of today, and I run towards the music room. I've ignored it for two years, but now, *right* now, I must be with her piano.

I force the door and rush to open the window. Fresh air streams in, along with the light.

It's so much worse than I thought.

Nothing's been touched.

Lesson plans, rotas, photographs, posters, concert bills, reviews – they all still line the walls.

They were supposed to have been taken down, my cousins packing it away until I could face it.

I slump down onto the worn red leather piano stool and lift the instrument's lid. My fingers run over the ivory keys. I have not been blessed with my mother's talent, but that hadn't stopped her trying to force the music out of me all those years ago.

Muscle memory kicks in. First, scales and arpeggios. Next, exam pieces learned so diligently by heart. The grades fall away, and my mother sits beside me, clapping to keep time as always.

That's a demi-not-a-semi-quaver, darling, do keep up!

Tears fall onto black enamel.

The removal men are coming in a few hours.

Because it's time.

Because this was her life. Her piano. It was never meant for me.

I replace the cover and turn to the walls. It takes ages to remove the pieces of print she painstakingly stuck there. Eventually, when the walls are bare, I bundle the heavy pile of memorabilia into my handbag.

I cradle the forgotten picture frame close to my heart, before slipping it, too, into my bag. I follow my feet and pull the front door shut. My last act is to post my mother's keys through the letter box.

Too late, I remember the open window in the music room. My feet slow. Should I go back?

No. I can't. I've already posted the keys. I'd have to call someone for help. And, after all, the removal men are due soon. They can shut up properly for the last time.

I carry on, walking on music. Chopin lifts the warm summer air. It's only at the end of the road, as I prepare to leave Walnut Way for the last time, that I realise something's wrong.

My handbag's too light.

I unzip it and search desperately for the large pile of memorabilia I was so sure I had clung to, but it's no use. None of it's there, nor is the framed photograph. The bag's empty.

I look back at the house. The windows are still dark, but somewhere nearby my mother's laugh floats on the breeze. Like a hammer, the weight of the grief hits all over again.

Livvy Brinson recently completed her MFA in Creative Writing at Birkbeck, University of London, following the completion of her MA there in 2016, and her undergraduate degree at Cambridge in 2009. In addition to writing, she loves laughing, running, cooking veggie food, reading and playing board games with her mates.

FALLEN ANGEL

Jacqueline Haskell

I once had a dog called Betty and she was my voice and my familiar – for by day I am a healer. Perhaps most importantly, she was my hearing dog. People asked her if I took sugar; Betty was fond of sweet things, so she almost always said 'yes'.

When I was invited to contribute to the audio project *100 Voices for 100 Years*, it was not my voice that you would have heard reading this piece, but that of a very dear friend who kindly stepped in to read it for me: not my voice because, at the time, I could not hear mine – its volume, inflection, pitch, and so on.

But I know how important voice is. On the opening day of a Creative Writing MA at a well-known London university, the course director proclaimed that by the end of the first year we would all find that most elusive of attributes, our *writer's voice* (if we were any good, that is, he added darkly).

He explained how the quality and individuality of that voice could make or break us as writers. So I know how important voice is, but how can we define it? How important is it that when read aloud, you hear my voice and not someone else's? How might it change your response?

Wherein lies the power of this voice? In the sense and argument, the beauty, and the meaning, of the words themselves? The connection they forge between people of different cultures, religions and continents? The projection of our inner soul? It is, I believe, a combination of all of these, and more.

I now have a piece of metal, a cochlear implant, inserted deep inside my skull that does the work of my diseased inner ear; some hearing is restored, though it is not the hearing I recall from my childhood. Voices now resonate, Dalek-like, inside my head. I can hear birdsong, traffic, even music, which I was told might take years to become audible again, and for some unlucky people, might never do so.

In the beginning, though, I didn't wear the implant – it triggered headaches, I told people – and it did, and still does – but also, through my return to the clamour of the modern world, I came to appreciate the erstwhile silence.

I came to appreciate just how many of my true achievements occurred when I couldn't hear at all. Curse it though I did, my deafness sparked a creativity inside me: the writer's voice, the spiritual voice, the attention to the contemplative moment, that I have not experienced either before or since. Would I have become a poet if I could hear? Written my first novel? My second? Would I have left a lucrative career to retrain as a healer? Would I have been happier, felt more *heard*?

The science of the implant is, of course, nothing short of a miracle, and I am eternally grateful for it, and for the enormous achievements of all those who have made it possible, and who strive for the improvement of its already excellent performance, but if you cannot hear, you must first learn to endure, and then like, your own company; to become everything to yourself that others cannot; you must learn to carry your dreams inside your own internal voice. For in truth, we all have a voice, even if we cannot hear it.

Everybody loved Betty – even those people who professed to dislike, or even to be afraid of, dogs. Sadly, she eventually developed a health condition that meant she could no longer be a working dog, and she was rehomed as a 'fallen angel' with a new family, as a pet (we recipients never 'own' our assistance dogs; as with many other things in this life, they are merely on loan).

These days, more than six years on from the operation, and four years from the loss of the dog, I am back in the world, and I wear the implant most of the time, but sometimes, I long for Betty and the silence.

Jacqueline Haskell has an MA in Creative Writing from Birkbeck, University of London. Her debut novel *The Auspice* was a finalist in both the 2018 Bath Novel Award and the 2020 Cinnamon International Literature Prize.

Stroking Cerberus, her first poetry collection, is published by Myriad Editions as part of the Spotlight Books series, a collaboration between Creative Future, New Writing South and Myriad Editions to discover, guide and support writers who are underrepresented due to mental or physical health issues, disability, race, class, gender identity or social circumstance. Jacqueline works as an animal healer and lives in the New Forest.

MARY POPPINS ON STEROIDS

Olivia Chappell

Thwack!

So that's what it feels like when a Pritt Stick bounces off your head.

You are a teacher now.

You supposedly discover your 'teacher persona' in your training year: your alter ego for standing in front of thirty teenagers. A way of staying sane through seventy-five-hour weeks. A safety mechanism. Armour.

Mine fully emerged the following year. I'd trained in a secondary school nestled in the South Downs where the kids wouldn't say boo to a goose. But the year after, I landed in a West London academy, ready to dazzle and nurture young minds with my passion for Drama. Right?

'Miss, has anyone ever said you remind them of Mary Poppins?'

I even stood like her – feet in first position, hands clasped, a firm-but-fair demeanour. She just appeared. Something in me must have needed her joy and efficiency to override the chaos I felt. In the

South Downs, a disapproving frown from Mary was enough to silence any rogue calling out without raising a hand.

Glare. Spit spot. Child neutralised.

But not here. These kids were the Pritt-Stick-lobbing type.

A high percentage came from poor backgrounds. Many had unstable homes, fragile self-esteem and a lack of positive role models. Some days it was less 'Please put your hand up before calling out', than 'Please stop punching him and yelling the C word'.

Original me – pre-teacher, pre-Mary – had no stomach for confrontation. She chose the easy road every time. The road of obedience, of wanting to be liked.

Here, it was make or break. I had to grow a backbone, and fast. Mary Poppins had to become Mary Poppins on *steroids*.

My hardest class was the last lesson on a Thursday, a ninety-minute gauntlet. My drama studio was bright and spacious but the lack of desks meant it easily became a zoo, and every zoo has its leaders. Thursday's group had one particularly vicious hyena-like twelve-year-old (yes, *twelve*) who nursed a weekly vendetta.

On this Thursday, I'd put the usual hours into preparing the lesson, laying out incentives, meticulously choosing groups and so on, but my efforts seemed lost. About halfway through the class, my twelve-year-old nemesis slowly backed me up to my desk, looked me up and down and pushed his sweaty face inches from mine, and snarled, 'Aw Miss, don't make me *abuse* you.'

★

My training taught me to focus on the 'reasons behind the behaviour'. Whatever a student does – refuse to write a single word, or kick the classroom door in – we should focus on what might be going on in their life. Try to see a young person who could be unhappy at home or disguising a learning difficulty. But that rational brain is hard to find when you're in fight-or-flight mode with an angry teen in your face. The harsh urban environment beyond the gates had forced students to grow up and toughen up fast. They were slow to trust new faces and constantly fighting for power.

They smelled the weakness and fear in me. In that moment, I was the prey.

'Aw Miss, don't make me abuse you.'

The threat twisted out of him like acid. Hissing words with a stabbing gaze. He was desperate for a reaction, one I would *not* give him the satisfaction of getting. Teeth gritted, blood pumping, using everything in my power to remain unaffected, Ms Tough-Poppins calmly but firmly instructed him to leave.

Mary's invincible armour subsiding, I exhaled a shaky breath, held up my head, and finished the lesson.

In hospitals and tube stations you see posters: 'Our staff will not tolerate abuse.' Yet teachers are expected to just take it – it's 'part of the job'.

But to that twelve-year-old hyena, I say thank you.

Thank you for making me fine with someone not liking me.

Thank you for pushing me so far that I found when I will not accept it.

★

I'd love to say this was the only visceral moment, but it wasn't. That's young people for you; they're learning who they are. Sometimes they get it wrong.

It's not all doom. I had another student – let's call him Shane – who was failing badly. When I demanded he participate in his group work, he stormed out yelling, 'You're a shit teacher!'

Less than eighteen months later Shane got an A in his final GCSE performance. He's off to university soon, and now whenever I see him he nods with a knowing smile. Sometimes he even sneaks me a fist bump. Once, when I was having words with a younger student in the corridor, Shane marched up: 'Miss is a good teacher, you better behave for her.'

I was so lost when I started teaching, but most teens are far more lost. When you manage to get a kid who's not eaten breakfast and hasn't seen their mum in years to feel proud of themselves, it's magic like no other.

I'm back to freelance life now, and will continue to work with young people as much as I can. I'll never be someone who seeks confrontation, but now I know I can handle it. So: thanks, Mary Poppins – with or without the steroids – for teaching me that I have value and strength.

When your back's against the wall, literally or metaphorically, stand your ground: there is a version of you deep within that will stand tall.

Olivia Chappell is an actor and teacher. As an actor, she works in film, voiceover, theatre, television, commercials, radio, comedy, and has even done the odd musical. Sometimes, she also gets behind the camera. Find her at www.oliviachappell.com.

True to her word, Olivia continues to teach young people, as well as helping adults develop and strengthen their presentation skills. More at www.creativeutopia.org.

THE COLLECTOR

Diane Simmons

In 2015 my daughter Laura died just a few weeks after being diagnosed with stomach cancer. She was twenty-eight. Exhausted and lost, my husband, my son and my son-in-law all gradually returned to work and my younger daughter went off on a long-planned trip abroad. But I had nowhere to escape to. I am a writer, working from home, and I certainly could not write. There was no room in my brain for anything creative. I wondered at times what the point of me was.

When my mother died, she left a tiny collection of jewellery that my sister and I shared. I remember feeling sad for her that she hadn't owned more, that she hadn't had the kind of life where she needed pretty necklaces and extravagant earrings. I decided that in future I would ask my husband for jewellery for my birthdays and Christmases, so that when I died there would be pieces my daughters would enjoy inheriting. My two daughters often borrowed some of this jewellery for weddings and parties, sometimes squabbling over who got to wear what.

In the awful months that followed Laura's death, my mind repeatedly focused on thinking about the jewellery collection I had built up and I found it difficult to take in that there would no longer be any need for it to be shared when I died – that now, I only had one daughter, that all the jewellery would be hers. My son-in-law, just a few days after the funeral, had given me Laura's engagement ring to add to my collection and this no doubt added to the confusion in my mind. I often found myself picturing a grieving woman throwing her jewellery into the river – it no longer being needed.

That image prompted the first story I wrote after Laura's death and I was proud when it was published in the National Flash Fiction Day anthology the following year. In the months that followed I wrote other stories, some inspired by my grief, others not, and I have managed to carry on writing, have become much more prolific. In early 2019, *Finding a Way*, my flash fiction collection on grief, was published by Ad Hoc Fiction. I managed to stay focused and the following year I had a novella-in-flash published by V. Press and have since written two further novellas. I have also become a director of National Flash Fiction Day and the UK Flash Fiction Festival.

The story that started me being able to write again is called *A Collection*.

A Collection was first published by National Flash Fiction Day in its 2016 Anthology A Box of Stars Beneath the Bed.

A COLLECTION

I throw in the opal ring next. It makes little impression on the river, unlike the jade bracelet and the gold chain I bought in Marrakech.

The opal ring had been the start of my collection, bought just a week after Sophie was born. 'Something for me,' I'd reasoned, as gift after gift arrived for her.

The last piece I select is my mother's engagement ring. It's a diamond cluster, the only decent jewellery she'd owned. When she died, I cried as I surveyed the cheap beads and mean-stoned rings I'd inherited. It didn't seem much to show for a life.

So I'd started collecting – birthdays, Christmases, anniversaries, I asked my husband for jewellery, determined that Sophie would have an inheritance to delight in.

As soon as she took an interest, I allowed her to play with the cheaper pieces, let her rummage in my wardrobe for heels and hats to parade in. As she grew older, she borrowed necklaces for university balls, rings for friends' weddings, brooches for job interviews. 'Can I keep the sapphire ring?' she often begged. 'Or the opal?'

'You can have them when I'm dead,' I used to say.

So stupid. I should have showered my beautiful girl with everything I owned. Not carried on building a collection that would never be needed.

As I trudge back to the car, I look down at my left hand, twirl the ring on my middle finger. It's a ruby, antique, bought as a present for Sophie's graduation. She'd been so proud of her First and she adored the ring, had rarely taken it off. It doesn't look good on me. But I didn't hesitate when the undertaker handed it to me. I slipped it onto my finger, have kept it there ever since. It's the only jewellery I have now, the only piece I see any point in owning.

Diane Simmons is a co-director of both the UK National Flash Fiction Day (NFFD) and the UK Flash Fiction Festival. She has been a reader for the international Bath Short Story Award, an editor for FlashFlood and has judged several flash competitions, including Flash 500, Micro Madness and NFFD Micro. Her flash fictions and short stories have been widely published and placed in numerous competitions. *Finding a Way*, her flash collection on the theme of Grief (Ad Hoc Fiction), and her flash fiction novella *An Inheritance* (V. Press) were both shortlisted in the Saboteur Awards.

TWO HUNDRED YEARS AGO WE WOULD HAVE BEEN DEAD BY NOW

Louise Mangos

Much of my fiction, whether novels, short stories or flash fiction, contains morsels of my life, whether it's the settings or the characters. The shorter pieces often come from something more visceral, the strength of emotions and reactions. The following flash fiction could almost be classified as creative non-fiction. When it was first published with Reflex Fiction in 2017, it connected with a huge number of women on Twitter who were going through similar menopausal experiences.

If you think back a hundred years to when women were first allowed to vote, menopause was a taboo subject. The word itself was rarely uttered. 'A touch of the vapours' or more recently 'hot flushes' is an almost comic reference to only one of the radical changes in the female body once its reproductive system ceases to function. I hope my piece, along with the continuing fight for women's equality, signifies that there is now a more open attitude to the inevitable physical changes taking place in our bodies now that we are living longer.

TWO HUNDRED YEARS AGO WE WOULD HAVE BEEN DEAD BY NOW

Forty years of twisting hands inside her belly, dragging at her guts for five days every month, as regular as a Swiss train.

Three natural births, each round head inherited from their high-browed father, burning as they crowned, leaving their imprints on her cervix and her memory like the sear of a cattle brand.

Five years of crimson flames rising from her breasts to wrap around her throat like a hungry serpent. Five years of the softening of flesh between her hips where she used to be as flat as a carpenter's bench. Five years pressing her cheek against the cold glass of window-panes, and grabbing menus from passing waiters to use as fans. Five years peeling herself from sodden bed sheets, and standing naked in front of the open fridge in the middle of the night.

But most of all, it's the darkness in her head, the illogical anger and inexplicable shame. She spirals down, this feeling that her life is over. He no longer looks at her with hunger in his eyes. Someone needs to catch her in a safety net and persuade her that there is something worth living for.

Louise Mangos writes novels, short stories and flash fiction, which have won prizes, been placed on shortlists and read on BBC radio.

She has published two full-length suspense novels. Her debut psychological thriller *Strangers on a Bridge* (HQ, 2018) was a finalist in the Exeter Novel Prize and longlisted for the Bath Novel Award. Her second novel *Her Husband's Secrets* (previously *The Art of Deception*) was published in 2019 by HQ. Her short fiction has appeared in more than twenty print anthologies and magazines. She lives on a Swiss Alp with her Kiwi husband and two sons.

HALF SMILING

Rebecca Rouillard

I'm an optimist. A glass-half-full kind of person. I don't necessarily expect it, but I always hope for the best.

2018 starts well. In January I receive an amazing phone call from editor Debbie Taylor, telling me that I've won the *Mslexia* Women's Novel Competition. Two weeks after the competition results are announced in March, I have offers from several literary agents.

By April, I am halfway through editing my novel before my agent submits it to publishers. My book is set in the not-too-distant future and is about a brother and sister, called Ash and Ellyn, who live in a lighthouse. She's human, but he's a sentient, humanoid AI. Soon after the story begins, Ash's body begins to malfunction. It starts with just a numbness in his little finger and then spreads up his arm until one whole side of his body is affected. I imagine it like a human having a stroke.

I'm sure you've also heard the expression 'Life Imitates Art'. One Sunday morning I notice that one side of my tongue has inexplicably gone numb. By Wednesday the right side of my lip feels as though I've had an anaesthetic from the dentist. On Thursday morning my eye feels strange and I realise that my right eye isn't blinking. My smile is lopsided, my eyebrow only goes up on one side – I look like a rakish pirate. I lift both of my hands up in front of the mirror, like you're supposed to, to make sure that I'm not having a stroke. I'm pretty sure that I'm not having a stroke. My brain feels fine. But would you be able to tell if your brain wasn't fine? I call III, like you're supposed to, and she tells me to go straight to A&E and offers to call an ambulance for me.

'No, please don't call an ambulance, I can drive myself,' I tell her. 'I drove the kids to school half an hour ago.'

'Do not drive yourself,' she tells me.

I begin to feel less optimistic.

At A&E the doctors quickly establish that I am not, thankfully, having a stroke. But I do have something called Bell's Palsy – a kind of facial paralysis that affects the nerves on one side of your face, possibly caused by a virus. They prescribe steroids and anti-virals, but all you can really do is wait and hope that everything will go back to normal. It could take two weeks, they told me, or it could take a year. Occasionally it's permanent. The experience goes into my book. I keep writing.

I'm an optimist – I'm drinking soup through a straw but at least I'm half smiling.

Rebecca Rouillard was born in the UK but grew up in South Africa. She has a Creative Writing degree from Birkbeck, University of London, and was the managing editor of the Birkbeck Writers' Hub for four years.

Rebecca's writing has appeared in various online and print anthologies and her novel won the 2017 *Mslexia* Novel Competition. She currently works as a school librarian in south-west London and is writing children's fiction. You can find her on Twitter as @rrouillard or on her website: www.ninepmwriter.co.uk.

WORTH SO MUCH MORE

Abda Khan

When I was asked to contribute to this fantastic anthology, I had not intended to send in a poem. I am a novelist by choice (lawyer by profession), and I have almost finished writing my third novel, and am already thinking about my next one. I do also write poetry; however, I very rarely share it. It is too personal, too private. It makes me vulnerable for all to see. It gives the reader a window into my life, and into my heart and mind. It allows the reader to scrutinise me, to examine my thoughts in a very intimate way, maybe feel sorry for me, perhaps even judge me, although I hope that doesn't happen!

Sharing my experiences about the practical barriers and difficulties I have faced and overcome in life is something I can do quite easily. Writing about profoundly personal trauma, disclosing details about some of the times in my life when I have been at my lowest, I find much more difficult, almost impossible. So, for me, sharing this poem, 'Worth So Much More', is in itself a huge act of bravery.

People end up suffering from depression for all kinds of different and often complex reasons. My depression came after many years of suppression of negative feelings which emanated from various traumas. I am not yet the 'finished article'. At fifty-one years of age, I am still a work in progress. Sometimes life doesn't give you the break you need, it doesn't allow you the freedom and space you deserve, but as day follows night, darkness is eventually followed by light. I feel a sense of achievement for having come such a long way, towards self-belief and a place of inner strength. I am still travelling along a, sometimes bumpy, road but as the journey continues, so too does my hope for a better future.

WORTH SO MUCH MORE

I don't recall when it started
Much less did I understand why
First, the little things seemed so tricky
As though I was a child again

Simple chores turned into mammoth tasks
My brain hurt thinking;
Why?
The mountain ahead grew taller and bigger
Feelings of stupidity festered inside
Overtaken only by the urge to cry

'Why are you so pathetic? Just look at you!'
The words ran around in my head
Unable to do or say anything right
My mind was awash with self-doubt
And my body felt hollow inside

I wonder what would happen? I asked myself
If I just stepped out in front of the bus
If I fell off the bridge and onto the tracks
If my car veered off to one side of the road
Would it all end? Finish? Stop?

I looked at my children, and with a jolt, I knew
I had to reach out, I had to get help,
Before I drowned without a sound

You are unwell, my dear, he said,
You must not be so hard on yourself
He looked and listened, he helped and healed
The scars buried deep rose up to speak
Of the traumas so raw, never allowed to heal

Depression, he said
You are depressed
Emotional wounds you have suppressed
So much that so that your brain now hurts
Your heart now aches, and your body now shakes

You must rest, and you must heal
You will recover, and you will feel
Your life is precious, it means a great deal

Whatever pain I have endured
Whatever injustice and cruelty came before
I will no longer allow it to define who I am
For I am worth so much more

Abda Khan is a lawyer turned writer, with two published novels: *Stained* (Harvard Square Editions, 2016) and *Razia* (Unbound, 2019). Abda was Highly Commended in the Asian Women of Achievement Awards 2017, won British Muslim Woman of the Year 2019, and was shortlisted for the Law Society Lifetime Achievement Award in 2020.

Abda is passionate about women's issues and is delighted to be able to contribute to this anthology. Her poem relates to her own experience of her battle with depression, and the journey towards self-worth and hope for the future.

ELECTED

Sarah Jones

It was actually a man who inspired me to get into politics.

When I was at university and I was nineteen, I got pregnant and I was facing life as a teenage single mum. I happened to watch the Conservative Party conference and there was a man called Peter Lilley, the Secretary of State for Welfare at the time, who made a speech based on a song from *The Mikado*, a Gilbert and Sullivan comic opera. The song was 'I've got a little list . . .' and he had adapted it to be all about the people he wanted to get rid of.

He said, *'I've got a little list of ladies who get pregnant just to jump the housing queue. They will not be missed. They will not be missed.'*

Everyone in the hall laughed and everyone thought it was hilarious that they were talking about how women who get pregnant when they're teenagers are basically worthless.

That made me so angry because I knew that I had something to contribute, and I wasn't worthless. So I joined the opposing party, the Labour Party.

Ever since then, it's fair to say that I have stood on the shoulders of women who have supported me through my entire career to the point where I decided to stand for election and to win. I certainly wouldn't have done it without the strong women around me, who have come before me, who have helped me.

From Dorinda Neligan who was a suffragette 100 years ago in Croydon, to Toni Letts who is the Mayor of Croydon and gives me loads of support, I have huge respect for all these strong women who have helped me to get to where I am. That's my story and hopefully, by sharing it, I can make sure other people who want to go on a similar journey are able to do it.

Sarah Jones is a British politician who has been the Labour Member of Parliament for Croydon Central since the 2017 general election. She was the first female MP ever elected in the borough, where she lives with her four children.

JUST A MUM

Antonia Abbot

Hi everyone, I'm Toni and I'm just a mum.
I don't have a real job,
I'm just a mum.
I've got three small daughters,
so I don't work,
I'm just a mum.

I've got a degree and that,
a good one,
but I don't do anything with it,
cause of the kids, see?
So I am actually capable of being a productive member of
    society.
I could be sitting in an office somewhere,
spoon-feeding an executive,
I don't even have to do that for my one-year-old.
She can feed herself.

I used to be a PA,

babysitting and organising really important people.

I'm sure it was quite an important job,

full of important tasks.

Although, I can't remember them right now,

baby brain – it never really goes away.

I'm sure on my first day I was nervous and frightened.

Probably not as frightened as that first time,

in the hospital,

after the messy bit,

the dangerous bit.

When everyone left, well everyone except the baby . . .

    and me

And the whole world contracted.

I was in charge.

Responsible.

Not for someone else's schedule,

for an actual life.

Scared.

Terrified.

Worried.

Tired.

Sore.

Really. Fucking. Sore.

But then,

you know that feeling?

The one you get when you fall in love for the very first time?

The one where you feel you're going to explode just by

thinking about them?

The Romeo and Juliet,

no one has ever loved anyone the way I love you complete

panic attacks just thinking about it,

kind of feeling?

Well,

when I looked at her,

all tiny and helpless

and utterly, terrifyingly beautiful

I knew then,

no matter what I had done until then,

from that moment on,

I was just a mum.

Antonia Abbot is a writer, poet and spoken word artist based in the southside of Glasgow. She has three daughters and started her writing career after the birth of her first child. Her children serve as a constant inspiration for much of her work, which contains a deep connection to motherhood but also looks at the human condition as a whole. She shows an ability to reach into the psyche and evoke an emotional response through her writing, much of which is a reaction to events that influence her and the world around her.

ONE IN TWENTY-THREE

Helen Rye

In October 2016 I won the Bath Flash Fiction Award with a story about the ongoing refugee crisis, *One in Twenty-Three*. I didn't really see myself as a writer; it was my first ever publication. It took me into the literary world and has opened doors for me ever since.

It was painstakingly researched and written with the utmost respect, but it still troubles me. It's a first-person narrative; I'm a white Westerner. I wouldn't do this now. Back then, I didn't know anything.

I wrote the original draft – a monologue – for a city theatre I was helping with, exploring people's relationship with the land. The Brexit vote had brought rising nationalism and hostility towards refugees in the UK, and I wanted to make people understand what was driving ordinary people from their land and into the sea with their children. I cried when I wrote it. At the performances, the audience cried too.

When I heard about the Bath Flash Fiction Award, I impulsively shortened the monologue to fit the word count and sent it. I was so surprised to see it on the longlist, I thought it might be another story with the same unlikely title. The night before the final results

I dreamt I came third, so I had a ridiculous tiny hope. I only kept on refreshing to see who'd come second and first out of curiosity. When my name came up in first place, the shock was intense.

One in twenty-three of those attempting to cross the Mediterranean via the most dangerous route, that year – while racist bile was spouted against refugees, and our government refused help to children in the mud of the Calais jungle – would drown. The details were based on real people's experiences of losing the home and land they loved. I hope I was amplifying their voices.

A few months later, celebrated Vietnamese poet and novelist Nguyen Phan Que Mai messaged me. She wrote that she'd wept over the story, that it was the story of her home, too. Her translation was subsequently published in Vietnam's top newspaper, *Hanoi Moi*, and in an anthology alongside work from authors such as Junot Díaz and Margaret Atwood. The royalties went to an educational fund for destitute Vietnamese children.

I cried like a weirdo, in the school playground, when congratulations over the *Bay Len* anthology were coming in, and messaged my writer friend to say I wanted to give the Bath prize money back because the story 'belonged to 10,000 dead people, not me'. The reality was that I was too broke, anyway; he talked me down. The story has since been taught in universities and included in a UK secondary school English textbook. The anthology fundraiser was undoubtedly a wonderful thing. Maybe these things justify its telling. I don't know.

I can't forget that it really belongs to the 10,000 people who had lost their lives at sea trying to reach Europe by the time I wrote it – and so many more since.

ONE IN TWENTY-THREE

Our land was beautiful. You should have seen the cherry blossom in the springtime, the foot of our mountain was clothed in it. And the sweetness of the figs in autumn — there is nothing like it anywhere.

Figs were our country's first gift to the world. Anzuki, Halabi, Bouksati, Oubied — such poetry there is in the names, and in the soft, ripened flesh you could taste the warmth of the sun that falls on the land of my grandfather's fathers.

We burnt the trees to keep our child from dying of cold, the winter after the power went down. My husband wept as he carried the branches from the orchard, but the snows were coming and we had nothing left to burn.

He spared one.

The last fruit was ripe on its branches and the leaves had almost gone, the day the rebels took him away.

I took my son to my sister in the city, but then the bombs came. They fell on the library. On the marketplace. On the internet café at the corner of the next street. On the hospital. On the people who were fleeing from the hospital.

Our lives compressed to the twelve-metre span of this boat.

I called my son Ocean, because once I loved the sea. Now our land lies scorched and turned toward the earth, and ten thousand have fallen like leaves beneath these waters.

Did you know that the fig is not really a fruit? No, it is a flower that has turned in on itself, so that all of the beauty and goodness lies hidden on the inside. All the colour that could in another life have become bright petals is wrapped in darkness, away from the world. But it is in there.

It is in there.

Helen Rye lives in Norwich. She has won the Bath Flash Fiction Award, the Reflex Fiction contest and third place in the Bristol Short Story Prize and Manchester Writing School's QMD Prize. Her stories appear in *The Best Small Fictions 2020* and have been shortlisted for the Bridport Prize, nominated for the Pushcart Prize and Best of The Net, and published in many journals and anthologies.

Helen is currently studying part time for an MA in Prose Fiction at the University of East Anglia, where she received the Annabel Abbs Scholarship. She is a senior editor at SmokeLong Quarterly.

VOICES TOGETHER

PLAY ON

Vanessa Hammick

Every now and then I meet an adult, fully grown and proper, who has decided to give acting a go. I immediately offer advice – the pros and cons of method acting, how to do fake tears, dealing with fame . . . But then I have to ask . . . 'What took you so long?'

I have loved performing since I was tiny. I spent my childhood in the world of pretend, watching films and re-enacting them whole, making up stories and performing for anyone who would watch (with mostly no one watching at all). It's not unusual to go through a phase of intense imaginative play, but my phase continues today, and I'm thirty-five.

My best relationships were formed through this invigorating hobby. My sister and I would gather the family to watch our circus performances – I remember tottering in my little socks on the circular pouffe in the lounge to enthusiastic, albeit amused, applause (we had to issue stern reminders that we were acrobats, and not clowns, when our limp roly-polys left us sprawling like mangled starfish).

At school, a best friend was made in Drama GCSE. As we struggled to forge our fledgling plays we butted heads, but, somehow, we knew to never take our disputes outside of the drama studio; nurturing an honesty and trust in our relationship that means we still make work together today. Another close friend took me to her amateur dramatics group – backstage we would create amateur dramatics of our own – the scintillating highs and lows of first crushes, kisses, broken hearts and riveting friendships. I met my first love doing a play, and my fiancé at a job in a theatre (and a few other 'loves' in between . . . but we don't need to mention them here).

Friendships made through drama felt intense and ephemeral. Even in my postgraduate diploma and acting training in my twenties, I experienced the same giddy highs and devastating lows more akin to being a teenager. It was wonderful and terrible; all very dramatic and exhausting. But the freedom, the exploration and expression helped me understand myself so well. Unpicking the motivation of characters helped me learn about my own motivations, and to truly understand what drives me. It was thrilling to learn to turn vulnerability into something potent and communicative. It was a relief to be in a class with others who felt it was important to do so.

As I moved into making more of my own work, it became harder wrought. After years of training and watching the incredible wealth of theatre we have here in London, the challenge of creating work that could stand up to it was insurmountable. Outside of the class, other issues come to the forefront – funding, space, tech fees – making a play went from something you could do in a living room to something that costs the same as a deposit for a flat just to get going! Now I wish I'd not been so hard on myself.

At the time of making a play it can feel like you put your whole life on hold to create the work, but, looking back, those plays are a distillation of my life at the time. I remember walking with a friend from Wales to London to create a piece with hobby horses; it was only a few years ago but my life was so different then, and I am so so glad that we captured that time in a heartfelt, personal play.

I'm guilty of judging myself so harshly for how little money I've earned and how little success I have had. I often feel I have failed. But I am still here, still making work. And looking back, what really matters is what the work meant and the friendships it gave me. It doesn't matter that I'm often broke, because that's priceless.

Vanessa Hammick is a writer, performer and community theatre maker based in London. She co-founded Croydon Cycle Theatre with Amy Foster.

OTHER PEOPLE

Jude Higgins

Ten years ago at sixty, I retired from my work as a Gestalt psycho-therapist, a career I'd followed for around twenty-five years. In my work, I often supported and encouraged people to follow their creative dreams so it was natural for me to think of new creative ventures after retirement. Fast forward a couple of years through an MA in Creative Writing and a partly finished novel and you'll find me in a workshop about flash fiction with writer Tania Hershman. I quickly became addicted to the form. And soon founded the Bath Flash Fiction Award with the aim of increasing knowledge of this exciting genre and getting others to read, write and listen to it.

I've often gained confidence in things I find difficult to do by organising events around them to motivate myself. In my early thirties I ran Assertiveness Training Groups for women. Even though I was shy, I was good at this and I did become more assertive. Running the Bath Flash Fiction Award means that I've read thousands of micro fictions in the last three years. It's had a big and positive effect on my own writing and I've had publishing success – a high point being the publication of *The Chemist's House*, my flash fiction chapbook. But so many other benefits have emerged, one of which is being part of the flash fiction writing community on social media and elsewhere. As someone with no children or extended family, the people in this large diverse group of worldwide flash fiction writers seem like a family group – a family with many shared interests. And I learn so much about different lives and cultures via the brilliant short fiction shared every day online. One positive outcome from the recent lockdowns has been connecting with more people on platforms like Zoom. My fictional micro piece *Other People* is about the way people can stay connected, even if they are alone. In 2017 the story won one of the monthly flash fiction contests run by the Word Factory, on the theme of Citizenship, Identity and Belonging.

OTHER PEOPLE

Since she's been alone, your friend in Australia helps rescue pilot whales stranded in shallow water. The woman down the road drives for a living with the radio on for company. That neighbour of yours, whose wife left last year, is excited by string theory and writes perfect algorithms.

You've just binned the old clothes from your previous life, mixed and matched a capsule wardrobe and begun collecting garden gnomes. You like those concrete mouldings of tiny, cheerful men. One's perched with a fishing rod at the edge of the goldfish pond and your favourite gnome is calmly smoking a pipe in a bed of primulas.

Sometimes, on a lonely night when the moon is full, you imagine those other people outside too. That woman you scarcely know has driven for miles hardly needing the headlights because the sky's so bright. In a quiet lane, she'll climb on to the roof of her van, lie flat and gaze at the Milky Way. Your neighbour, with his telescope focused, will decide that no equation can ever fathom the mysteries of the universe. On the other side of the world, your friend will be out in a boat watching rescued whales breach a moonlit ocean.

In the garden, you sit on a stone, motionless like the gnomes, not minding that your classic trench coat is creased, or your designer jeans are muddied. You tilt your face towards the sky while the man in the moon looks down. And you don't feel sad.

Jude Higgins is a writer, writing tutor and event organiser. Her flash fiction has been published in many anthologies and literary magazines including Fictive Dream, Flash Frontier, FlashBack Fiction, MoonPark Review, New Flash Fiction Review, Ellipsis Zine, Pidgeon Holes, The Cabinet of Heed and five National Flash Fiction Day anthologies. Her flash fictions have won prizes and have been selected for TSS's BIFFY50 in 2019 and 2020.

Jude's flash fiction pamphlet *The Chemist's House* was published by V. Press in 2017. She runs Bath Flash Fiction Award, is a director of Flash Fiction Festivals UK and the short-short fiction press Ad Hoc Fiction. More on Twitter @judehwriter or judehiggins.com.

LETTER TO MY
FOURTEEN-YEAR-OLD SELF

Alex Keelan

Remember when you were eleven, a friend told you what a blow job was? You didn't believe her, you said, 'no one would ever do that', you said, 'someone's having you on'. At fourteen you feel so far away from that eleven-year-old girl, so far away from yourself. Grief, pain, shame and alcohol have driven you to your knees, and it sucks, literally. Don't worry, you'll find out sex isn't a one-sided conversation; like all communication, you'll find your voice and your first words will be, not like that!

You're not fat! You'll waste too much of your precious time worrying about being fat, and waste even more of your precious time being pissed off at how much of your precious time you wasted worrying about being fat. Time you could have spent doing things that filled your heart with joy. It's not your fault, it's partly due to the cocky boy you go out with in high school, the mean one with impotence problems that he blames on you and your body, it is not you or your body. Be grateful for him, one December day, at school, giddy about Christmas, you'll have tinsel wrapped around your ponytail, he'll order you to take it out and say, 'you look a stupid

333

fucking bitch'. You'll keep it in all day at school, but, later, that night, you'll meet up with him at the park, with your hair down, he'll swagger over, kiss you, and tell you, 'that's better'. This will frighten you, how it makes you feel will frighten you. The way this boy reminds you of your violent stepfather will frighten you, it'll make you see how easy it is to mistake control for love.

Soon after, he will dump you, again, this time you won't go back. This will drive him crazy, he'll tell the boys at school to spit at you, he will write horrible things about your body on the school blackboard, he'll be so mean you won't go out with anyone else for three years . . . and you'll have the time of your fucking life! You'll dance, you'll drink, you'll wear whatever you like and speak to whoever you like. Some men in your seaside hometown won't like it, they'll call you a bitch, a slag, a dyke, a whore. When a guy in Oz nightclub tells you it's because you act like you're God, it isn't, carry on dancing. Don't go home in a taxi crying.

I'm sorry to say, no one is going to rescue you, no one will discover you, no one is going to walk down the street of your council estate, see your inner brilliance, and whisk you away, it doesn't work like that. You'll save yourself; it takes longer but it will feel so good. You'll take the risks, do the scary shit and be brave, that's how it works, for nearly everyone.

Believe it or not, you'll be a youth worker, for a short while, and you'll stand in front of a group of thirteen-year-old girls that think female masturbation is sick and fucking disgusting, you'll stand in front of them, with your Catholic toes curling, you'll stand in front of them with your heart pounding and tell them it's brilliant actually and without it they will never know what *they* like. Yes, secret, you will burn in hell, masturbator you, will stand in front of a group of confused thirteen-year-old girls that hate their vaginas so much they let men fuck them till they are bruised and bleeding, girls that believe sex is only to pleasure men, girls that have sex with men in telephone boxes, in parks and in skips, girls that say to you, 'ewwww, do you do it?' You will stand tall and say YES I do and I love it! The sky will not fall in and God will not strike you down. You will go home and cry that night after work, not for you but for the state of the fucking world. It'll all be worth it, though; those young women will decide to call their youth group Women that Wank!

Don't wait for permission to create, you'll spend your early twenties telling people you're not creative, mostly because you can't draw, stop it! Everyone is creative, the older you grow the more you'll come to realise that you are one step removed from all the creatives and artists you love, that step is self-belief. You'll eventually believe in yourself and go on to write poetry and theatre and even share it with the world.

You will fall in love with a kind man and have two, kind, funny, lovely sons. Yes, I said sons, all your sisters will have daughters, but the universe knows what you need, your house will be full of men and it will be, mostly, joyful!

You will go through a phase of reading your boys their favourite bedtime story every night, you'll find it boring and repetitive and not understand the appeal for them. It's just a story about a family going on a bear hunt, they come across easily navigated obstacles, a shallow river, a forest, a muddy field. Each time they encounter a new challenge, they say over and over again that '*they can't go under it, they can't go over it, uh oh, they have to go through it*'. This will eventually become your mantra. So, in light of this, my final words, even though I have given you all this advice, you can't go under it, you can't go over it, uh oh, you have to go through it. And it's OK, sometimes it's even fun.

Alex Keelan writes for stage and screen. Her short film *Maid of Stars* won Best Short at the Lift-Off online festival 2020 and audience choice runner-up for InShort film festival 2019. Her play *The Loves of Others* won Best Comedy at Manchester Fringe Festival 2017. Her work has been produced at the Edinburgh Fringe, Oldham Coliseum, Hope Mill Theatre, 53Two, Garrick Theatre, and for BBC Radio 4.

Alex passionately believes the world needs more women's stories, and she is co-founder of Vignettes, a platform for producing new writing by Northern women. You can find Alex on Twitter @AlexTKeelan.

OUT THE ATTIC

Eliza Beth Stevens

How Jo March inspired me to take my own stories out the attic and make a career in the arts.

I am woman. Daughter. Sister. Friend.

Raised by strong women, I am the image of my mother with the unchanging sense of justice to match. The graft and hard work, not to mention humour, from my grandmother, also make up a huge part of who I am today. I carry these likenesses with me, wear them with a great sense of pride. I've always been taught that I can do whatever I put my mind to and I have always known my own mind.

I often say, in only a partly joking fashion, that when I was a young girl, I pretty much based my entire personality on Josephine March from *Little Women*. Like Rachel from the TV show *Friends*, I read it every Christmas and have a whole list of reasons why I believe it to be the perfect representation of how women's ambition comes in a variety of forms and that each of those are equally valid. Unlike Jo, though, I haven't always aspired to be a 'world renowned writer'. I always sang a bit, read a lot, but I always fancied myself being a lawyer or a vet.

Over the summer of my nineteenth year, I was involved in a series of theatre productions which all centred female voices, a notion that was relatively new to me. Shocking, I know. Jo March would not have been impressed. First was *Blue Stockings*, Jessica Swales's play depicting the first female students of Cambridge, then *Everything Is Possible*, a community theatre project with York Theatre Royal and Pilot Theatre. This time, we were representing the women who fought for our right to vote. These projects found me a community of people that were eager to tell stories, not just perform. Being there, wearing my suffragette colours and appearing through the mist outside of York Minster was one of the most memorable moments of my life so far. I wasn't doing this to be on stage any more, I was doing it because of my duty in representing the women who came before me and fought for my right to vote and be educated.

This was the series of events that led me to believing I could have a career in the arts. Or to put it another way, these events gave me so much drive and determination that I decided there was no other option for me. I was determined to spend my life telling stories because these projects taught me that my voice was important too. That I could make a difference.

I went to drama school and wasted no time in getting started on those goals straight away. By this point, I had already decided that being solely an actor was not for me. Tired of swooning in roles that required me to play a literal prize for men and withered by being told to lose weight for a gig or that I was 'not really pretty enough', I decided the way to really make my difference was to be a director and writer. I wanted to be creative in my own right and I wanted to make space for other women to do so too. In my first year of drama school, I launched my company Out The Attic on International Women's Day with an event I called *The Storyteller Social*. The idea was that this would be a regular space for local creatives to share their work in whatever way they see fit. The company's name links back to Jo March too – named because Jo needs to get out of her attic to create authentic stories. We also produce original theatre and our debut production, . . . *that's what she said*, exploring sisterhood and race through six girls' verbatim (true) experiences on a girls' holiday to Ibiza, is now being commissioned and marks the company's professional debut.

I am still an actor. One about to graduate, and at the very beginning of my career. And that is a very exciting yet very scary place to be. This industry is incredibly flawed and it can sometimes feel really daunting. But I feel strong and confident knowing that I am in charge of one tiny little corner of that. Out The Attic gives me and all the other women involved that little bit of agency to input our own stories into the ether. Ones that deserve to be told. Ones that deserve to be heard. I no longer feel pressure to morph into what this industry wants me to be if the desired end result does not reflect who I am or what I stand for, because I have my own space to create and tell stories that do. And most importantly I get to use my privilege to facilitate others to do the same.

So thank you, Jo March, for your unapologetic ambition and for inspiring me to write my own stories as well as listen to and learn from those of the women who came before me, to take them out the attic and into the world.

339

Eliza is a director, actor, writer and film maker from Yorkshire, based in Liverpool. She is a recent graduate of the Liverpool Institute of Performing Arts. She is also the founder and artistic director of Out The Attic, a 'platform for the stories of women and those unrepresented throughout history', and their event *The Storyteller Social* which runs monthly in the city and has debuted in Manchester, Yorkshire, California and New York. She most recently directed the company's debut production . . . *that's what she said* in Liverpool and her debut short film *Alone, Together* is due to start filming in 2021.

YOU SAY TOMATO

Damhnait Monaghan

When I first moved from Canada to the United Kingdom I knew there would be challenges. But I didn't think language would be one of them. Both countries spoke English after all.

Well, after seventeen years over here I've adopted my fair share of vocabulary and expressions that wouldn't cut it back home. For eleven months of the year I proudly carry the torch for knickers and take the lift in Marks and Spencer. But as soon as I hit Customs in Toronto, I'm all about flashlights and elevators. And I'm wearing underwear under there.

My life as a linguistic double agent has been labelled way too stressful by one of my Toronto friends, but to me it's a no-brainer. Wait, do you say that here? I guess I'm trying to say it's easy peasy. Although I make the vocabulary fit the geography, it happens almost unconsciously. I guess I'm just a cultural chameleon.

It isn't always straightforward. When it comes to 'down there' as a British doctor once described the general area, I now live in the land of the euphemism. When I first moved over a GP once said to me, 'Does it hurt when you spend a penny?' I had no idea what he was talking about. I was completely in the dark and only after repeated questioning did the penny drop. Although, I hasten to add that I did not spend it in his office.

Sometimes I accidentally say a British word that I've already decided I can't pull off. It just spurts out in a sort of cross-cultural Tourette's syndrome moment of madness. And I'll be looking around and thinking, 'Was that me? Did I just say that?'

It happened recently at my daughter's netball match. One of her teammates scored an incredible goal. Her mum was standing beside me and I blurted, 'Cracking goal!' And then I flinched. Cracking? Not that there's anything wrong with it. In fact, I rather like it, it's a cracking word. But in these situations, I find myself wondering . . . was it OK, did I use it in the proper context? Can I get away with it with this Canadian drawl? (As one of my British friends describes my accent.)

But the mum beamed at me and said, 'Wasn't it just.'

So, I'm officially adding cracking to the list of British words I can use with authority.

But no matter how long I live in the UK there are certain words I will never use in their uniquely British context. Toilet, for starters. As in:

Where's James?

He's in the toilet.

I always find myself hoping James is *not* in the toilet because to my Canadian ears that will forever mean the thing you flush and not the entire en suite. But just because I don't say it doesn't mean a character in one of my stories can't, provided she's British of course.

I heard Tessa Hadley speak a few years ago and she said that the

New Yorker had asked her to Americanise some vocabulary in a short story. But she was adamant that the London couple in her story couldn't possibly buy diapers or a stroller for their baby. It had to be nappies and a pushchair.

And as a reader and a writer I agree. Otherwise, it just doesn't ring true. So, you never know. When that fictional British character of mine is *in* the toilet, maybe she'll even spend a penny.

Damhnait Monaghan was born and grew up in Canada but now lives in the south of England. A former teacher and lawyer, she is an award-winning flash fiction writer with numerous publication credits.

Damhnait's novella-in-flash *The Neverlands* was voted Best Novella in the 2020 Saboteur Awards. Her debut novel *New Girl in Little Cove*, inspired by the years she spent teaching, was published in 2021 by HarperCollins Canada and Graydon House Books (USA).

TO THE WOMAN WHO CALLED ME BORING

Eloise Williams

I am quiet.

I've always been shy, and I struggle with anxiety, but I am also at my most happy when I am doing quiet things.

When I was young, I was afraid of the dark, school. Monday mornings, the Sunday night theme tune to *Last of the Summer Wine* – knowing that it tolled the start of another week filled with requests to put my hand up and contribute.

For most of my adulthood, I was even more afraid. Of saying the wrong thing, of people not liking me, of using my voice, of not being interesting. When you called me boring, I thought you were right. I thought I had nothing to say. Nothing worth listening to.

I am naturally quiet in a world where loudness is celebrated. Where we are encouraged to join in with discussions, answer questions, give our opinions on everything – often, it seems to me, without needing to put much thought into what we are saying, as long as we are saying something.

I'm a slow processor. I like to deliberate before I voice. I like to weigh up the options, see what people think on different sides of arguments, contemplate the big things and give time to all the tiny things too.

In my early twenties I went to drama college and hid behind dramatised versions of people who only said witty, erudite, applaudable words. It wasn't the best place for an introvert with anxiety and I struggled at first, but then we were given the task of writing something. I wrote a monologue. I have lots of thoughts in my head, the monologue said to me as I wrote it. They are worth sharing. They are worth waiting for, but to find these thoughts you need to spend time in the quiet places.

I'd found a way to speak through my writing. I could spin words in different colours. Say outrageous, funny, important things. Gentle, sad, beautiful things. I could speak with my soul and give myself time to ponder before I bared all.

At the grand old age of forty-eight, I've only recently accepted that being quiet is not the disease I'd thought it was. It is a gift. In the quietness there is a watchful truth.

I give lots of public readings of my books now, and though I will always feel a rush of nerves before sharing, these are words that I've thought about and crafted and which mean something to me. I can discuss them with the people who want to listen, and I'm interested in hearing their responses. Meaningful words are exchanged. We don't just reside in the landscape of small talk and noise. With honesty comes connection, kindness and respect. Respect for my voice and the voices of others. Respect for the quietness which I fought against and now embrace.

So, to the woman who called me boring, you are your own worst enemy. Look in the mirror again, Eloise. Listen to yourself. Know that there are interesting things happening in that quiet space. That's where you can best hear yourself. In that quiet reflection there is you.

Eloise Williams is a writer. Having worked as an actor for more than a decade she turned to writing to save her sanity. She is the author of four books for young people – *Wilde*, *Seaglass*, *Gaslight* and *Elen's Island*, all published by Firefly Press – and is the inaugural Children's Laureate Wales 2019–21.

Eloise's work with young people encourages them to use their own voices. She is learning to do the same.

ENOUGH JUST TO BE

Jessica Hayles

In Honour of Ena Lindsay RIP

When I think of women and I think of achievements and I think of me, I have many. Achievements. But they're small.

Are they not enough? Do they not compare? I haven't achieved great things. I haven't overcome anything huge. I haven't changed the world in a way I'd like to, but I'm still proud. I still feel like I have. That every day or every week or every year I have. And I am. We are.

When I think of women and I think of achievements and I think of me, I just can't award me mine. I feel it's not where it's due.

Yes I work hard. Yes I'm friendly. Yes I jog. I have a degree. I have GCSEs. I followed my dream job. I travelled the world. I gave up smoking. I learned to not need my father. But all this achievement feels like it belongs to other women. Other women in my life who gave me that opportunity. My mother. My sister. My grandma. My nan.

My nan. Now, she has achievements. I know she sees an achievement in me. Sometimes at a distance. A generational distance. A cultural distance. A linguistic distance. But me.

My nan came all the way from Jamaica. She left her family in a tired house in rural Jamaica and travelled the 7,360 kilometres from Kingston to Bristol for me. For our family. She tells of a banana boat, a tough journey yet exciting. That's an achievement.

She tells of receiving quite the opposite of the grateful and welcoming response she was expecting, that had been sold to her. By 'keeping me 'ead down, and paying no one no mind', for me.

She tells LITTLE of the hardship she experienced in Jamaica; so poor, so desperate, so needy after 250 years of slavery, for me. She doesn't want to dim me. She tells of the jobs she's done for years and years here. The cleaning, the hospitals, the sewing, the cooking, the motherhood, the struggle, the adversity, for me.

And what I see is a woman with a great spirit. A vivacity for life. A charm and cheek that makes everybody bright. She picks up the phone and screams 'Good morning my friend' before she knows who's calling.

She banters the butcher. The toddler. The homeless man. The preacher. She has a love that's grown with her achievements. It escaped. A woman who has achieved so much when having so little. In the face of daily difficulty . . .

When she looks at me, I see her see what she's achieved.

She's modest, don't get me wrong. She cannot see it in herself, she sees it in me. And that's OK.

She can't write of her achievements. Literally. She can't write of mine. But I can.

Together we have many. Because she let me be.

Jessica Hayles is an actor, voice artist and curious citizen of the world. She is of mixed British and Jamaican heritage, and grew up in Bath and Bristol. She is interested in social and racial justice, human rights and human behaviour.

Jessica has a BA from the Royal Welsh College of Music and Drama. She has over a decade of experience performing in the UK's top theatres – from Shakespeare to modern dramas to immersive site-specific productions – as well as various TV, film and video game credits including *Doctor Who*, *Endeavour*, DC's *The Flash*, and *Swan Song* with Mahershala Ali.

I AM NOT SUPERWOMAN

Lesley Traynor

Single mother.
Classed as trash.
Written off by the Government.
Went back to work when babies only twelve weeks old;
but still.
Not Superwoman, just a single mum

Drove children to clubs, fixed broken boilers, leaking gutters,
picked up children.
Not the school run.
Read Harry Potter with my children.
Studied the Reader's Digest Manual.
Wrote a novel, like another single mum.
I wasn't Superwoman, just a single mum.

My father walked ten miles every day, then fell.
Motor Neurone Disease.
No Superwoman could cure that!
Then this woman fell.

Fell down through ladders that skimmed the high cornice,
false in their security.
Concrete absorbed conscientiousness,
absorbed the power to walk and speak.
A cruel mimic of what had killed a father;
but this was no disease.
Superwoman! Felled!

Pace of life slowed to a shuffle,
communication faltered,
a challenge to follow a thought,
form words that forbade pity.
Life is short, became the new mantra.
Within a locked world,
I walked a past life. Ethiopia.
Found a path through that war-torn country,
one trod without fear.
I survived.

I taught myself to walk, to talk,
creativity flowed. The written word, art, film.
Publications, exhibitions, commissions.
No barriers.
How many other women fought the Gatekeepers?
2016, Edinburgh Fringe.
Called for women to read their work on the street.
Speak their truth, their way.

No censorship, no self-censorship.
No barriers.

Women With Fierce Words;
a sisterhood of writers.
Their Fierce word, one that empowered;
a signpost for others to find their Fierce word,
their voice.
We are all Superwoman

Lesley Traynor is a Scottish writer published nationally and internationally. A chapbook of her poetry *Thrawn* was published by Dreich in 2021. She has an MLitt in Creative Writing and is the former director of the Scottish Writers' Centre and a Trustee of the Federation of Writers (Scotland).

She won the 2019 Edinburgh International Book Festival memoir writing prize, and was shortlisted for the 2019 Beyond Borders International writing prize. Passionate about supporting women's voices, she founded the inclusive collective Women With Fierce Words in 2016. At the Paisley Book Festival 2021 they reflected on their disrupted 2020 lives. More on Facebook @womenwithfiercewords and Twitter @latraynor.

THE AMBASSADOR

Julia Woollams

People say they don't like labels but we all use them. I don't immediately identify as a 'writer'.

Graphic designer – yes.

Woman – maybe (although I still feel like a girl).

Mother – that's a newish one, and still getting used to it.

Lesbian – I dislike the term, so let's say gay.

Wife – yes (as 'partner' just confuses people).

Croydonian – absolutely.

Blogger – yep.

And that's where the writing comes in, I suppose. Although
admittedly words and pictures have always been intrinsically inter-
twined in my day job as a designer. So perhaps it was inevitable that
I set up the Croydonist with my wife Angela.

The Croydonist. We're a blog about (you guessed it) Croydon.
Celebrating the culture in our borough. Always in a positive light.
Because, well, Croydon has had enough negative press over the
years, hasn't it? Labelled as violent, chavvy, common. Every town
has bad points, but it just so happens ours has a whole heap of good
points too.

We're an ever-growing collection of the best bits of our borough, according to us. From cocktails and cuisine, to quirky culture, and cool Croydon people, we write about it only if we genuinely like it. It turns out there's a lot to like.

So how did we get here? I'm a Croydon native. I remember the Whitgift Shopping Centre before they put a roof on it. I remember when my beloved 50 Pence Building was called the NLA Tower rather than Number One Croydon. I grew up thinking NLA stood for National Lego Association, because, as well as looking like a stack of 50ps, it also looked like a stack of 50ps built out of Lego.

I digress.

When I went to art school and got a job in a design studio, I spent a lot of time telling friends and colleagues how good Croydon truly was. Defending its honour:

Did you know it has a windmill?

We're only fifteen minutes from Gatwick. The same from Central London. Half an hour from Brighton.

It's the birthplace of punk. And dubstep. And grime.

We weren't just home to Kate Moss, but a whole host of famous souls, from Stormzy to Sue Perkins, via Ronnie Corbett and Sir Arthur Conan Doyle.

We had London's first airport. It's now a museum.

We've had a mushroom farm. A saffron farm.

Did I mention the world-renowned street art?

Oh, and Queen Elizabeth I liked to come for a visit. In our crocus valley.

That's what Croydon means – Crocus Valley.

I could go on.

Angela is a Croydon convert. It took me one year to persuade her we should set up home together in Croydon. It wasn't until we created a Croydon travel guide for her friends coming for a weekend visit that we realised we should perhaps set up a blog promoting our hometown. We wondered, would we have enough content? We laugh about that now.

Would we have enough time? Debatable – but we love doing it so you can always find time for things you love. Would people read it? Amazingly it seems they do.

And here we are, going strong nearly five years later. Ambassadors of Croydon.

Let's add that as a label.

By day, **Julia Woollams** is a graphic designer and branding consultant at her creative agency 31% Wool where she works with clients across a variety of sectors to help make a positive social difference. By night she writes and designs for the Croydonist – a cultural blog promoting her hometown, Croydon, which she co-founded with her wife Angela. They are also planning their second Croydon-based indie music festival called Cro Cro Land which launched in 2019 to bring guitar bands back to the birthplace of punk. Julia's writing on branding has also been published in *Graphic Design for Everyone* (DK, 2019). Find out more at croydonist.co.uk or 31percentwool.com.

RELENTLESS VOICES

SEPTEMBER

Emily Garside

September always feels like the time to start again. The compulsion to buy school supplies and start fresh hangs in the air. For someone who has spent far too many years in education, both as a student and a teacher, it's a feeling I can never quite shake.

In September last year, I walked out of a job, at the end of yet another fixed-term contract, and said, 'Never again.' I was not going back to another office job I hated. I was going to try, one last time, to do something I wanted to. This school year was going to be the one that changed things.

A few weeks became a couple of months. No sign of anything or anyone who would employ me. Christmas retail temping came around. A chance to work in a bookshop, a childhood dream. And while it wasn't exactly a dream job – as retail jobs rarely are – it was enjoyable, a sense of camaraderie among colleagues. We were all a bookseller and something else. A director, many writers, or just people still looking for their path. And so, when I had to sell my old boss a book, it didn't feel so bad. So what if she thought she'd been right all along and I'd never amount to much? I knew all of us behind that counter were something else as well.

As the darkness of December drew in, I gave in. I went to an interview for an admin job. It felt like the eyes of the world were pressing in on me to 'get a proper job'. And so, I went to the interview. It was a disaster from start to finish and still I got the job.

For a month in the admin job nobody talked to me. I wish that was an exaggeration. I'd sit, eight hours a day, and only be directly addressed when someone wanted something. Eight hours of isolation, and whispers if it looked like I was daring to use the kettle. Temps aren't allowed coffee.

Within a month I was called into the office and promptly fired. For having too 'substantial' a Twitter profile. And thinking I was too good for their job. And January was the darkest month I have known. In February I gave in and signed up to a temping agency. One that had been nice to me many years ago in another bout of unemployment. They gave me a job that started the next day. I cried all the way there. I was scared – that people would be unkind again, that I wouldn't last the day because they'd find something wrong with me as everyone does. On the way home, I cried because they were so nice.

It's not perfect. I wear a uniform and occasionally get shouted at by the public. I have to call people Dr So-and-So every day while they have no clue I also have 'Dr' before my name. It pays minimum wage. But it's the best thing to happen to me in a long while.

Because for a few months I have been able to hit pause on just searching for something, anything, to pay the bills, and concentrate on doing the things I've always wanted to do. Because while my paid work was falling apart, I was getting closer to my real goals and my dreams. But I was too busy concentrating on the rest of it falling apart to notice.

In September, weeks after I lost my last 'proper' job I got offered my first play commission. In December while I was busy selling books to other people, I signed a contract for my first book.

I was going to write the book of my research, a book on the play I had loved and researched for a decade. I might not be an academic any more, but I was writing the book I became an academic to write. I was going to write the play I'd dreamed of writing instead of doing my PhD.

Jobs will always come and go. In ten years of fixed-term contracts I've learned that much. Eventually you will find something to pay the bills. But ten years of waiting for the door to open a crack has taught me opportunities to do the thing you've always dreamed of don't come along every day. And when one does you have to kick it the rest of the way in.

September felt like starting again. By December I felt like giving in. In February I had given up. In March I got a chance to chase the things I need to. 'Never again' sometimes takes a few false starts to get there.

So, I'll take the uniform, and minimum wage, the being invisible until someone wants to shout at me, I'll take the fact that I pretend not to be a Doctor while so-called real doctors think I'm a dumb receptionist. I'll take all that to go home and be a writer.

Emily Garside is a writer of many kinds including but not limited to academic, journalist and playwright. Having originally been a historian, she pursued a theatrical academic career following training in Montreal (not with Cirque du Soleil, being naturally very unco-ordinated). On completing an MA at RADA, Emily spent a number of years as an academic and lecturer, receiving a PhD from Cardiff Metropolitan University. Emily continues to teach at the University of Wolverhampton and Bishopsgate Institute and teaches writing workshops for a range of organisations including London Playwrights Blog.

Emily is literary manager for Forest Theatre Company and chair of the Board of Trustees for Taking Flight Theatre. She is a long-time participant in the 14/48 theatre festival and her debut professional play *Don't Send Flowers* was staged in 2019. She continues to write for the stage.

SHAMELESS ACTIVISTS

Jane Riekemann

I was sixty when I became a political activist. On 23 June 2016 I sat up all night in disbelief as the results rolled in until David Dimbleby announced at 4.40 a.m. we would be leaving the European Union. I cried for hours. Tears of sorrow and rage. The anger has stayed and twenty-two months later still fires me up to spend the bulk of my week campaigning to stop Brexit. Within a few days of the vote, I'd joined the steering committee of non-party-political community group Bath for Europe, which initially seemed like a support group for those equally dismayed at the way the country was heading. Over the past few years, I've yelled myself hoarse on protest marches, helped bring speakers such as Professors Michael Dougan and A.C. Grayling to Bath, thrown myself into the 2017 general election campaign which saw Liberal Democrat and pro-EU Wera Hobhouse replace the sitting Tory to become the first female MP for Bath.

But mainly I write. I chair our media group – we are the voice of our local campaign and it's up to us to get the message out. So now, for the most part, I'm producing press releases, articles, leaflets and writing letters. Not much time or room in my brain to create fiction, especially short stories, my real passion.

In the past, I've taught Drama, English and Creative Writing in secondary schools, both in the UK and abroad. I co-founded and run an international short story award, the ninth edition of which has just closed, and in between penning political pamphlets, I'm reading the stories that have been sent in and just relishing the chance to escape to other worlds. Even dystopian ones seem less bleak than our present one.

But one thing I've learned is you're never too old to become a fighter. Having sat on the political fence for most of my life, through trying to respect the opinions of others and not wishing to offend, I now place my blue beret-ed head firmly above the parapet and wait for the shots to ring out. Most Saturdays I'm in our city centre handing out leaflets and asking people if they're happy with the way Brexit negotiations are panning out. I've been called 'scum', a 'traitor' and been trolled in the comments section of our local paper. The younger me would have been embarrassed to have attracted so much attention, but my sixty-two-year-old self was enormously proud of a blurry picture of me and others in the *Daily Express* last September, with the caption 'Shameless . . . activists'.

I've often thought about why this is the fight I've chosen over so many other worthy contenders; for example, I didn't go to the Iraq War protest in 2003. But, as well as considering this a disastrous national decision on so many levels, I do have a personal reason. My husband is German and, though he's lived here for seventeen years, has been sick with worry about his status – possibly like the three million other non-UK EU citizens in our country. The immigration issue has pushed us towards a more hostile environment where foreigners, not just those from the EU, feel unwelcome and that includes those who moved here as Commonwealth citizens more than half a century ago. I was born in Brixton in 1955 and some of our neighbours were part of the Windrush generation; in fact, the area in front of the library was renamed Windrush Square in 2005 to recognise the contribution they made to the community. I loved the buzz of multi-ethnic Brixton with its Caribbean market, reggae, gospel and later Motown sounds, and am now horrified at the hurt and suffering inflicted on people such as former neighbours, their dependants and all those who came to our country to make a contribution. Until the tide turns and I feel my country's been reclaimed, I'll keep fighting and hope other women join me.

A former teacher of English and Drama, **Jane Riekemann** lived in the US and Germany for seventeen years before settling in Bath, Somerset, in 2001. With like-minded writers, she launched the international Bath Short Story Award, which will celebrate its first decade in 2022. She also runs the Creative Writing classes for a local arts festival.

Stopping Brexit had been her main goal and, with that in mind, she ran the media group of bathforeurope.com. Although the UK has left the EU, the campaign for closer alignment with our European neighbours continues and Jane still considers herself a 'shameless activist'.

NORA DAVIES' MOCK EXAM AND MINE

Miriam Elin Jones

I doubt Mr Smith – whose real name has been changed just in case he feels like Googling himself one rainy Thursday afternoon and catches me ranting here about something that happened well over a decade ago, that I *still* can't really properly get over – even noticed I was sat in his class taking that Sociology mock exam that day. He probably didn't even blink while decorating my essay with his red pen, sort-of following whatever marking scheme he had at hand.

I was that quiet kid, who said nothing, never raised a hand, and sat right in the back row hidden away – more often than not, directly behind the prim and proper Nora Davies (name also changed) who ALWAYS made sure her voice was heard – and I was often forgotten about and left to my own devices. That strange kid with a bad fringe, wearing black nail varnish.

Mr Smith, however, rushing through my mock exam, noted that I deserved 38 marks out of the designated 40 for my timed essay writing, and begrudgingly wrote 'Good Effort' at the bottom of the paper.

Which I thought nothing of. Yeah, it was a good effort, until I rocked up to class the next day, faced with Nora Davies, yet again in front of me, bragging to the girl next to her about how well she'd done. Over her shoulder, I saw ARDDERCHOG – excellent – in big BOLD letters on the page, with . . . with . . . a 35 out of 40.

Now, this was something I struggled to comprehend. Bad feedback for a good mark, and glowing feedback for an all right mark. And the only thing I could come up with was that Mr Smith just didn't like me.

Well, he definitely didn't like me after what I did next.

'Sir?'

The usually noisy class fell eerily silent.

For I – me, of all people – had raised my voice.

And as I asked why my high mark wasn't considered spectacular enough, Mr Smith's usually assertive, slightly cocky manner crumbled, as he couldn't quibble with the case I'd presented in front of him.

And as I asked, realising I'd shocked all seventeen of my fellow students, who ranged from footballers, rugby boys, a few girlie girls and a fellow emo kid, into silence, I realised why I'd had that 'Good Effort' for my work.

You see, Nora Davies had asked for it. Put herself out there. Practically left an apple at Mr Smith's desk, making sure he knew she was there. Striding into the classroom, blonde-highlighted ponytail swishing, announcing she had just left choir practice.

I, on the other hand, dragged my feet about the place, shuffled, too scared, too shy to raise my hand, so frightened of saying the wrong thing, getting an incorrect answer even when I knew perfectly well I was right, and yet, I always wanted to be found. To be spotted. For someone to notice I could put together a good essay.

And no, I will neither forgive nor forget that Mr Smith accidentally – there was no malicious intent really – made a mug of me that day. Because it took me that 'Good Effort' at the end of my rather well-written essay (if I do say so myself) for me to raise my voice. For me to start talking. For me to put myself out there for the 'well dones' and 'fantastics' that I've worked for since. I haven't quite got the essay framed up on my wall – it's kept safely in a drawer to this day – but I thank Mr Smith. That mock exam reminds me occasionally that I've always got to ask for – and sometimes demand – what I want and deserve.

Miriam Elin Jones is a writer, playwright and translator from Carmarthenshire. Her most recent work has been published in the *Adref* (Cylchgrawn Cara, 2020) and *Seren Wib a Storiau Eraill* (Y Lolfa, 2018) anthologies, and she has been part of Theatr Genedlaethol Cymru's New Playwrights' Group since 2018.

In 2020 Miriam Elin completed a PhD thesis discussing the development of Welsh-language science fiction and continues to publish academically. She still has the unfairly marked Sociology essay from 2009 stowed away in her desk drawer – just to remind herself that she can see her inner potential, even if others can't.

BRUISE

Sallyanne Rock

Content warning: this piece contains references to domestic abuse.

Six years after leaving an abusive relationship, I was in the middle of
family court proceedings, after taking action to keep my two young
daughters safe. My daily life at the time revolved around Social Services, police officers, solicitors, mental health workers, counselling
sessions and school interventions, all while trying to hold onto a
full-time job. I had developed an anxiety disorder as a result of the
stress and was on medication to treat it. I had also enrolled on the
Women's Aid Freedom Programme, in which I was unravelling
twenty years of domestic abuse.

I had been in a new, non-abusive and loving relationship, but we
couldn't maintain it against the backdrop of the situation and it
broke down. I didn't have the option of breaking down. The court
process was still ongoing and I had my daughters to look after. That
was when I began to write.

I wrote down feelings in lines, making sense of the overwhelm by
finding words for the tangled mess of it all. Whenever my emotions

felt unbearable, I would get out the laptop or my phone, and let the words pour out. I wrote through my anger, my frustration, my desperation and grief. I carried on when my tears blurred the poems. It became my catharsis.

Around the same time, a friend had a flash fiction piece printed in a magazine that published new writing by women. She encouraged me to send some of my work there too, so I submitted a couple of poems. They weren't accepted for publication, but the editors provided some positive feedback.

The poetry I was writing at the time was raw and emotional. I didn't consider form or think about imagery or internal rhyme. It was more about getting feelings out of my head and onto paper. But I was really getting into reading online lit mags, and discovering new poets, and new poetry styles I'd never come across before. I learned how to craft my own poetry into something others would enjoy reading.

I haven't stopped writing since. I've had poems and stories published online and in print. I've read my work at open mic nights and had some really encouraging comments. I've applied to volunteer with a young writers' group, so I can pass on some of my passion. I go to as many local poetry events as I can, and I've made new friends who are writers and poets. It's a wonderfully encouraging and supportive community and I love being a part of it.

I was proud to have a poem published recently in a charity anthology. My youngest daughter took a copy to school to show her teacher, who asked me, 'So, is this what you *do*?' At the time I was embarrassed and brushed off the question, telling him about my nine-to-five office job. But it stuck with me, and now, I think I'm at the point that I can say, 'Yes, this is what I *do*. I'm a writer,' or, 'Yes, I'm a poet.' It might not be what pays the mortgage, but it *is* what I *do* and it makes me who I am.

While I was in the abusive relationship, and for many years after, I felt worthless, stupid and incapable. I can't apply those words to myself any more.

First published in Whirlagust: The Yaffle Prize 2019 *(Yaffle Press)*

A BUTTERFLY SENSES HER ENEMY

I wait – pinned
in folded symmetry:
these new markings bloom
blacker than the last.

I listen for danger to slip
into the night
before I unclutch my breath
and moment-sleep
in the lavender half-light.

Memory fades
like an imprint behind the eyelids,
reappearing in a tape-reel flutter.

In the morning,
when your waking body turns towards me,
my shoulder blades flinch closed
before even your breath can reach
between them.

Sallyanne Rock is from the Black Country. Her poetry appears in various journals online and in print, including *Eye Flash*, *Finished Creatures* and *Away With Words*. She has worked as an assistant writer in her local young writers' group, and has recently facilitated workshops of her own. Her pamphlet-length manuscript *Control* was shortlisted for publication in 2019 with Against the Grain Poetry Press, and also commended in the Paper Swans Poetry Prize 2019. She was the recipient of the Creative Future Writers' Award Gold Prize for Poetry 2019. Find her on Twitter @sallrockspoetry.

THE STONE

Sandra Arnold

On April 6, 2002, my youngest daughter, Rebecca, died of a rare appendix cancer at the age of twenty-three. For a whole year afterwards I couldn't say her name and the word 'died' in the same breath. Though I am a writer, and at that time was a teacher of writing, I had no words to describe this cataclysmic event in the life of my family. I could no longer read novels, listen to music, or watch films. I stopped dreaming. It hurt to breathe. It hurt to be inside my skin. I woke at night with my heart beating hard against my ribs. Large gatherings of people with their noisy laughter and banal chatter suffocated me.

The silence of my home, my garden, the warm breaths of my cats and dog and goat and horses, the quiet paddocks, the river walks and the mountains provided no refuge. They were all empty spaces that reverberated with Rebecca's absence. This new territory was so bleached of colour, so arid and alien, so lacking in anything recognisable that I had no language to negotiate my way through it.

New Zealand, where we live, is a beautiful country, but after Rebecca's death my husband and I needed to leave it for a while. A desert country seemed the place that best reflected our inner landscape and so we were drawn to work in Oman in the Arabian Gulf. We decided to immerse ourselves in the culture of this alien land that held no memories of the life we'd known.

On our way to work in Oman, we stayed briefly in England, the country of our birth, and with my brother I returned to the scenes of my childhood. This bridge to the past connected me to the present and showed me possibilities for the future. The year in Oman allowed healing to continue in circumstances we could never have imagined. I kept a diary to record our experiences there. By the time we returned to New Zealand we were ready to face the future. I began a Master's degree in Creative Writing which explored through fiction themes of loss and grief. The first story I wrote for this was called 'The Stone' and is based on an experience we had when we camped on the beach in Oman on the second anniversary of our daughter's death. It has been broadcast on national radio, included in an anthology of the best New Zealand fiction and also in a Medical Humanities journal from the University of Otago.

After my Master's degree I began a PhD in Creative Writing to research the topic of parental bereavement. Finally, after I completed my thesis I was able to live with my grief.

THE STONE

This morning we'd watched the sun rise over the sea because we needed to see colour spill over the earth. We walked past deep holes dug by nesting turtles and over the tracks their flippers had gouged in the sand. We found piles of broken eggshells at the bottom of the holes.

'Let's hope one of them made it to the sea,' Chris said. He picked up a stick and drew a heart in the sand around a cluster of empty shells.

'What a waste,' I said, counting around two hundred eggs.

'Part of a cycle,' Chris said, writing our initials inside the heart.

We peeled off our clothes and waded into the sea. Seabirds circled and dived. Floating on my back in the warm salty water I thought of a friend who once described the hours he'd spent in the sea after his boat capsized. The world became the boat he was clinging to and only that moment had any substance. He said he felt outside of time. I never fully understood what he meant, until now.

Outside of time. This day. This time. Two years ago. New Zealand.

Rebecca asks for music to be put on. She discusses a racehorse with our friends John and Sue and tells them she wants to train a white horse when she gets better. She asks me several times who came through the door and I say there's no one else here, just the seven of us. She touches everyone and checks their names, then asks Sue, 'What sound does a bear make when it's stung by a bee?' We think it's a riddle, but Rebecca says she doesn't know the answer either.

The two nurses decide to leave as she seems so much better. She's laughing and joking. Her face is a better colour. I say goodbye to them on the porch. When I go back into the living room Sue is telling Rebecca she and John will stay overnight so Chris and I can get

375

some sleep. Rebecca thanks her then nestles the side of her face into the chair and closes her eyes. As I sit down opposite her I see her chest is still. We put our faces close to her mouth and nose and feel the tiniest whisper of air. Chris finds a pulse in her neck beating very faintly. My heart is beating hard. John and Sue slip outside and wait on the veranda. The nor'wester roars through the trees whipping up the autumn leaves. Chris and I hold Rebecca's hands.

Beneath the hills wild horses graze in the moonlight. The lead mare lifts her head. Colts and fillies stop chasing each other's shadows. Foals stand closer to their mothers. The old ones stop grazing. They all watch the lead mare, and wait. The earth holds its breath. Rebecca's pulse flutters like a moth's wing, and is gone. I go outside to tell John and Sue and they say they know because the wind has died.

I don't sleep that night and next morning I move around as if trapped in glass. In the middle of a conversation with my two other children, a sound slides from my throat. It rises to a wail. Wave upon wave of wailing, from a place deep inside my body. Chris, Susannah and Benjamin can do nothing but hold me. A fantail taps on the window. As Rebecca's friends start arriving the fantail circles round their heads.

Chris knelt on the sand with the sea up to his chin. A seagull flew over our heads, its keening breaking the silence of the deserted beach.

'Do you remember,' I said, 'when I was in labour? You suggested playing Scrabble to keep my mind off the contractions? Then you put your hand in the bag of letters and brought out an R.'

'Coincidence,' Chris said. Then, 'Ouch!'

He reached down and brought up a stone. 'No wonder it cut me. It's covered in limpets.' He turned it over. His brow creased. He held it out to me. In the middle the limpets had dropped off, leaving behind a raised pattern of white calcification in a perfectly formed R.

Sitting under the stars in front of our campfire I hold the stone and stare into the flames.

'In ancient Persia when someone first saw oil trickle out of the desert they didn't understand what it was,' I say. 'They thought it was some kind of water and when it ignited they believed the fire was sacred. They didn't believe the flame just went out. They thought it died, like the soul leaving the body.'

Chris points to the sea. The sparks from the agitation of the algae have become flashes of light that run along the length of each wave. The sea is ablaze with white fire. A large dark shape emerges from the water. A giant turtle. She drags herself across the sand, stopping to check out sites to dig a hole, then makes her way to our tent and starts digging beside it. With a sigh, she begins the long process of shovelling out sand with her front flippers. We edge closer, and by the light of the moon we watch her lay her eggs.

After two hours she covers her nest with sand, turns around and heads back to the sea. We follow and watch her swim away. Pieces of moon float on the water where she disappears beneath the waves.

Sandra Arnold is originally from County Durham and lives in New Zealand. She has a PhD in Creative Writing from Central Queensland University, Australia, and is the author of five books including three novels, a non-fiction work and a collection of flash fiction.

Her work has been widely published and anthologised internationally and placed and shortlisted in various competitions. She has been nominated for the Best Small Fictions, Best Microfictions and the Pushcart Prize. She was awarded a residency at the Robert Lord Writers Cottage in Dunedin, New Zealand, in 2019 to complete a new collection of flash fiction. More at www.sandraarnold.co.nz.

DROPPING THE BALL
(HAS NEVER FELT BETTER)

Ashby Young

I'm fourteen and the world has revealed more to me than I am ready for. I'm caught up in the drama around me: friends becoming enemies becoming friends with knives behind their backs, boys kissing girls with clumsy mouths and unpractised words picked up from the web pages they're too young to be visiting.

The changing room before PE is the stadium for stage-whispers and conspiracies. We are fourteen and we're just learning how to weaponise our eyes, searching for safety in the hunching of shoulders and quick changes. There is a game to be played here, as we toss insults like netballs and pretend to revel in the hurt we cause without reprimand. I am fourteen and desperately forcing my heart to flutter when I sit next to the boy with sandy hair in Maths class, I am fourteen and playing hide-and-seek with the brightest girls' glittering eyes as they exercise their new roles as predators. I'm fourteen and realising just how much of a crime it is to take up space.

I'm fourteen and not sure when the laws of interaction changed. We don't know who's refereeing, but all of us are slipping into the positions we've been assigned. I only know half of the rules, but that's

OK because some of us don't even have the kit. They're quickly elected as prey. They're *loners*, and *weirdos* and *spazzes* and I'm so sorry every time I hear the accusations and don't raise my voice.

My role is one of the fragile few hovering in no man's land, and I'm terrified to misstep into enemy territory and become Other. I'm mastering the value of silence; my stance as the ever-supportive defence to the venting of my friends keeps me on the team.

(Part of me wishes for the spotlight, wonders what it's like to have all eyes on me. It sounds exciting, it sounds *terrifying*.)

And then something shifts. Maybe I miss the basket, maybe I look for too long at the girl with a soft pixie cut and a distinct lack of belonging. But the red card is raised. Sharp-arrowed insults find a new target, and my friends stop giggling gossip into my ears. In the changing rooms I'm not a part of the whispering any more. I'm supposed to hear it anyway, I know how this game works, but suddenly I'm booted off the field and onto the bench.

I'm fourteen and I'm hurtling towards my breaking point when – just as any teen drama dictates – the rebellion comes in all its spiteful glory.

I'm arriving at school one morning with a dare on my face and my own, newly shorn, pixie cut ('a *boy* cut', the hairdresser grimaces, and that in itself holds its own thrill). In the library at lunchtime I write pages of angst-ridden poetry filled with all the words I swallow down. It isn't my voice yet, there's a performance even here; but the lines aren't anyone else's either, so I claim them with clawing hands.

Eventually, the changing room cannot touch me. I'm sixteen and realising that the girls around me, the ones who chose my label, don't know what they're doing either. There's no room to be hurt by '*lesbian*' once I understand how they're manufacturing personalities for the rules that declares this is just how girls are; we should compete and hate and fight and flinch.

I'm eighteen years old and it's New Year's Eve. I'm in my sister's house, surrounded by her friends – *my friends*. I've begun to pave the way to who I hope to be. Love sits as a blanket over us all. (There is grief too. I'm learning that there is space for both at once.) It's almost midnight – or past it. I've just confided in them that I haven't shouted or raised my voice, maybe ever.

They pull me from the sofa and we're outside. Something in the night is scratching me raw, and that's OK. They squeeze my hand – a reminder that this is real – before letting it go and screaming. It sounds to me like a prayer. Like the chanting of a thousand spectators as I line up my shot. The air is burning.

It doesn't take long, or it takes an eternity, but I'm joining in.

The words aren't recognisable, but my throat is ablaze, and something about this is *radiant*. I think maybe this is reincarnation.

Because fear and competition and roleplaying be damned, we're here. Me, and my friends, and my lighthouse of a sister, finally yelling back at the gaze I cowered from. I think about my silence. I let myself grieve, I let myself rejoice.

I ensure that the world hears it all.

I put the rule-book away. I refuse to be ashamed of the space I fill.

Ashby Young is an eighteen-year-old English and Creative Writing student at Royal Holloway, University of London. After spending their life anxiously awaiting the day they were whisked off into a magical world, they eventually decided to start creating their own.

With a specific interest in free-verse poetry, Ash tries to document the journey of coming to understand their identity, with the hope that their writing will find others who in turn feel less alone. Ash's knowledge of sport resides solely in its use as a metaphor.

SAME SH!T DIFFERENT CENTURY

Suffragette City

In 2018 we – Hannah Monkley, Amy Trend and Amy Towle – created a podcast called *Same Sh!t Different Century*. The podcast came about after we attended the Women's March in 2017, dressed as suffragettes, brandishing a placard saying 'Same Shit. Different Century' and an image of us went viral. We wanted to make the point that it's 100 years since the first women were given a vote, yet there's still so much that we need to do for women's rights in this country and over the whole world.

We all know each other as we work in a historical costume house in London. One day over lunch we were planning on attending the Women's March and Hannah half-jokingly suggested we should go as suffragettes. Amy Trend replied, 'Actually that's a really good idea, we should definitely do that!' The idea was born and we set about designing our costumes and creating our placard, ready for the march.

It really was such an amazing day. The best day. It was so inspiring, empowering and overwhelming. We had such a great response from everyone we saw. We had mothers coming up to us and saying that their children, little girls, had no idea about the suffragettes as they had never been taught about them in school, but now wanted to learn more. It just felt so great to share their stories. We managed to make a few more people aware of what women in history had been through to get us to the point we are today, and it felt amazing.

During the march, so many people took our photo and an image of us ended up going viral. Off the back of that, Sarah Mower, who writes for *Vogue* and organised the fashion element of Port Eliot Festival, tracked us down via Instagram and invited us to join her at the festival to talk about suffragettes and protest fashion.

We jumped at the chance. We knew quite a bit about suffragettes already, as we had done lots of research before the march to prepare ourselves with answers to any negative comments (the suffrage movement wasn't as diverse as it could have been and many women campaigned only for the rights of white women). However, obviously now we had to go and give this talk, we upped our game and did mountains and mountains of research on them. The more we researched, the more we wanted to learn. You'd be reading up on one woman and hear someone else's name; then you'd want to learn about them as well; then you'd read their story and you'd think I want to know more about this as well. It's never-ending.

At the festival we were given about an hour to talk. It was amazing and we loved every second of it, but we were a bit disappointed that we didn't have time to talk about everything we researched and didn't get to tell all of these amazing stories. We really wanted to get these women's names out there. You know, get them some recognition. So we decided to start a podcast to continue the conversation. We were a bit apprehensive as we knew nothing about audio recording, editing and podcast hosting sites. We had to learn the technology from the very beginning, but we managed it.

It's been such a positive experience so far and we've had some great feedback. It's been lovely to hear praise from people and thrilling that everyone else seems just as interested in these women as we are. If we can teach just one person something inspiring, then it's worth doing.

In each episode we try to link the theme of the podcast and the issues we talk about back to something that is happening today. For example, we wanted to cover the sometimes lack of intersectionality in feminism. Every story we read about and research is just so inspiring; well, it certainly inspires us to go out there and be a little bit more politically active. In the words of the suffragettes: Deeds not words. It is amazing how much of this is still happening today. Prisoners are still hunger-striking, women are still denied control over their own bodies, there are still places with inadequate disabled access and people are still being subjected to horrific police brutality. It just goes to show there is still such a long way to go.

It really is the same shit, different century.

Amy Trend, **Amy Towle** and **Hannah Monkley** work for the internationally recognised historical costume house Cosprop, which has provided costumes for many award-winning productions including *Downton Abbey* and *The Durrells*.

In January 2017 they took advantage of their costuming skills to make a bold statement at the Women's March dressed as suffragettes. The reaction they received was unprecedented. After being photographed numerous times, their image was shared all over social media, reaching a wide community and endorsed by celebrities including The People for Bernie Sanders, Dita Von Teese and Mark Gatiss, ultimately featuring in articles in the *Guardian* and Vogue Online.

WHEN YOU GROW UP

Louise Houghton

My three-year-old nephew wants to be a dustman. He is fascinated by recycling and how it all works and I truly hope he does do something within that industry, even just briefly, just to live out his childhood dream.

For a child, there are no limitations, no gender restrictions or any other boundaries standing in the way of what their heart desires. So why don't more of us trust our three-year-old self to know what we were put on the planet to do?

From as young as I can remember, I had a dream to pursue a life 'front of camera'. I remember being four years old and standing on tiptoes peering through the window into the drama club that I was too young to join and wishing the days away till I could go. That feeling of determination has never left me. Maybe because I am a Taurus and like a bull, but maybe also because I was so clear on what I wanted to achieve in life, that I wouldn't let obstacles stand in my way.

As a child, my parents helped me go to every amateur dramatics club there was around. But, when it came to me going to drama school, they wanted me to get my A Levels, then a degree to 'fall back on'. Without their financial support I could only follow the path they chose for me, but I knew this was not my story.

When I moved to London after university to stand on my own two feet, my parents began to accept that I wasn't going to give up. Through a chance encounter, my dad actually helped me get some work experience at a production company and the ball started rolling. I was soon hired as a production assistant and after a year I was presenting a show that was broadcast on Sky Sports. I was travelling Europe and living the dream, of sorts, but I still wanted to go to drama school. So, when I got accepted with a scholarship, I was off! Life was progressing nicely and I earned a living juggling presenting for a Sky channel and acting in sitcoms and dramas for BBC, Channel 5 and BBC Wales.

Working in this career, though, was a lot harder than I ever imagined. There is so much uncertainty with it, but I always tried to trust my path and every door that opened along the way. It was this trust that saw me end up in Berlin working for a German network, DWTV. It was a big challenge for me because I wasn't a journalist, but this job gave me a noteworthy foundation and reputation that meant it wasn't long before requests came in for me to host award shows and other live events around the world. I was even presented with the opportunity to move to America, but as with every step on my path, there were hurdles to overcome in pursuing this next stride – and this was one of the biggest.

After getting my visa in motion, my sister, who I lived with in London, had a stroke. This changed everything. She was my best friend, and I became her carer. I didn't even want to go to Berlin, let alone America. Luckily though, after a few years, she pulled through and encouraged me to take a trip to LA to see how I felt. I remember waiting for a taxi outside LAX airport and bursting into tears. I knew I had to do this for me.

I think when you open yourself up to your path, things somehow fall into place. I felt like LA was the place I was meant to be, but as the initial months there passed by, I had doubts. Why had I left a stable job, my lifelong friends and dear family? For what – the sunshine? The inner trust in myself had become more challenging to believe in. Was I just following a silly childhood dream? Could I really 'make it' out here? I had to basically start over and rebuild my career from scratch.

Four years down the line and I am proud to say I have now worked with Universal, ESPN, CW and Cellar Media. I have continued travelling the world hosting live events and developed a real passion for our planet and the environment. I have even explored my spirituality, and in the summer of Covid, when all live events were on pause, I finished my master training in Reiki energy healing. I learned to surrender to what will be, to be proud of myself and give myself some much-needed recognition.

After three months back in the UK caring for my mum, who also unfortunately suffered a stroke, I have just returned to LA to film a scene in the movie *Pray For Me* and to get my teeth into a new show called *America's Next Investment*. I am due to co-produce this show as well as host it and I have just realised why I am so excited. For so many years I fought to pursue my dream of working in the entertainment industry. I always followed my gut instinct and now I am excited to be able to support entrepreneurs raising capital for their business ventures and ultimately fulfilling their passions and dreams.

My career may not look exactly like I had imagined as a child, but I am now able to appreciate what I have achieved and I'm proud of myself for not having given up on my dream.

As for my nephew: if his passion for recycling continues, there are so many avenues to explore within the industry that I really do hope he doesn't 'bin' the idea of working in this field. *(Pun 100 per cent intended!)*

The key in life is to believe. Believe in yourself. Believe in your world and believe that you can do what your three-year-old heart desires.

Louise Houghton is a British host, broadcast journalist and voice-over artist. She works internationally on film, TV, online and at a variety of live events. These include anything from award shows and gala dinners to press conferences and launch events. She is best known for her seven years hosting DWTV's daily live lifestyle magazine show, *EUROMAXX*.

Currently based in LA, Louise is working for Universal, ESPN, Cellar Media and developing a new show called *America's Next Investment*. She met Miranda at drama school and is honoured to be part of this project. More information about Louise can be found at www.louisehoughton.com or social platforms @louisehoughton.

I ACHIEVE, YOU ACHIEVE, WE ACHIEVE

Tania Hershman

She does not expect to be recognised
from one occasion to the next, feels
her face easily forgotten, is amazed
when not only her but something she's said
is remembered. This chips away at her
conviction of insignificance, but *ohsoslowly*

like the ancient lichen which grows one centimetre
every hundred years. She suspects neither of them
can change shape or pace, or let go
of what they cling to.

I wrote this poem a few years ago, and was so – what? embarrassed? ashamed? – of the feelings in it that I couldn't even say 'I do not expect . . .' I had to step into the third person to get close to this sensation of such unmemorableness. When the collection that contains this poem came out and someone said that this poem spoke to her, it seemed like a miracle.

But the suspicion 'she' has in the poem turned out to be wrong. I did change shape and pace: I learned to expect to be recognised and remembered. Not because I have achieved great fame, but because I began to accept that I am a person people enjoy meeting and talking to, and want to meet and talk to again.

Interlude: I have to stop writing and go off and do something else because even that sentence made me wonder at my hubris, at my boastfulness.

I'm back now, and, speaking of boastfulness, in 2018 I was commissioned by *Mslexia* magazine to write an article about women writers and bragging. I interviewed my friends and found that each has her own way to talk about her achievements on social media or in person. Writing the article made me bolder. I doubt if I will ever describe my own book as 'a masterpiece', as Angela Carter did in a letter to a friend. But when good things happen, I tell people, and I find a way to phrase it, to talk about my achievement, in order to pass on the permission to do anything you want to do in the way you want to do it.

I recently read a *Guardian* profile of the captain of the victorious US Women's Soccer team, Megan Rapinoe, who is described at the victory parade after winning the 2019 World Cup, lifting the trophy and shouting, 'I deserve this!' Imagine yelling 'I deserve this!' Imagine even thinking it!

I grin as I imagine it. I am a woman who works, who writes, who teaches, who helps others to write. More than that, I am a woman who lives as she wants to, joyously alone, writes exactly what she wants to in the way she wants (short stories, poems and strange hybrid forms), earns money from writing and receives invitations to keep doing it, performing it, publishing it and talking about it.

As one of the co-founders of the On This Day She Twitter account, where we put women back into history one day at a time, I understand how privileged I am to be able to do and have it all. I will never yell 'I deserve this!' because the world owes me nothing. I am simply grateful. But I don't 'feel my face easily forgotten' any more.

I see and I am seen. I have achieved myself.

Tania Hershman's poetry pamphlet *How High Did She Fly*, joint winner of Live Canon's 2019 Poetry Pamphlet Competition, was published in November 2019, and her hybrid physics-inspired book *and what if we were all allowed to disappear* was published by Guillemot Press in 2020.

Tania is also the author of two books of poetry and three short story collections and co-author of *Writing Short Stories: A Writers' & Artists' Companion* (Bloomsbury, 2015). She is co-creator of @OnThisDayShe and co-author of the *On This Day She* book (John Blake Books, 2021), and has a PhD in Creative Writing inspired by particle physics. Find her at www.taniahershman.com.

END NOTE

SCAFFOLDING

Miranda Roszkowski

The following piece was the final one in our run of 100 back-to-back stories (though we added a few special podcasts afterwards). Writing it was scary and joyful, much like the project itself. I am including it here, because as I've put the book together, several years later, many of the conversations I've had with the writers have reminded me of the importance of revisiting your successes. Even if you feel you were a different person, even if it was a different world. No one can ever take your achievements away.

'I can't do it. I have nothing to say.'

Me – on a Friday in May 2018 after a particularly existential rejection, knowing that in two days I had to share my five-minute story of 'achievement' for the *100 Voices for 100 Years* podcast I had set up.

It's not always easy to ask people for something, but in this case that was the whole purpose of the project – providing the platform for others to share work. And they did – every day for 100 days, I broadcast amazing female storytellers who shared their poems, stories, thoughts, desires, fears and – above all – achievements. It wasn't always smooth and things often didn't run as I had expected them to. Life got in the way, for my contributors as it did for me. Somehow I always managed to adapt, and when I reached out there was always someone who could help, whether that was to help me with technology, by stepping up to tell their story ahead of schedule, or through emotional support.

Every day I was surprised that the project I had dreamed about was a reality, growing, improving, building momentum. And as it grew I knew I wanted to speak myself.

On that Friday, I just had to do it. Even if it felt like I had zero to contribute, I would have to think of something.

I listened to that day's podcast. It was the perfect antidote to all the negative things I was thinking. I emailed the writer. 'I understand,' she said when I told her what was going on for me. I knew she did. Later that day, on social media, another one of my contributors reposted the piece she had recorded less than a week before, a piece that was full of struggles and hope. 'I am so far from optimistic now,' she said, needing a reminder of that other version of herself who had been able to recognise all the great things that she had done.

Neither this contributor nor I had fundamentally changed from the people who one day, seven days, 100 days before, had felt invincible. When things are going well, for me at least, I remember all the steps it has taken to get there. My achievements feel solid, like scaffolding holding me up. When something knocks me, I feel like I'm in free-fall. So asking people to talk about something they have achieved isn't as straightforward as it seems. I didn't know what to expect when I sent out the first call for submissions but I thought there might be more stories about bungee-jumping. Instead, the stories are beautifully crafted, vulnerable and in many cases about resilience. Some people came forward like a shot. Many needed persuading. One or two lost heart halfway through.

Are we, as female-identifying people, conditioned to avoid blowing our trumpets? Or is it that our mouths don't know how to form the words to show our pride – because we don't see other women doing it? Is it because the stories that we are told, even if they are about women, are not quite relatable because they are written by men? I think that this could be true, and that's why it was so important for me to have this 100-strong chorus of stories and storytellers.

So on that Friday, even though I had nothing to say, I sat down and made a list. And the longer I thought about it, the more I realised I had to be proud of.

'Do you think I should do it?'

Me – four months earlier, mid-January 2018, speaking to my housemate late on a Sunday afternoon.

I had drafted an email to my contacts – almost every single one I had picked up in the last ten, twenty years of my studies, social and working life. People with whom I had toured to the outer reaches of the UK in a rusty van, people who I had met in the swimming pool, people whose birthdays I knew off by heart, people who had performed at the spoken word night I ran for three years, people who I had never met in person. Tutors, lovers, friends. Everyone who was important. I had so much to lose, in my head at least, if they thought it was a stupid idea.

'Really? Should I?'

'Do it,' my housemate said and I pressed send on the message which contained the seed of my idea. Within thirty minutes people I respected hugely had replied with encouragement.

'I have to do it now.'

I could not have done it without help. It was often hard-going – for a start I had never created a website, I still know nothing about audio files. I asked a couple of friends who have podcasts. I asked a friend of a friend about websites. I asked a stranger in a shop. I found I was not afraid to ask. I found I was not afraid to get things wrong. I didn't have time. I was working full time, writing a book, building a relationship, supporting my flatmates through some bad times, I was trying to work out what was going on with my sister's wedding. Instead of worrying about getting it wrong, which I do – so much – I put that to one side, and when I didn't know how to do something, when I was overwhelmed, when I needed a hug, I just asked.

'I did it.'

Me – 17 May 2018.

I hope the project touched people and made them think. We had listeners in Vietnam, the US, all over Europe. And even if it is all down to the high-quality writing I was lucky to source, I did create the platform, block by template block, and I am hugely proud of that.

We all need a leg-up. I took a chance on people I didn't necessarily know before, and they delivered – sharing their beautiful stories, and being open to my suggestions when I had thoughts on the structure or which angle they should use to frame their experiences. Other publishing channels might not take so many risks but it doesn't mean your writing is bad, your voice is worthless. Hopefully others will create similar projects, platforms, initiatives that we can all take part in.

I didn't plan out every detail before I started. I was shameless in my ambition and in pursuing writers, surprising myself above all others. I wasn't already well known or backed by a big organisation. Turns out you don't always have to be. You just have to have a go.

Leap and maybe someone will catch you.

Or maybe you can swing off that scaffolding.

COPYRIGHT NOTICES

ACKNOWLEDGEMENTS

I owe huge thanks to so many people who helped make this book. From the colleagues and friends who replied to my email about an overly ambitious podcast in January 2018 to tell me to go for it, to the Pankhurst Centre in Manchester and all our amazing local speakers, who helped us make our crowdfunding launch event worthy of the former residents of that historic building. And huge, wild thanks to my friends, family and more than 500 supporters who believed in this enough to fund its publication.

But I would be nowhere without the amazing writers who shared my ambitions for the project and lent their words, first to the podcast and now the book. Many of you who were strangers before are now my friends. To all 104 of you: your support, counsel and humour has taught me so much. Special thanks to the four or five of you who pushed so hard for this book to get funded. A team of wonder women.

Thanks also to Claire Nicholas for the push on that Sunday night to send the email that would change everything, and to Katy Guest, Imogen Denny, Cassie Waters and the team at Unbound for making this book a reality.

Thank you Dave, for all the hugs and for being the bolt in my scaffolding.

And the biggest thanks of all to the women who went before, who fought so we could have the freedoms we (sometimes) take for granted. Your voices resonate through all of us.

NOTE ON THE PROCEEDS

The contributors of *100 Voices* have generously decided to donate their profits to charity. All of the author profits from the book will be going to Rosa UK, a grantmaking charity that funds grassroots women's organisations working to make the UK a fairer, safer place for women and girls. You can read more about their important work at rosauk.org.

Unbound is the world's first crowdfunding publisher, established in 2011.

We believe that wonderful things can happen when you clear a path for people who share a passion. That's why we've built a platform that brings together readers and authors to crowdfund books they believe in – and give fresh ideas that don't fit the traditional mould the chance they deserve.

This book is in your hands because readers made it possible. Everyone who pledged their support is listed below. Join them by visiting unbound.com and supporting a book today.

Penelope Ball

Ros Ball

Ros Ball

Wesley Ball

Emily Bamford

Nicola Bannock

Donna Barbour

Hilary Barkway

Caroline Barnard

Hilary Barratt

Zena Barrie

Susan Barsby

Emma Beechey

Seona Bell

Lyn Betts

Susmita Bhattacharya

Martha Marie Bicket

Genevieve Binefa

Gina Birch

Liz Bishop

Astra Bloom

Will Bond

Ruth Boreham

Tracy Borman

Kim Botly

Eliza Bott

Sarah Boyd

Alice Bradshaw

Cynthia Brickell-Hayton

Lorna Brightmore

Livvy Brinson

Matilde Broberg Ekstrom

Pippa Brush Chappell

Elizabeth Bruton

Geraldine Buckley

Lucy Buckley

Viv Buckley

Geraldine Buckley (Snr)

Barbara Buettner

Matthew Bulgo

Laura Burgoyne

Alica Burgz

Sarah Burnett-Moore

Johanne Burns

Alex Burton-Keeble

Ellie Butler Church

Michael Button

Rebecca Buxton

Gail Cahill

Ewan Callaway

Robbie Carnegie

Ali Carroll

Liz Carroll

Jo Carruthers

Victoria Chamberlain

Julia Chappell

Katy Chappell

Olivia Chappell

Alexia Charisi

Sofie Charleson

Laura Clee

Rebecca Clee

Isabelle Clement

Liz Clifford

Michael Coates

Tamasin Coates

Collingham Real Ale Festival

Ellie Constantinou

Tanya Conyers-Silverthorn

Nick Cooper

Angella Cooze

Gail Cornish

Peta Cornish

Megan Corton Scott

Ben Cottam

Jackie Cotton

Gemma Coughlin

Melanie Cox

Helen Craven

Deborah Crawford

Sarah Cromwell

Rachel Cussen

Louise David

Christine Davidson

Branwen Davies

Helena Davies

Ellie Dawes

Susan Dawes

Ayisha De Lanerolle

Annelies De Wilde

Mal Dee

Anna Deibel-Jung

Becky Dennis

Emily Devane

Liz Dexter

Francesca Di Mattia

Jason Dickerson

Olivia Dickinson

Rebecca Dilg

Emma Dixon

Carol Dodgshon

Samuel Dodson

Melangell Dolma

Hannah Donaldson

Lisa Donoghue (from Mark and
   Christina)

Catherine Donovan

Eugene Doyle

Florence Doyle

Jane Duffus

Joe Dunthorne

Hannah Durham

Jo Dwyer

Sharon Eckman

Jane Elliott

Jane Elliott

Kate Ellis

Sarah Ellis

Ruth Emery

Katie Emmerton

William Emmett

Nadia Etchingham

Kate Etheridge

Alison Evans

Nathan Evans

Richard Evans

Sarah Evans

Mels Evers

Kieran Falconer

Quentin Falk

Barbara Farrell

Adam Farrer

Hazel Farrow

Louise Farrow

Marcelle Fawcett

Barry Featherston

Chelsea Felstead

Fred Fernandez-Armesto

Joe Ferris Castle

Maria Filippidou

Robert Fisher

Carmel Fitzgerald

Cheryl Fitzgerald

Sarah Flowers

Eimear Flynn

Elizabeth Folarin

Amy Foster

Jenny Foulds

Sarah Frances Armstrong

Craig "Jiggy" Francis

Sarah Franklin

Melissa Fu

Cate Fuchter

Lee Furness

Liz Gale

Mair George

Laura Gilbert

Caroline Gillespie

Maria Godebska

Emma Gold

Daniel Goldstein

Jo Goodbody

Ann Goodman Smith

Lucy Goose

Jenny Gordon

Caroline Gourlay

Scarlett Graham

Fiona Grant

Jessica Gray

Sarah Green

Georgia Gregory

Michaela Greibach

Anya Greig

Heather Griffin

Judith Griffith

Katy Guest

Emma Halliday

Emma Halliday - This
    Vulnerable Life

Vanessa Hammick

Tom Hancock

Vicky Hannah

Tianna Hansen

Ben A Harvey

Jacqueline P Haskell

Sophie Haydock

Jane Healy

Angela Heathcote

Keith Heddle

Sarah Hegarty

Ada Henden

Hannah Hewins

Holly Hewins

Amanda Hickling

Ben Higgins

Jude Higgins

Alison Hitchcock

Sara Hodgkinson

Eliza Hogermeer

Rees Hollie

Holly Holmes

Suzi Holmes

Helen Hood

Dawn Hooper

Russ Hope

Ruth Hopkinson

Melanie Hopwood

Debbie Horne

Sarah Horsman

Katy Hoskyn

Louise Houghton

R Houldsworth

Joanna Howard

Julie Howard

Natalie Rachel Howard

Lianne Howard-Dace

Nathalie Hudson

Nick Hunt

Jennifer Jackson

Joseph Jarman

Adam Jefford

Judy Jefford

Tom Jefford

Rachel Jeffrey

Louise Jensen

Tulika Jha

Angela John

Hannah Johns

Holly Johns

Katherine Johns

Jennifer Johnson

Ozlem Johnston

Laura Jones

Michael Jones

Ray Jones

Eleanor Katz Castellano

Paula Keatley

Stef Keegan

Miranda Keeling

Cliff Keller

Freya Kelly

Peter Kent

Aaron Keogh

Aliyah Keshani

Aliyah Kim Keshani

Ben Kettner

Abda Khan

Dan Kieran

Tracy King

Alastair Kinross

Amy Kinross

Sue Kinross

Vyvyan Kinross

Stella Klein

Pamela Kleinot

Sander Kooij

Cara Krmpotich

Sharmila Kumar

Alex Kung

Chloe Lack

Michelle Laker

Harriet Lander

Felicity Lane

Lloyd Langford

Clare Laws

Bahar Lawson

Jill Lawton

Emma Laxton

Andrew Leach

Emilia Leese

Hannah Leniston

Ruth Leonard

Leonora Letchworth

Mary Levitt-Hughes

Anthony Lewis

Chris Limb

Georgina Lippiett

Bronwen Lloyd

Jonathan Lloyd

Keith Lloyd

Vikki Lloyd

Lou Lockwood

Molly Lockwood

Carina Lorriman

Claire Lowdon

Simon Lucas

Rosaleen Lynch

Louise Macdonald

Cat Macfarlane

Jill MacKenzie

Tina MacNaughton

Sabrina Mahfouz

Andrea Malam-Alexander

Andrea Malizia

Louise Mangos

Martin Marlowe

Emily Martyn

Sheila Martyn

Karen Maxwell

Con McCartney

Lawrence McCrossan

Sophie McDermott

Peter McDonald

Stella McGourty

Emma Mcilwee

Lily McLeish

Kirsty McQuire

Ciara McVeigh

Jan Mead

Alex Mendes da Costa

Baron Mendes da Costa

Dave Mendes da Costa

Elsbeth Mendes da Costa

Thomas Mendes da Costa

Christine Metcalf

Sarah Metcalf

Caroline Methuen

David Middleton

James Millar

Rosanna Millinchip

John Mitchinson

Linda Moffat

Damhnait Monaghan

Carole Moore

Jide Morakinyo

Sarah Morgan

John Moriarty

Simon Moriarty

Sue Morón-García

Fionnuala Morris

Madeleine Morris

Sarah Mosedale

Sarah Myers

Vikiy Myers

Trinidad Navarro

Carlo Navato

Colin Nelson

Zoe NervousNeutrino

Chris Newsom and Jasmine
    Milton

Gary Nicol

Emma Nisse

Alice Noakes

Sally Noonan

Tom Norton

Rosie Newman

Jane O Shea

Lisa O'Hare

Jessica O'Leary

Rachel O'Riordan

Suzanne O'Sullivan

Katharine Oakes

Hayley Oakley

Laura Oates

Sophie Odenthal

Daniel Okubo

Christine Oliver

Vanessa Onwuemezi

Dixie Orford

Jeremy Osborne

Pages Cheshire Street Bookshop

Juliet Palfrey

Christina Palmer

Julia Palmer

Tegan Palmer

Helen Pankhurst

Nikolas Papanastasiou

Sarah Parker

Steph Parker

janice parsons

Michael Payne

Esme Pears

Siobhan Pena-Taylor

Hannah Perkins

Jodie Perks

Dr Nicola Phillips

Celia Phipps

Jonathan Pickard

Dave Pickering
Clair Pollard
Justin Pollard
Conrad Pollock
Diana Pollock
Gabrielle Pollock
Tamara Pollock
Megan Poole
Celia Popovic
Tabitha Potts
Andrew Poulton
Clare Price
Miriam Price
Nicholas Price
Marianne Privett
Jessica Pulay
Holly Race
Sarah Rae
Gita Ralleigh
John Ramsey
Laura Rathbone
Daniele Rauso
Sarah Rayment
Mary Reece
Carmel Reilly
Matthew Reiss
Emma Rhind-Tutt

Gerry Richards
Laurence Richards
Mary Richards
Victoria Richards
Jane Riekemann
Lisa Ritchie
Amanda Roberts
Jane Roberts
Claire Robinson
Jane Robinson
Gaby Robinson-
    Wright
Stephanie Ross
Anne Roszkowski
Luke Roszkowski
Mark Roszkowski
Miranda
    Roszkowski
Sandie Roszkowski
Rebecca Rouillard
Angelique Rowan
Graham Rowan
Jaimie Rowan
Usha Rowan
Esther Rowe
Reshma Ruia
Lisa Rüll

Sevil Rush
Charlotte Rushton
Ana Rutter
Patla S
Natalie Salaman
Annie Salmon
Julie Salmon
Laura Sanson
Chris Savory
Aindreas Scholz
Holly Seaward
Stefanie Seddon
Caroline Selai
Shaggy
Jessica Sharman
Rebekah Shaw
Jane Sheehy
Jeanette Sheppard
Angela Shoosmith
Diane Simmons
Maggie Singleton
Francesca Skelton
Sue Sloan
Sam Smethers
Bob Smith
Lynn Smith
Ronald Smith

Val & Bob Smith

Alex Standen

Vivienne Stark

Hilary Statts

Linda Stevens

Anne Summerfield

Leanne Summers

Lizzie Summerskill

Bex Sutton

Mai Saroh Tassinari

Louise Taylor

Polly Teale

THE 125 ARTISTS (David,
    Sarah, Rebecca, Adam,
    Molly and Jo)

The Development Team
    Unbound

Jacqui Thomas

Sam Thomas

Jen Thornton

Lucy Titley

Pippa Tolfts

Louise Toner

Sabine Tötemeyer

Hannah Tovey

Simon Townend

Tessa Trabue

Luke Tredget

Gareth Turkington

Natalie Twum-Barima

Stevie Tyler

Sue Tyley

Chris Udenze

Manoja Ullmann

Richard Van Noorden

Zach Van Stanley

Kerry Vevers

Benjamin Victor

Jaroslava Vik

Annie Vincent

Debbi Voisey

Rachel Voldman

Tamara von Werthern

Angela Wallis

Stephen Warren

Ali Wates

Fiona Webb

Eris Westlake

WGYTC

Alice White

Nicholas White

Ed Whiting

Andy Wiener

Hannah Wilgar

Lucy Wilkins

Alex Williams

Ruth Williams

Catherine Williamson

Flora Williamson

Adam Wills

Alex Wilson

Ken Wilson

Lucinda Wilson

Simon Wilson

Marianne Windham

Laura Windley

Teri Wishart

Gretchen Woelfle

Julia Woelke von Werthern

Lara Woolford

Julia Woollams

Karis Wright

Maureen Wright

Emma Wyatt

Heather Wyatt

Heledd Wyn

Jennifer Yong

Alex Young

Emily Young

Isabel Young

Debbie Young-Somers

Robyn Zaza

Jacqui Zinkin

Lucy Zion Thatcher

Tanya Zybutz